C000049044

WORLD CHRISTIANITY SERIES

Eastern Europe is a volume in the *World Christianity* series published by the Missions Advanced Research and Communications Center and, for the first time, by MARC, an imprint of Monarch Publications.

The Missions Advanced Research and Communication Center (MARC), in an effort to motivate the Church in the world to the task of evangelization, produced thirty-five country profiles in 1971. These profiles attempted to describe the status of Christianity in those nations. They were subsequently used at the International Congress on World Evangelization held in Lausanne (LCWE) in 1974. Since that time, other countries were added, and older profiles revised. In 1978 the profiles were collected by sub-regions, and material on unreached groups was added to the text from the Unreached Peoples Database. This volume, with its new format, is the work of many people at Keston College. The publishers express their gratitude to them all.

The information contained in this volume is part of the MARC/ LCWE attempt to display the task of world evangelization in a way that will help the Church identify and evangelize the peoples of the world in their historical context and reality, and to recognize the political division of the world into nation-states.

World Christianity: Eastern Europe

EDITED BY PHILIP WALTERS
Foreword by Michael Bourdeaux

Missions Advanced Research & Communication Center

Monrovia, California

MARC

Eastbourne

Copyright © Keston College 1988

First published 1988

All rights reserved.
No part of this publication may be reproduced or
transmitted in any form or by any means, electronic
or mechanical, including photocopy, recording, or any
information storage and retrieval system, without
permission in writing from the publisher.

Front cover photos:
Left, top and bottom — Tony Stone Photolibrary—London
Right — Photo Library International

British Library Cataloguing in Publication Data

Walters, Philip
    World Christianity : Eastern Europe.
    1. Eastern Europe. Christian Church, to 1974
    I. Title
    274.7

    ISBN 1–85424–065–X

Keston Book No. 29

Published in support of the Lausanne Committee on
World Evangelisation

Co-publishers:
MARC International, World Vision International,
919 West Huntingdon Drive, Monrovia, California 91016, USA

Printed in Great Britain for
MARC, an imprint of Monarch Publications Ltd,
1 St Anne's Road, Eastbourne, E. Sussex BN21 3UN by
Richard Clay Ltd, Bungay, Suffolk.
Typeset by Watermark, Hampermill Cottage, Watford WD1 4PL

CONTENTS

FOREWORD

I am delighted to be associated with this volume in the *World Christianity* series. The sections on the various countries and denominations have been written by specialists drawing on sources of information of all kinds: religious literature (both official and unofficial) coming out of the countries concerned; archival material; and their own (and others') first-hand experience. In particular, full use has been made of the material and knowledge accumulated at Keston College.

This book attempts to set out the facts about Christian witness in Eastern Europe in a clear and orderly manner. It is perhaps the most comprehensive introduction to the subject since the second edition of Trevor Beeson's *Discretion and Valour* in 1982. It is a much-needed book: so much has happened in the last four or five years. In the Soviet Union, Mr Gorbachev's policy of *glasnost* or 'openness' has meant a much freer discussion in the Soviet press and media of religious themes and even of the persecution of believers. All kinds of changes have been promised which should enable Christians and other religious believers to play their full part, as loyal Soviet citizens, in the processes of *perestroika* or 'restructuring'. Now we may look forward to the fulfilment of these promises.

The Christians in the Soviet Union and Eastern Europe will continue to be centrally involved in developments in their countries in all spheres—religious, political, cultural, economic. All those concerned with the future of Eastern Europe can turn to this timely volume for their basic information about the position of the Christian communities there today.

Michael Bourdeaux
Keston College
May 1988

INTRODUCTION

KARL MARX DESCRIBED RELIGION as the 'opium of the people' and suggested that under socialism people would no longer need drugs. Where his followers have come to political power, they have generally sought to hasten the process whereby religion 'withers away'. Yet despite this long term objective, the practical policies adopted by the Communist governments in the Soviet Union and Eastern Europe have varied considerably, both from country to country and over the years, depending on a variety of considerations: the different denominations involved and their own traditions of relations with the state, foreign policy, internal politics, economic conditions within the country, ideological preoccupations, nationalist pressures. To the casual observer the believer in Yugoslavia would appear to have the same rights as his or her counterpart in Western Europe; in Albania religious practice has been forbidden since 1967.

The first successful socialist revolution occurred in Russia during the course of 1917, where the Bolsheviks led by Lenin used a popular revolution to seize power. Lenin shared Marx's view of religion as both illusory and an instrument of class rule. Before the revolution Lenin had argued that under socialism the state would remain neutral in matters of belief, whilst the party would seek to convince people of the falsity of religious views. In practice the whole state apparatus was quickly brought into play against religion, in particular against the Russian Orthodox Church, which was perceived by the Bolsheviks as one of the central pillars of the old régime. Over the next decade Soviet policies towards religious groups fluctuated. Some previously persecuted groups enjoyed considerable freedom, whilst others, notably the Orthodox, suffered constant harassment. From the late 1920s, however, all religious groups suffered under Stalinist terror, and on the eve of the Second World War it appeared that institutional religion in the Soviet Union was on the verge of extinction. During the Second World War, however, conditions improved dramatically. Stalin realised that in order to win the loyalty of the significant proportion of Soviet citizens who were believers, he would have to woo the churches with concessions; and since that time, the major denominations have enjoyed a sometimes precarious toleration. The authorities have realised that unless believers are given some measure of official toleration, all religious activity will go underground and be impossible to monitor or control. They are also able to use the church hierarchs to endorse specific aspects of Soviet policy, such as the campaign for world peace.

The major denominations are allowed a church hierarchy, some training facilities for priests and a restricted number of publications; but none of these concessions has any legal guarantee. The only legalised unit is the parish with its registered place of worship. Nevertheless, a campaign such as that of 1959–64 under Khrushchev, when thousands of churches were closed illegally, is always possible. The authorities expect believers to confine their religious activities within a very restricted framework as the price for registration, and many evangelical Christians have taken the decision not to seek registration from the state at all, preferring the freedom of the outlaw to meet, worship, evangelise, baptise their children and so on. Anti-religious pressure is constant throughout the education system and in government propaganda at all levels, and there is systematic discrimination against believers in all jobs except the most menial. Conditions for religious believers are probably worse in the Soviet Union than in any other East

European country except Albania.

Mounting religious dissent and a significant religious revival since the late 1960s have presented the authorities with increasing problems. Since the accession of Mr Gorbachev and the introduction of the policy of *glasnost* ('openness'), there has been increasing discussion in the press and media of religious issues. There have been regular promises that the laws on religious activity are to be revised fundamentally; but at the time of writing no actual *perestroika* ('restructuring') has taken place.

In Czechoslovakia, strong pressure on the churches has been a constant feature of communist policy for nearly forty years, apart from a brief period in 1968–9. The situation here for Catholic priests, Protestant pastors and the average believer is almost as difficult as in the Soviet Union.

In Hungary, there has been steady improvement in the official status of the main Churches since the early 1970s. An accommodation has been worked out whereby the Churches have received concessions in theological education, church building and the publishing of literature; but the price which the church leaders have paid in compromising with the requirements of the régime is too high for many believers.

In Bulgaria, the Orthodox Church enjoys a good deal of toleration, partly because of its historical championing of Bulgarian freedom against the Turks. In Romania, the Orthodox Church is similarly identified with the aspirations of the state, and under the strongly nationalist régime of Ceausescu it is able to maintain a relatively high profile in society. In both these countries, however, the authorities use the official churches to discipline religious activists, and there have been spates of arrests of religious dissenters during the 1970s.

The situation of the church in East Germany is unique. The government itself follows closely the Soviet line, but the Protestant Church has a distinct and influential role to play within the socialist state, and conditions for believers are in most respects better than in any other East European country, except perhaps Yugoslavia. The churches have close links with their sister churches in West Germany; and the need to repair the evil legacy of Nazism has tended to unite the churches with the government in a common cause. At the same time, the church as an institution is independent of the state, which has no direct or indirect say in church appointments.

The position of the Catholic Church in Poland is also unique. Having the allegiance of 90% of the population, it has always been an autonomous unit with its own structure and organisation, and despite the efforts of the communist authorities to restrict its practical role within society, it has remained free from government control and able to function as the guardian of moral and spiritual values. The importance of the church in shaping events in the Solidarity period took the world by surprise; and it will doubtless continue to play a central role in guiding further social and political development in Poland.

Yugoslavia and Albania are distinctive in that neither country is a Soviet satellite, and this has meant that the policy each country has pursued towards religion has been quite autonomous. In both countries the population is a mixture of Catholics, Orthodox and Muslims. In Yugoslavia, religious practice is tolerated within very widely defined limits, while Albania is the only state in the world where religion is illegal, and all public expressions of faith are savagely punished.

Whilst there has been no shift in the basic ideological hostility of the Eastern European Communist Parties to religion, a certain 'normalisation' of church-state relations has developed. Violent assaults on the churches from the late 1920s to the early 1940s in the Soviet Union and in the late 1940s and early 1950s in most of Eastern Europe met with varying degrees of success in breaking the institutional resistance of religious bodies, and have allowed the various governments to rely more on control, co-option of church leaders and 'education' in later years. Though in most of Eastern Europe, with the possible exception of Poland, the balance of power lies firmly in the hands of the state, the less overtly coercive approach of recent years has raised a number of problem areas in church-state relations. At the centre of these usually lies the question of what is properly owed to Caesar.

One area which causes problems in all Eastern European countries is that of peace and military service. Most Soviet and East European church leaders are expected to be assiduous in promoting official peace policies; but in countries such as East Germany and Hungary groups of believers have initiated a more even-handed peace debate and have tried to give primacy to their religious convictions, rather than to the particular political line promoted by their governments. When such groups encourage or are associated with conscientious objection, they often come into conflict with both state and church leaders.

Another area where difficulties regularly arise is that of religious education and literature, both subject to considerable restrictions in the USSR and Eastern Europe. In the Soviet Union parents may bring up their children as believers and those churches permitted training institutes may educate future priests and pastors; in Hungary optional religious education classes are available in schools in certain circumstances. The same variations may be found in the field of religious literature, with a great shortage of Bibles in some countries and virtually free availability in others. Other forms of religious literature generally remain in short supply throughout Eastern Europe and believers have often sought to make up the deficiency by producing their own material, often at the risk of imprisonment.

A third area of tension is the question of national identity. The governments of Eastern Europe are very sensitive when a particular Church is closely identified with the aspirations of a particular national group. Poland provides the most obvious case: the Catholic Church is the repository of Polish national identity. Within the Soviet Union, the Republic of Lithuania provides a similar case: since the 1970s, the Catholic Church in Lithuania has become intimately involved with the national struggle for freedom from Russian domination.

All the countries of Eastern Europe, except Albania, possess: central church organisational structures and hierarchies of officially-recognised clergy who are expected actively to endorse the social and political line pursued by the state (only in Poland has this expectation been unfulfilled); relatively small groups of active dissenters who reject most if not all state control of religion and restrictions on religious activity and who often criticise the morality of the ruling ideology and even the legitimacy of the régime; and, between the two, a graduated spectrum of church-goers who are more or less satisfied with the opportunity for limited religious expression at the price of remaining second-class citizens. In the countries with harsher régimes, the latter group tends to comprise mostly old people. In some instances all three types of believer will unite in a coherent movement to pursue religious liberty, but for this to happen special conditions are needed.

The problems facing the churches in the Soviet Union and Eastern Europe have not, however, led to a decline in the number of active believers. Particularly in the more repressive countries, many if not most religious denominations have seen a substantial increase in membership since the 1970s and some have experienced charismatic renewal movements. External pressures are stimulating not only a quantitative but, more importantly, a qualitative growth in the churches of Eastern Europe.

It is obvious that religion is here to stay as a factor in communist societies. As the only legalised form for alternative ideological commitment, the churches and other religious bodies equally obviously are in a unique and potentially powerful position. Until recently, however, their importance has been seriously underestimated by political and sociological analysts in the West.

CHAPTER 1

The Soviet Union

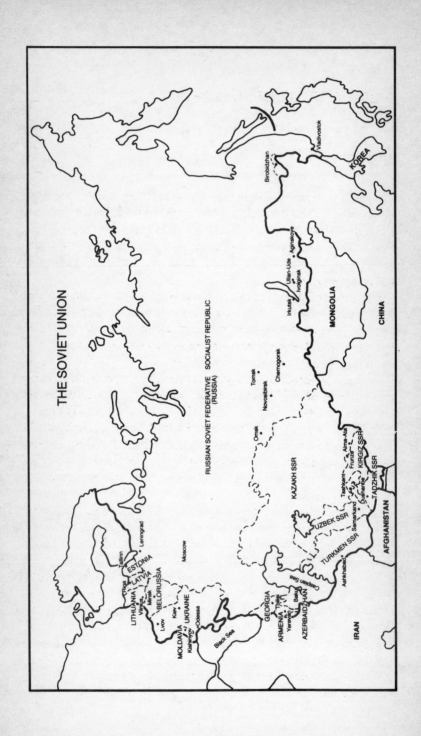

THE SOVIET UNION

RUSSIAN SOVIET FEDERATIVE SOCIALIST REPUBLIC (RUSSIA)

MONGOLIA

CHINA

KOREA

Vladivostok

Birobidzhan

Irkutsk
Ulan-Ude
Ivolginsk
Aginskoye

Chernogorsk

Tomsk
Novosibirsk

Omsk

KAZAKH SSR

UZBEK SSR

Alma-Ata
Tashkent
Frunze
KIRGIZ SSR
Samarkand
Dushanbe
TADZHIK SSR
TURKMEN SSR
Ashkhabad

AFGHANISTAN

IRAN

Caspian Sea

Baku
AZERBAIDZHAN
Tbilisi
Yerevan
ARMENIA
GEORGIA

Black Sea

Odessa
Kishinev
MOLDAVIA
UKRAINE
Kiev
Lvov
BELORUSSIA
Minsk
Vilnius
LITHUANIA
LATVIA
Riga
ESTONIA
Tallinn

Moscow

Leningrad

THE SOVIET UNION: OVERVIEW

The country

Covering a larger land mass than any other single political entity, the USSR stretches over 10,000 kilometres from the Eastern Pacific shores to Central Europe and includes eleven time zones. Within this vast territory are to be found a wide variety of natural phenomena: climate, relief, vegetation, natural resources.

For over half the country the average annual temperature is 0°C. Yet, though the Soviet Union is generally known for its winters, during which temperatures in some parts may fall below −60°C, the southern regions of Central Asia experience annual summer averages of around 25°C.

In terms of relief and vegetation the country is equally variegated. Most of the European and Russian parts are relatively flat, broken only by the Urals, which rise to a maximum height of 1,900 metres. On the southern borders, however, lie considerable mountain ranges, including the Central Asian Tyan-Shan mountains rising to heights of over 6,000 metres and the Caucasus, where Mount Elbrus reaches over 5,600 metres.

The predominantly lowland areas of the USSR are in turn characterised by a rich diversity in vegetation and soil, ranging from the Arctic tundra of northern Russia and Siberia, through the forests of central Russia and the black-earth zones of Ukraine and southern Russia, to the semi-tropical regions of southern Georgia and the arid steppes and deserts of Central Asia.

Possessing some 16% of the world's total land area, the Soviet Union is richly endowed with natural resources, including as much as half of the earth's iron-ore deposits. Other minerals with which the country is plentifully supplied include manganese, copper, lead, zinc, mercury, gold and silver. It also has considerable energy deposits, of which coal, oil and natural gas are the most significant.

While size brings many advantages, it also brings problems. Many of these resources are not easily accessible; large areas are unsuitable for agricultural production (owing either to excessive cold in the north or to shortage of water in the south); and vast distances in combination with a far from adequate transport system have led to considerable difficulties in supplying some parts of the population.

The people

In public discourse the terms 'Russia' and the 'Soviet Union' are all too often used interchangeably, though they in fact mean different things. According to Soviet writers, the 'Soviet Union' (or Union of Soviet Socialist Republics) is a multi-national state made up of over 100 nationalities and divided administratively into fifteen republics based on major national groups. Russia, or the 'Russian Republic', is just one of these fifteen republics, albeit the largest.

This confusion has arisen for a number of reasons. In the first place the roots of the USSR lie in the old Russian Empire. More importantly, Russians are the largest ethnic group within the country, comprising at the last census some 137.4 million of a total population of over 262 million. Additionally there are another 51.6 million Slavs (Ukrainians and Belorussians), who are all too easily identified with the Russians. Finally, of course, the confusion of 'Russian' with 'Soviet' stems from the fact that the Russians are dominant politically within the USSR, exercising a considerable degree of control, even in republics where the titular nationality provides the formal political leadership.

Less well-known is the fact that the second largest group in the Soviet Union after the Slavs is the Turkic peoples, of whom there are over thirty-five million. Of these the best-known are the Uzbeks, Kazakhs, Azeris, Turkmen, Kirghiz and Tatars. Together with some three million Tadzhiks of Iranian stock, these peoples of Muslim background are the most dynamic element in the population. The birth-rate of these groups has been declining at a much slower rate than that of the Slavic and European elements in the population, and their share in the population is rising. Thus between 1970 and 1979 their share rose from 16% to 18% and is projected by some experts to reach 24% by the end of the century. The proportion of younger people in the Turkic-Iranian population groups is hence much higher than in the other ethnic groups, and this has another important consequence: they are likely to provide over a third of the conscripts entering the Red Army by the year 2000.

Other significant groups include the Baltic peoples (Estonians, Latvians, Lithuanians and Karelians), who have much in common with the peoples of Scandinavia and Northern Europe; the Caucasians (Georgians and Armenians), with their long historical and cultural traditions; the Mongols (Buryats and Kalmucks); the Jews; the Moldavians, who have more in common with the Romanians (whose language, though not alphabet, they share); and the Germans, who settled in Russia during the eighteenth century but were deported to all corners of the Soviet Union during the Second World War. There are many smaller groups of hunters and fishermen in the far north; and even Greeks and Koreans are to be found among the hundred or more nationalities inhabiting the Soviet Union.

Brief history

The origins of the modern Soviet state can be traced back to the ninth century, if not earlier. The nomadic peoples who traversed the southern steppes were gradually displaced in the fifth and sixth centuries by Slavic groups. Then in the ninth century, Norsemen led by Ryurik established political ascendancy over the Slavs and in subsequent centuries merged with them. During this period the town of Kiev and its Grand Prince gained pre-eminence, and in 988 Vladimir of Kiev accepted

Christianity in its Byzantine form. For a century and a half the town flourished politically and culturally until internecine struggles between the various princes undermined the Kievan state at a time when new foes threatened.

By 1240, the independent existence of virtually all the Kievan and other princedoms had been brought to an end by the Mongol invaders. Despite their reputation for the brutal destruction of those they conquered, the Mongols preferred indirect forms of rule, relying on the payment of tribute, conscription of Russian vassals and the reservation of the right to confirm new princes in their posts.

It was during the Mongol overlordship that the town of Moscow grew in importance, and in 1380 the Muscovite Prince Dmitri Donskoi inflicted the first serious defeat on the forces of the Khan. Though the Mongols were able to sack Moscow two years later, they were gradually pushed back and by the late fifteenth century had ceased to pose any threat to the Muscovite state. They had, however, bequeathed to the Russian state what one historian has called 'a certain absolutist and autocratic framework', which was reinforced by the tendency towards autocracy already present in an imperial system modelled on that of the Byzantine Empire.

Over the next two centuries the fortunes of Moscow declined under Ivan IV or 'Terrible' and his immediate successors until in 1613 Mikhail Romanov was elected tsar and a measure of stability was regained. The seventeenth century witnessed two developments that were to be of great significance for the future of the Russian state: the final consolidation of serfdom, and the schism within the Orthodox Church that led to the creation of the Old Believer movement. (This we shall discuss later).

Under Peter the Great (1682–1725) considerable effort was made to modernise and westernise Russian life, with the tsar himself encouraging industrialisation, education and science. These reforms and modernisations were not accompanied by an alteration in traditional forms of rule, however. Education produced a frustrated group of intellectuals willing but not permitted to participate in government. Limited social and administrative reforms carried out during the nineteenth century failed to satisfy this group, more extreme members of which assassinated the reforming Tsar Alexander II in 1881 and overthrew the autocracy in 1917.

Lenin and the Bolsheviks added to the Russian autocratic tradition the Marxist belief that a perfect social structure could be established. In pursuit of this goal they launched a radical programme of social reform and of violence against those who resisted. Though experience served to moderate this programme during the 1920s, under Stalin rapid industrialisation and the collectivisation of agriculture were accompanied by mass purges and terror in which millions died. Since the death of the dictator in 1953, mass terror has been abandoned as a form of rule, though coercion remains a significant feature of Soviet society. Under Khrushchev, Brezhnev and Gorbachev, however, there have also been some attempts to achieve economic development, aimed at meeting the consumer needs of the citizen and thus ensuring his loyalty.

The economy

Marxist theory suggested that the first socialist revolution would occur in the economically developed capitalist world, yet the Russian Empire in 1917 was relatively backward. Moreover, the Bolsheviks inherited an economy further weakened by three years of war.

Initially, the young revolutionary government favoured a policy described as 'War Communism'. In part this was a response to the conditions created by the civil strife which split the Empire apart in the years 1918–21, but it also represented an attempt to move rapidly towards the achievement of communism. It entailed the nationalisation of all property, the allocation of resources by the centre and the requisitioning of peasant produce. By 1921, however, it had become apparent that the state lacked the ability to implement effectively such complete control over the economy and, more importantly, that it was politically necessary to placate the peasants, who formed the majority of the population. Thus Lenin and his colleagues pushed through the 'New Economic Policy', which gave a greater degree of freedom to private enterprise and allowed the peasants to sell their goods in the free market.

This more relaxed economic policy came to an end in the late 1920s when Stalin launched a programme of rapid industrialisation that attempted to bring the economy under central control. This has determined the structure of the Soviet economy ever since. Simultaneously, ran the campaign to collectivise the peasantry; a process completed by 1938, but at the cost of millions of lives, through famine and the dispossession or arrest of up to 4½ million so-called 'rich peasants'.

The basic economic priorities of the Soviet state are determined by the Communist Party and enshrined in successive 'five-year plans'. While the Party sets out the basic goals, their detailed working out is the task of the state planning agency Gosplan. This body consults with the various economic ministries and enterprises, but once the plan is worked out, it becomes—at least in theory—binding on all institutions involved in economic matters. In other words it is the state which determines what shall be produced rather than the 'market'.

The basic advantage of this system of centralised planning is that it enables the state to divert quickly considerable resources to major development projects or to meet defence needs; its basic problem—extreme inefficiency in the meeting of consumer needs—would appear to stem from the fallacy of the official belief that the centre is fully aware of the economic 'needs' of the populace.

In recent years some attempt has been made to improve the working of the economy, whether by reducing the number of targets that industrial firms have to meet, by allowing enterprises more say in the use of their profits, or by giving greater incentives to those involved in agricultural work. It remains to be seen how effective these will be.

Social conditions

The Bolsheviks came to power in 1917 with the intention of

transforming a backward, superstitious and predominantly rural society into one based on modern industry and a scientific understanding of the world. To this end they effected economic change, provided a wide range of social services, and made full use of education and propaganda.

An initial target for reform was the family. Women were given equal rights under matrimonial law; divorce was made much easier and abortion permitted. Though divorce and abortion were again restricted under Stalin, since his death they have once more become freely available. Indeed by the late 1970s, the divorce rate was approximately 34,000 per 100,000 and the annual number of abortions at six million exceeded the number of live births.

Though the position of women has changed and improved in many ways since 1917, the fact that 44% of women work has not prevented the continued male orientation of society. In many cases economic necessity forces women to work, yet because cultural attitudes have not changed they are still expected to be good housewives and thus, in effect, work a 'double shift'. This fact, taken together with poor housing conditions and the high incidence of alcoholism in Soviet society, has not helped in the preservation of stable families.

In the field of education, considerable progress has been made since 1917. Literacy has risen, at least according to official estimates, from under 30% to 99%, and a minimum period of education for all was established by the mid-1930s. At the present time compulsory education begins at the age of six and lasts for a minimum of nine years. At fifteen pupils can then go to either vocationally or academically orientated schools, from where the most gifted go into higher education. At all levels a major task of the teachers is to socialise future citizens and in higher education institutes courses in both Marxist theory and scientific atheism are obligatory.

Universal medical care is provided free for all citizens, and the number of doctors (70% of whom are women) is high in comparison with the West. Though extensive immunisation has reduced the incidence of many diseases, as late as 1970 there was a major cholera epidemic; in 1975 it was also revealed that 8.5% of hospital beds were allocated to tuberculosis patients.

Considerable problems appear to have arisen with regard to infant mortality, which rose from 22.9 to 27 per thousand in the period 1971–4, after which time statistics were no longer published. While conditions have undoubtedly improved considerably over the last thirty years, the overall quality of care would appear to be poorer than in most Western countries, a major reason being the great shortage of modern drugs.

Political life

Formally, the USSR is governed by 'soviets', or councils, existing at every level of the political system. Deputies to these bodies are elected by adult citizens, though there is only one candidate for each seat. The Supreme Soviet, which meets in Moscow, is responsible for passing laws, though the extent of its real power is perhaps indicated by the fact that it is rarely in session for more than ten days a year. More important is the Council of Ministers, the government of the Soviet Union. This body comprises nearly 100 ministers with responsibility for the economy, law and order, social services, etc.

To understand Soviet political life, however, we need to look beyond these bodies and appreciate the central role of the Communist Party. It is the Party that established Soviet rule and has dominated the USSR ever since, and it is the Party that determines the general direction of policy affecting every political, social and economic issue.

Though Party organisations exist at every administrative level, real power in Soviet society rests with the Central Committee and the Politburo. The latter body generally includes around a dozen members and is headed by the General Secretary, at present Mikhail Sergeyevich Gorbachev. Under Stalin the General Secretary was a dictator, but since the 1950s, Soviet leadership has tended to become more collective in nature.

The Party ensures its dominance in Soviet society by two mechanisms. Firstly, through the *nomenklatura* system: the effective right to vet those appointed to all important positions from government ministers down to headmasters. Secondly, Party committees at all levels have the right of *kontrol*, or checking that the institutions and economic enterprises within their area have carried out instructions or fulfilled their plan.

The nature of political life in the USSR differs greatly from that in the liberal democracies. In the first place there are no free elections, though since Gorbachev came to power, there have been suggestions that contested elections may be allowed in future. At the time of writing, however, voters are faced with a single candidate whose selection is vetted in practice by Party organisations—though not all those elected are Party members.

Also absent is the broad framework of civil rights that the citizens of a liberal democracy take for granted. Though most of these rights are guaranteed by the Soviet constitution, rights are understood as something granted by the state rather than as in any sense 'inalienable' or 'God-given'. Moreover, those who have claimed those rights have frequently been imprisoned. Though many prisoners of conscience have been released since Gorbachev came to power, in April 1988 there remained at least 200 documented cases of people imprisoned for their religious faith.

In charge of this coercive aspect of Soviet life and charged with responsibility for rooting out dissenting elements is the Committee for State Security, better known in the West as the KGB. This body has agents and informers in every institution within the Soviet Union, and while its effectiveness can be exaggerated, the knowledge that its representatives may be everywhere is sufficient to prevent most citizens from indulging in any active pursuit of political freedoms.

THE STATUS OF CHRISTIANITY

The religious complexion of the country

First Christian contacts
Tradition, reliable or otherwise, records that Christianity was

brought to the Caucasus by the apostle Andrew. From history, we know that there were Christian communities on the shores of the Black Sea by the third century, and that over the period 350–450 AD the small Armenian and Georgian kingdoms formally accepted Christianity. Soviet archaeologists have also discovered evidence of Christian activity from about the fifth century in Central Asia, later an area to be dominated by Islam.

During the tenth century the Kievan state developed extensive contacts with Byzantine Christianity. Under Prince Igor (913–45) expeditions were mounted against Constantinople with varying degrees of success, but after his death the relationship between the two states was dominated by trade. Under the sponsorship of the Byzantine Emperor, Igor's widow Olga was baptised, though her personal faith appears not to have greatly influenced the populace of Kiev. Under her grandson Vladimir (980–1015) a pagan revival was initially encouraged as a means of uniting the feuding local cities.

Ironically it was the same Vladimir who in 988 inaugurated the Christianisation of Kiev. Though this change of religion brought diplomatic advantages, including marriage to the Emperor's sister, his conversion appears to have been genuine. Certainly he took seriously the dissemination of the faith among the population, inviting in Byzantine clerics and building churches. Under Yaroslav the Wise (1035–54) this process was taken much further, with the appointment of bishops, the emergence of monastic communities and the erection of the great Cathedral of St Sophia in Kiev. By the end of the eleventh century, organised Christianity appears to have taken firm roots in Kievan Russia.

Non-Christian peoples

Few people realise that the world's fifth largest Muslim community is to be found in the USSR, in the republics of Soviet Central Asia. This is also one of the oldest Muslim communities, with roots stretching back to within fifty years of Muhammad's death, though the full conversion of the Turkic groups took place under the fourteenth-century Tatar Khan Uzbeg. The area has a rich Islamic heritage, traces of which are still to be found in architectural and literary remains. One of the most authoritative collections of *hadith* (traditions about the Prophet) was produced by al-Bukhari who, as his name suggests, came from the town of Bukhara (in what is now Soviet Uzbekistan). During the twelfth century religious life was greatly enhanced by the emergence of Sūfī movements based in the towns of Bukhara and Merv (the present day town of Mari in Soviet Turkmenistan). Most noteworthy of the great Sūfī masters was Baha ad-din an-Naqshbani (c 1318–89), who founded an order that is still active in much of the Islamic world.

From about the sixteenth century the Russians began to penetrate Islamic Central Asia, utilising both trade and military might, and by the 1860s the Tsarist Empire had effectively conquered the area extending to contemporary Iran and Afghanistan. Initially the Orthodox tsars attempted the forcible conversion to Christianity of these people, but most of them resisted. Consequently, under Catherine the Great (1762–96) the emphasis moved towards control, with the establishment of a Spiritual Directorate for the Islamic peoples. Nevertheless, in the mid-nineteenth century further efforts, this time of a predominantly educational rather than forceful nature, were made to convert the Muslims of the Russian Empire.

The October 1917 Revolution led to a harsh assault on Islam in the Russian Empire, though after a few years some concessions were made to the predominantly Muslim peoples of Central Asia and elsewhere. During the late 1920s, however, religious courts and schools were closed and the giving of alms discouraged, while in the 1930s Stalin launched a more brutal campaign with the mass closure of mosques and the imprisonment and execution of mullahs, combined with an outpouring of virulent anti-Islamic propaganda. The traditional way of life was totally disrupted by the liberation of women, the introduction of pig-farming (pork is forbidden by Islamic tradition) and the abolition of the Arabic script.

The Second World War helped to save institutional Islamic life, as it did the institutional life of other major religious denominations. Four Spiritual Directorates were established, the most important being that for Central Asia and

Kazakhstan, based in Tashkent. Mosques were reopened, two training institutes permitted to function and a small number of government-selected Muslims were allowed to perform the *haj* (pilgrimage to Mecca). Islam again came under attack during the Khrushchev period (1958–64) but since then a certain modus vivendi appears to have been achieved. The régime remains hostile to all religious faith and attacks it in print as well as placing many obstacles in the way of those wishing to practise their faith. Yet it permits a limited number of mosques to exist and in recent years has granted permission for the opening of some new mosques, bringing the total to about 500.

Alongside the official Islamic establishment there exists a whole range of unofficial and uncontrollable practices, from the more orthodox Sūfī brotherhoods to syncretic practices associated with magic wells or holy places. These are frequently attacked by the Soviet press; and when they are found, the unofficial mosques associated with them are closed down and the mullahs imprisoned.

Finally, we should note that in recent years Soviet Muslims appear to have been affected by growing Islamic assertiveness in the wider world and more particularly by events in Iran and Afghanistan; but it is difficult to predict what the long-term effects of this influence will be.

There are about 1.8 million Jews in the USSR, though it is not known how many are active believers. The identification of the Jews with their spiritual and cultural heritage appears to have grown since the formation of Israel in 1948 and the Six Day War of 1967. Increasingly discriminated against, many of them sought emigration, and during the 1970s thousands left, though from late 1979 it became increasingly difficult to do so.

The religious needs of the Jews are served by an estimated sixty-nine synagogues, of which half are located in the Georgian republic. In more recent years there have also sprung up groups of Jewish believers seeking to explore their faith and heritage, and unofficial Hebrew teachers have been imprisoned.

Mainly in the regions close to Mongolia, several hundred thousand people of Buddhist background are to be found. Very little is known about their religious life and estimates of the number of active lamas range from thirty altogether to one in every village.

In some of the more remote parts of the USSR traditional religious practices, such as ancestor worship or the cult of the bear, are still to be found. In recent years some of the Eastern religions have made some inroads among the population, most notably the Hare Krishna cult, which appears to have thousands of followers; they have been subject to considerable persecution since about 1981.[1]

The state's attitude to religion

History

The official ideology of the rulers of the USSR is Marxism-Leninism. Karl Marx's philosophy was clearly atheistic: in his view, ideas about God are created by men and are thus illusory. He also saw that religion can easily be used by exploiting elements in human societies in order to encourage the oppressed to accept their fate and look forward to relief in the next world.

The Russian revolutionary Lenin followed Marx in his analysis of religion, though his critique was often considerably harsher: on one occasion he spoke of religion as 'spiritual booze'. Yet Lenin was also concerned to demonstrate that believers could live under socialism and argued that the attitude of the Communist Party and the state towards religion was different. The attitude of the Party was unashamedly atheistic and it would carry out active propaganda against religion; the attitude of the latter, however, was neutral in matters of religious belief. Nevertheless, Lenin consistently maintained that a combination of social transformation and education would eventually lead to the 'withering away' of religious belief.

In practice this overwhelmingly hostile attitude to religion has been reinforced by the 'totalist' nature of Soviet ideology, with its claim to provide a full understanding of the world and of the means by which it can be transformed. This claim to infallibility means that alternative belief systems have no long-term validity, and it appears also to mean that unless the Soviet system changes its very nature, no real freedom can be granted to the churches, although their circumstances can vary in difficulty at different times. Certainly if we examine the history of church-state relations in the USSR, we find a persistent hostility manifested towards religion, even during more 'liberal' periods.

Within a year of coming to power the Bolsheviks had launched a harsh attack against the Russian Orthodox Church, tainted in their eyes by its association with the old régime. The 1918 Decree on the Separation of Church from State and Church from School deprived the Orthodox Church of both its privileged status and its property. In denying religious organisations the status of a person at law, government placed the local parish church on a lower footing than virtually any other social organisation. Simultaneously active laymen and priests were subject to abuse in the press, harassment, arrest and, in some cases, execution. For a time the newly elected Patriarch Tikhon was held under arrest and the authorities encouraged a radical 'Living Church', prepared to compromise with the new régime. Gradually, however, the Orthodox hierarchy under the leadership (from 1925) of Metropolitan Sergi moved towards political loyalty vis-à-vis the Soviet state.[2]

Though harassment continued throughout the 1920s, it was not until 1929, in the context of Stalin's attempts to industrialise and bring the Soviet Union under tight political control, that a new and more brutal assault was launched against all religious groups. Over the next decade institutional religion was to be virtually wiped out in the Soviet Union, while thousands of clerics and laymen died in labour camps. Mass church closures were given some legal basis by the 1929 Law on Religious Associations (see p 31), but the prime characteristic of this campaign was its arbitrariness.

Only the outbreak of war appears to have saved organised religion. The secular authorities had been aware for some years that although they had almost succeeded in destroying institutional religion, they had made very little impression on the loyalty of believers to their faith. Then the unexpected Nazi invasion in 1941 was seized on by religious leaders as an opportunity for them to demonstrate their patriotism. They declared their support for the war effort, and the secular authorities in turn realised that they did indeed need the support of the whole population at this critical time. Persecution was therefore abruptly halted. The Orthodox Church was permitted to hold a synod, to publish a limited amount of literature, to resume theological education and to reopen some churches. Similar concessions were granted to other religious groups. In late 1943 the state Council for the Affairs of the Russian Orthodox Church was formed, and soon after the Council for the Affairs of Religious Cults, dealing with all other religious groups. In 1965 these were to merge into the Council for Religious Affairs.

This more moderate policy continued after the war, though restrictive legislation remained in force, arrests still took place and anti-religious propaganda and education continued unabated. Then in the late 1950s General Secretary Khrushchev, who did much to open up Soviet society in other areas, launched a vicious campaign against all religious organisations. They were forced to accept a greater degree of state intervention in their internal affairs; thousands of places of worship were closed; and religious activists arrested.

In many ways this campaign was counter-productive, for although it led to the halving of the number of religious associations, it also produced a strong resistance to state policies from believers. Thus by the 1970s, the state faced not only a religious dissident movement affecting many religious groups, but also a revival of interest in religion among the wider Soviet population.

Current practice

Formal religious life within the USSR today is basically regulated by the 1929 Law on Religious Associations (amended in 1975), as interpreted by the Council for Religious Affairs (CRA). The latter body has representatives at the centre, but also in the provinces, responsible for making all the major decisions affecting the churches.

The basic religious unit, and the only unit formally recognised at Soviet law, is the local religious community or 'association' of at least twenty adult members. Each such association must apply to the local authorities for registration; when such an application has been received, the local authorities make a recommendation and pass it on to the CRA in Moscow for a final decision. In theory this registration will be granted as long as all the paperwork is in order, but in practice there are a number of limitations that allow considerable scope for arbitrary refusal. Thus groups whose members have been guilty of legal violations or 'anti-social activity', or whose teachings are deemed to have a 'superstitious character' (which may cover anything from allegations of ritual murder to speaking in tongues), stand no chance of gaining registered status. During the 1960s and 1970s numerous *samizdat* (literally 'self-published') documents reached the West, detailing some of the problems facing those seeking to register religious associations. Believers involved were often told, for example, that the buildings they had in mind were unsafe or 'too near a school'. If they still proved persistent, the more active believers were threatened with job dismissal or psychiatric internment.

Nevertheless the state has adopted a more flexible attitude to registration with some groups. Since the early 1970s, Baptist communities have been permitted to register more freely; over 500 have done so. This should be seen as a concession wrung from the state by the emergence of a strong dissenting movement among the Baptists. For the authorities it is greatly preferable to have legally functioning religious associations over whom some surveillance can be exercised than to have a healthy underground church movement which is far harder to control. Other groups to benefit from this flexibility have been the Lutherans, Mennonites and Muslims. Many unofficial groups have, however, chosen not to register under conditions that they feel unduly inhibit their practice of the faith.

Since Gorbachev came to power it appears that the overall decline in the number of places of worship has ceased. The complaints of believers have been supported in the Soviet press, with many articles reporting on the way officials have blocked legitimate attempts to open churches. Nevertheless, there has been no indication that the thousands of churches closed against the will of believers will be reopened.

Once a community has gained registration, it still needs to find a building and a priest or pastor. In theory this should not be difficult. By law religious communities are permitted to acquire free of charge or lease property owned by the local authorities, and there are plenty of disused churches in the USSR. In practice all sorts of difficulties are placed in their way, with safety rules often serving as a convenient pretext. Similarly it should be relatively simple for local congregations or central religious organisations to appoint priests or pastors, but in fact the CRA representatives frequently complicate this procedure by refusing to recognise the person in question or ensuring that an unworthy individual is kept in place. Thus some believers have complained about being unable to remove priests who are drunkards or mercenary.

Even should these hurdles be overcome, religious communities are subject to constant state interference in their affairs, ranging from the harassment of those who bring their children to church, through the monitoring of sermons, to the fining of members who organise meetings in their homes. For those outside registered communities these problems are magnified greatly, with fines commonplace and imprisonment not unusual for those who organise illegal activity.

As noted, the only religious institution recognised by Soviet law is the local religious association. Nevertheless, since the Second World War, many of the major denominations have succeeded in setting up various central administrative bodies and institutions, such as theological seminaries and official journals. Only the Baptists and the Orthodox have central administrative structures covering the whole of the USSR, however, and other denominations, like the Roman Catholics, have none at all.

At the level of church leadership state control is, if anything, even more thorough than at local level, though in theory church and state are separate. From leaked official sources we know that all appointments to church leadership are controlled by the Council for Religious Affairs. One such document dealing with the Russian Orthodox Church noted that 'Not one consecration . . . takes place without the careful checking of the candidature by the responsible members of the Council in close contact with its commissioners and appropriate interested bodies'. Moreover, those church leaders who are too resolute in the defence of the faith or who prove particularly active in preaching are subject to sanctions, ranging from warnings to dismissal.

The CRA also exercises control over admission to the limited number of theological seminaries and over all religious publications, as well as briefing those clergymen permitted to travel abroad or to meet foreign delegations.

Religious believers do not only face difficulties in direct connection with their religious activities. The entire Soviet educational system is permeated by the atheism of the official Marxist-Leninist ideology. Religious education is forbidden in schools, and such information as is provided about religion is highly tendentious. Teachers are required to bring up their pupils as materialists and to ensure that lessons given in any subject have at least some atheist content. At university level, courses on scientific atheism are compulsory in all faculties and students must pass examinations on atheism and materialism. Atheist propaganda is systematically promoted in factories, clubs and cinemas; atheist articles and programmes appear in the mass media; atheist lectures are given and workers are expected to attend them. Throughout the Soviet period, efforts have been made to devise and promote non-religious rites relating to birth, marriage and death, with varying degrees of success. The commitment to struggle against religion is taken very seriously by the Soviet authorities.

Even if atheist education and propaganda have very little effect on the beliefs of a committed Christian in the Soviet Union, the obligatory adherence to atheism means that a very wide range of educational and vocational opportunities are closed to the believer. It is rare for a known believer to succeed in completing higher education, and jobs of any degree of responsibility are usually ruled out in advance by the requirement that they be occupied only by Communists—and hence by atheists.

THE VARIOUS CHURCHES

The Russian Orthodox Church

History

The Russian Orthodox Church celebrated its thousandth anniversary in 1988. Although there were Christians in the area earlier and legend has it that the apostle Andrew was a missionary there, it was in 988 or 989 that Prince (later Saint) Vladimir of Kiev adopted Christianity in its Orthodox form from Byzantium. The Kievan Chronicles relate how Vladimir, having decided to adopt a state religion, sent ambassadors to different countries to sample their various faiths. The emissaries to Byzantium are said to have reported that the worship of the Orthodox Church was so beautiful that 'We knew not whether we were in heaven or on earth'. Vladimir had his subjects baptised and cast the statues of the old pagan gods into the River Dnieper. From then on, and after the centre of power moved to Moscow, Russian Orthodoxy was the national Church and the dominant form of Christianity; and over the centuries it became ever more closely bound to the rulers of the land, even at times of serious conflict between church and state. The Church inherited from Byzantium the Constantinian concept of 'symphony' between church and state, which survived until 1917. The great men of the Church and leading figures in national life were often one and the same. The Church's history has been inextricably bound up with that of the Russian people and with other peoples—notably the Ukrainians, Belorussians and Moldavians—and it has exerted a profound influence on Russian culture.

From the sixteenth century onwards, Orthodoxy expanded eastwards. Monasticism has always been a central feature of Orthodox life, and it was the monks who were the Church's missionaries. A monk would feel a call to live for a time in solitude in order to deepen his prayer life, and would move east and north into the forests. As time passed, and he grew in spiritual wisdom, disciples would gather around him, and a monastic community would grow up. The first of these was St Sergius, one of Russia's best-loved saints, who founded the monastery at Zagorsk. Even today this is Russian Orthodoxy's spiritual centre. Then another monk would feel the call to move east alone, and the pattern would repeat itself. In this way Orthodoxy spread throughout Siberia as far as the Pacific Ocean, and on into Japan, Alaska and California.

In the eighteenth century, Peter the Great—the reforming, Western-orientated tsar who sought to modernise Russia— made the Church into a state church. Since 1589, the Church had had its own patriarch, or head (previously it had been headed by a bishop appointed by Byzantium), but Peter refused to appoint a new one. He transformed the Church into what was virtually a government department, appointed a procurator to oversee it, and curtailed its authority and self-government. The Church was closely identified with the tsarist system, especially under the last monarch, Nicholas II, and therefore the Bolsheviks opposed it more fiercely than other religious groups. The fact that the Church was so closely linked to the autocracy has tended to obscure what might have turned into a renewal movement within the Church at the turn of the century. A number of leading Marxist thinkers converted to Orthodoxy. This suggests that, despite its subjugated position, the Church had managed to retain enough spiritual vitality to attract some of the most learned men of the time. Discussion of possible reforms within the Church was lively, but this promising development was cut short by the Revolution.

After the October Revolution in 1917, the Church enjoyed a very brief period of relative freedom, while the new Bolshevik government was occupied with more pressing matters. Earlier in 1917 it had finally succeeded in convening a council to discuss important issues in the life of the Church, and to elect a patriarch, and this council continued in session after the Bolshevik takeover. However, Church property was soon nationalised by the 1918 Decree on the Separation of Church and State. Moreover, the first of many bishops was murdered while the council was in session, and increasingly during the 1920s and on a massive scale during the 1930s, nearly all the bishops and clergy and incalculably large numbers of faithful perished in the labour camps or were shot.

The Soviet state attempted to neutralise the Church by the creation in the early 1920s of a rival body, the so-called 'Renovationist' (*obnovlencheskaya*) Church, also known as the 'Living Church'. It was headed by Orthodox priests, talented in many ways, who gave unstinting support to the socialist cause. For some years it enjoyed the full support of the secret police, who confiscated over two-thirds of the churches of the Patriarchal Church and handed them over to the Renovationists. Bishops and priests refusing to recognise the Renovationists were arrested and imprisoned. These very facts compromised the movement in the eyes of the faithful, who stayed away en masse from Renovationist churches and remained loyal to the Patriarchal Church. Though it survived into the 1940s, the Renovationist movement was a spent force long before. The state had lost interest in promoting it by the end of the 1920s, and from then on worked to achieve its purpose through the Patriarchal Church. The state had put strong pressure upon Patriarch Tikhon, who was elected in 1918, to declare his loyalty to the Soviet régime. After a period of imprisonment, he did indeed issue a statement to this effect in 1923. He died in 1925, and there are still those who believe he was murdered. His successor, Metropolitan Sergi (Stragorodsky), was not directly appointed by either the council or Patriarch Tikhon, and his legitimacy as head of the Church was (and still is) hotly debated. Sergi was also imprisoned, and after being released, in 1927, issued a declaration of loyalty to the Soviet State. Since that time the Patriarchal Church has been completely subservient to the state. Many thousands of faithful left the Church in opposition to Sergi's declaration and went underground; they formed various groups which in time became known as the True Orthodox Church or True Orthodox Christians.

By 1939, after many years of persistent persecution, the Russian Orthodox Church had virtually ceased to exist as an institution. There were only four ruling bishops at liberty, and very few of the thousands of churches remained open for worship. Theological education, monasticism and religious publications had long ceased. This situation was reversed owing to an unforeseen historical event: Hitler's invasion of the USSR. Stalin found that he needed the support of the Church leaders to kindle popular support and patriotic fervour for an unexpected war. The Orthodox faith, though suppressed institutionally, had remained alive in the hearts of the people, and the banner of Orthodoxy had to be lifted to rally them to the defence of the nation. Moreover, in the areas under German occupation local believers spontaneously began to reopen churches and monasteries and people who had lived without them for years flooded back to them. All this made it clear that the people had not abandoned their traditional faith, and after the war the policy was to permit the Church a legitimate, though very closely controlled, existence, so that the state could maintain surveillance. A further factor was the flourishing church life which existed in the western areas of the present-day USSR which were annexed after the war.

In September 1943, the three senior hierarchs of the Church were invited to a meeting with Stalin, after which the Church was restored to an official and public existence. It continued to give the unstinting support it had already demonstrated for the war effort. After the war, theological education was resumed, some monasteries reopened, and publication of religious literature, albeit in tiny quantities, recommenced. Overseas contacts grew from 1944 onwards.

The Church continued to enjoy the benefits of these improvements in institutional church life during the 1950s, but the status quo was severely disrupted by the anti-religious campaign of 1959–64. This was the initiative of the then leader of the Soviet Union, Khrushchev. It was a marked aberration in what could otherwise have been seen as a reasonably consistent pattern of relations between church and state in the post-war period. Floods of virulently anti-religious literature were published; some Orthodox priests publicly defected to atheism and published statements denouncing their former faith; bishops, priests, monks and nuns were tried and imprisoned on fabricated 'criminal' charges, perhaps as many as 15,000 Orthodox churches (more than half) were closed and have not since been reopened; and theological education was severely curtailed. The anti-religious campaign ceased abruptly with Khrushchev's sudden removal from power, but many of the losses sustained by the Church, above all the closed churches, have never been rectified.

Voiced dissent within the Church began tentatively as a protest against the anti-religious campaign, and gained strength when two Moscow priests, Frs Nikolai Eshliman and Gleb Yakunin, addressed an Open Letter to Patriarch Aleksi (1945–70) in 1965. The dissent took the form of protests to both state and Church leaders, pointing to the Church's lack of freedom and to the overly compliant attitude of Church leaders towards the state. During the 1970s the amount of *samizdat* reaching the West increased steadily, young Orthodox Christians set up informal discussion groups to provide a forum to voice their concerns, and Christians were active in working for human and religious rights: in 1976 Father Gleb Yakunin formed the Christian Committee for the Defence of Believers' Rights. In the later 1970s the Soviet authorities moved determinedly against leading dissenters (as they did against dissenters in other areas of Soviet life), and by the early 1980s it was clear that the human-rights movement, together with the brief flowering of East-West détente, had been effectively stifled.

The régime under Brezhnev continued the pragmatic policy of allowing strictly controlled freedom for official church life, partly for its propaganda value abroad and partly as a counterbalance to its continued harsh treatment of dissenters. The state continues assiduously to promote the Church's foreign contacts, from which the government derives a limited but worthwhile benefit. The Church's leadership under the present Patriarch, Pimen (1971–), goes along with this. The leadership changes after Brezhnev's death in 1982 made no difference, except that treatment of dissenters became even harsher. Not only active dissenters, but also Orthodox who possessed Christian literature, or met in study and discussion groups, were repressed. Since Gorbachev came to power, active harassment has decreased, but there are reports that study groups are afraid to resume meetings.

Church structure and associated institutions

According to Soviet law, the church exists only as a series of local communities which have no legal relationship to one another or to a hierarchy. The fact that a central administration does exist is purely de facto and has no legal basis. This central administration is called the Moscow Patriarchate. The chief governing body of the Church is the National Council (*Pomestny Sobor*), which is composed of the bishop, a priest and a layman from every diocese. It meets to decide important matters and to elect the Patriarch. Under Soviet conditions, the National Council may meet only with state permission, and there were three during the Soviet period—in 1918, 1945 and 1971. A fourth was held in 1988, the millennium year. In between Councils, the daily business of running the Church is the responsibility of the Holy Synod. This consists of the Patriarch as chairman, five senior hierarchs who are permanent members, and three other diocesan bishops who serve in turn for six-monthly periods.

The Moscow Patriarchate has the following departments: the Department of External Church Relations, responsible for all foreign and ecumenical relations; the Publishing Department; the Education Committee, responsible for the theological schools; the Commission on Questions of Christian Unity; and the Chancellorship, or business management, under which come the Economic Management Department and the Pensions Committee.

There are theoretically seventy-three dioceses within the USSR, but currently only fifty-seven diocesan bishops. The diocesan bishop is responsible for the pastoral care of all the parishes in his diocese, and in theory reports directly to the Patriarch. In addition to the diocesan bishops, there are suffragan or deputy bishops. There are three main clergy ranks in the Orthodox Church: deacon, priest and bishop. Deacons and priests may be married or unmarried. Unmarried and widowed priests may become monks and only monks are eligible to become bishops.

The number of functioning parish churches in the Soviet Union has declined drastically since the Revolution. At present there are probably no more than 6,500. This is clearly grossly inadequate for a Church which numbers around fifty million people. While large city churches may have several priests, small village churches often have to share a priest between two or more congregations, which means that many of them have services as infrequently as once a month. The parish, in the eyes of the law, is a religious association such as exists in all denominations. It consists of a minimum of twenty believers, who elect a three-person executive committee responsible for the day-to-day running of the church and with considerable influence. The religious association employs a priest, who is concerned only with the spiritual side of parish life. He is not allowed by law to attend meetings of the religious association, and may not have anything to do with financial matters.

The Church receives no financial assistance from the state. Its income is derived from collections at church services and the sale of candles, neck crosses and similar small items of worship (which it manufactures). The amount of the Church's income is unknown, but it is certainly hundreds of millions of roubles a year. It appears to be quite sufficient for its needs. Since the Church is prohibited by law from charitable and missionary activity, it cannot give away its income for these purposes. Its income is therefore spent on salaries and pensions for clergy and church workers, on the payment of taxes (up to 81% on the Church's commercial operations and up to 69% on the salaries of the clergy), on 'voluntary' donations to the State Peace Fund and the Historical Preservation Fund (often as much as 20% of the parish's gross income), in the upkeep of church buildings, and on the theological schools, the Publishing Department and the Department of External Church Relations. The latter finances the many Church representatives who travel abroad and gives lavish hospitality to foreign visitors.

The Church has three theological seminaries (at Zagorsk, fifty miles north-east of Moscow, Leningrad, and Odessa) and two academies (at Zagorsk and Leningrad). The four-year seminary course provides basic theological training for parish priests, and the four-year academy course more advanced training. There is also a correspondence course for parish priests who have been ordained without seminary training. The number of theological students at present is something over 2,000 of whom about half are correspondence students. There are eight monasteries and eleven convents. One monastery, the Danilov Monastery in Moscow, was returned to the Church only in 1983, and has now become its main administrative centre, as well as housing a community of monks. However, this represents a vast decline, since monastic life was such an important element in pre-revolutionary Russian life. There are only three monasteries on Russian soil: in Moscow, Zagorsk and Pskov, and one newly-opened convent, near Yaroslavl. There are no monastic communities east of Yaroslavl.

The monasteries are administratively and financially separate from the rest of the Church. They receive no funds from the Moscow Patriarchate, and subsist on the donations of believers, which are substantial. The monasteries are not mentioned in Soviet legislation on religion and therefore have no legal existence; they could be closed by administrative procedures at any time.

The Church prints a small number of small-circulation publications on state printing presses, subject to state censorship. There is a monthly journal, the *Journal of the Moscow Patriarchate* or *Zhurnal Moskovskoi Patriarkhii*, published in Russian and English, and a Ukrainian journal, *Pravoslavny visnyk* ('Orthodox Herald'), as well as occasional editions of prayerbooks and liturgical books in small but slowly increasing quantities. It has an occasional publication entitled *Bogoslovskiye trudy* ('Theological Works'), of which twenty-four editions have appeared. It also produces an annual calendar. In 1988 publication commenced of the *Moscow Church Herald*, a monthly news-sheet containing attractive colour photographs of church life.

The Church publishes occasional, very small editions of the Bible and New Testament. It seems likely that only 280,000 Bibles and 150,000 New Testaments have been printed since the Revolution—clearly utterly inadequate for the Church's membership.

The Russian Orthodox Church has an extensive and growing range of ecumenical contacts. It is currently engaged in a continuing series of discussions with the Roman Catholic Church, the Anglican Church, Lutheran Churches, the non-Chalcedonian Churches of the Middle East, and others.[3] It periodically hosts inter-religious peace conferences in Moscow attended by religious groups from around the world. It joined the World Council of Churches in 1961 (after at first displaying a marked lack of interest in doing so) and is its largest single member (by number of adherents). It is also a member of the Conference of European Churches and of the Prague-based Christian Peace Conference.

Church membership

No comprehensive statistics are available from either state or Church sources on the composition of the Church, and even its total membership remains a secret. However, some scattered information may be derived from many sources.

Russians are almost certainly the largest ethnic group within the Church, although it is also strong in Ukraine, where it has the greatest concentration of open churches. Belorussians have traditionally been the third ethnic component of the Orthodox Church. There is also a strong concentration of Orthodox churches in Moldavia. Other areas with centres of Orthodoxy are to be found in the three Baltic republics, particularly Latvia and Estonia. Before the Second World War 17% of ethnic Estonians were Orthodox, but nowadays it appears that the majority of Orthodox in the Baltic republics are Russians moved into these areas as part of the régime's Russification policy. Russians also form the majority of the small Orthodox populations in Soviet Central Asia and Azerbaidzhan, which are predominantly Muslim. It is difficult to estimate the size of the Orthodox population in Siberia, since there are so few churches there, and therefore it is also difficult to estimate how many of them are Russian settlers and how many are native Siberians.

The two main groups within the Orthodox Church are the relatively small number of urban intellectuals and the large mass which is basically derived from peasant stock. This is a continuation of the pre-revolutionary pattern, and reflects the fact that Russia never developed a middle class. The Soviet 'middle class' of managers, skilled workers and technocrats is on the whole uninterested in religion.

The impression given by Soviet sociologists of religion is that members of the Orthodox Church are predominantly female, elderly and poorly educated. The work of these sociologists must be treated with care, because there are ideological pressures upon them to produce the results desired by the Communist Party. In fact, however, the picture may be substantially true. For some time now there have been more women than men in Orthodox churches—but this is partly due to the sex imbalance in the population as a result of heavy male casualties during the Second World War. More elderly than young people can be seen in churches—but this is partly because young people risk losing their job or place in higher education if they are known to be regular church attenders. The same factor of discrimination is part of the explanation why education levels of Orthodox believers appear to be low. In recent years evidence has been accumulating of the attraction of Orthodoxy for the young and the well-educated, but this has yet to be reflected in Soviet sociology.

It is likely that the number of adherents to the Church is not less than fifty million. These cover the whole range from merely nominal believers to deeply committed Christians. Even nominalism, however, means something in a country where any expression of interest in religion may attract unwelcome attention from the authorities.

There are probably just over 6,000 active parish priests, that is, roughly the same as the number of churches. There are usually about seventy (diocesan and suffragan) bishops. It is not known how many deacons there are at present, but an official source in 1974 reported that there were fewer than 600.

The number of religious is unknown. In 1970 the same official source reported that there were 1,275 monastics, of whom three-quarters were nuns. It is reportedly very difficult for anyone, especially a young person, to become a novice. There are, however, reports of monks and nuns living a monastic life 'in the world', having taken monastic vows secretly. There is no way of estimating their numbers. There are also reports of people, sometimes whole families, living in obedience to an elder (*starets*) or 'spiritual father' resident in one of the monasteries.

This is a pre-revolutionary tradition: a *starets* is a person of spiritual wisdom and insight, usually acquired by living in solitude for lengthy periods. He is not appointed by the Church but acclaimed by the people, who will begin to come to him in greater and greater numbers, seeking advice. There is an unknown number of *startsy* in the Soviet Union at present: their names and locations cannot be published until after their deaths.

Current growth trends

There is a strong impression among all observers of the Russian Orthodox Church, both inside and outside it, that it is growing, but there is no statistical basis for this impression and no figures of any kind can be given. There have been persistent reports for over twenty-five years now of people from all walks of life converting to Orthodoxy. These include middle-aged and older people, but mostly young people, particularly young intellectuals.

By far the most significant development, however, has been the conversion to Orthodoxy of members of the creative intelligentsia. By this we mean not just highly-educated people, but the thinkers, writers, philosophers, artists, poets and others who believe themselves to be carrying on the traditions of the Russian intelligentsia of the past and creating a post-Marxist future, and so the fact that many of them are finding answers in Orthodoxy is of great importance. The conversion of such people to Orthodoxy not only contradicts Marxist theories about religion—which is true of anyone's conversion—but also reverses the trend of the Russian intelligentsia away from the Church. This trend began in the middle of the last century. The bulk of the intelligentsia rejected the Orthodox Church in which they had been brought up, and which they regarded as backward, intellectually inadequate, and subservient to tsardom. They did not think it held the answers to the questions they were asking about the future of their society. For those answers they looked to the West and embraced the rationalist ideas of the Enlightenment. Such great thinkers as Khomyakov, Solovyov and Dostoyevsky spoke out against this attitude, and propounded the virtues of the Orthodox faith, but their words fell upon stony ground. There seemed to be no reason why the Russian intelligentsia—in common with any other secularised intelligentsia—should ever return to the Church. There was a move in this direction by some members of the intelligentsia at the turn of the century, when a number of leading Marxist thinkers converted to Orthodoxy. However, most members of the intelligentsia did not follow the example, and the impulse towards renewal that they brought to the Church was quickly truncated by the Revolution. Today's Orthodox intelligentsia regard these thinkers as their spiritual forebears.

None of this, however, is intended to suggest that the conversion of an intellectual is intrinsically more important than anyone else's conversion. It is undoubtedly the strength of faith of the ordinary people, the survival of the faith in families, and the unrecorded conversions of average folk that has kept the Church alive. Though vast numbers of them suffered and perished in the labour camps during the 1920s and 1930s, alongside most of the clergy and nearly all the bishops, there still remained millions who flocked back to the churches and monasteries reopened under German occupation, causing Stalin to change his policy on religion. Today it is still the millions of faithful throughout the Soviet Union who make the Russian Orthodox Church one of the largest, most resilient (and well-financed) churches in the world. They have preserved the faith, the traditions and—latterly—the institutional structures which, in the post-Stalin years, have enabled the constantly growing stream of members of the intelligentsia, both young and old, to embrace Orthodox Christianity.

Orthodoxy in Russia has always drawn its spiritual strength from the common people. Princes and bishops have rallied the people in times of national crisis, and members of the intelligentsia have produced the works of theological and philosophical depth which have done so much to enrich Christians of other nations, but the solid bedrock of popular piety has given the support for the princes and bishops, and, very often, the inspiration for the intelligentsia. The greatest spiritual leaders in the Russian Orthodox Church have always been the simple peasants, the monks and saints, who gave up even the little they had for a life of humility and asceticism, the two hallmarks of the distinctively Russian brand of kenotic Christianity.[4] It has been this self-denial, this uncomplaining acceptance of hardship and suffering, that has kept the Church not only alive but vigorous, despite the attempts to destroy it. Millions of devout believers clung fast to their beliefs, despite appalling physical and spiritual deprivation, enabling their church to weather persecution of a scale and intensity never before seen in history. In time this will come to be seen as one of the greatest miracles of the twentieth century.

There are several reasons for the growth of interest in religion, including Orthodoxy, in the Soviet Union. Probably the most important is disillusionment with Marxism-Leninism. As people became aware that it did not function as it was supposed to even at the most basic level, in the economy, let alone provide any spiritual satisfaction or reason for living, they began to search for a system of beliefs that would give meaning to their lives. They found—and are still finding—many different answers, but for many the path to truth lay through Orthodoxy. Another reason for their quest was the lack of appeal of atheism, which did not provide them with a positive or adequate view of life. In particular, it failed to provide a satisfactory answer to the problem of death. The strong religious element in Russian culture, which we have already mentioned, is another cause of interest in religion. As people began to look back into their past to establish a sense of their own identity—which Marxism-Leninism did not give them—they encountered Orthodoxy at every turn. In particular, people come to Orthodoxy through reading the great nineteenth-century authors, above all Dostoyevsky.

Another factor has been the growth of nationalism in most parts of the Soviet Union, which is very often linked with growth of interest in religion—for example, Islam in Soviet Central Asia and Catholicism in Lithuania. The vigorous growth of Russian nationalism recently has led many to develop an interest in Russian Orthodoxy.

The return of intellectuals to the Church began at the end of the 1950s, grew gradually through the 1960s and more rapidly during the 1970s, and continues today. There are two main reasons why it began when it did. The first was that young people at the end of the 1950s belonged to the first generation under Soviet power that had leisure to think. Since 1917, the population of the USSR had endured war, revolution, civil war, large-scale famine, political terror, war again, and then the final years of Stalinism. These conditions—while they unquestionably strengthened the faith of many through appalling suffering—were not in general conducive to any movement by unbelievers towards the Church. The second reason was 'destalinisation', which was started by Khrushchev's famous 'secret speech' to the CPSU (Communist Party of the Soviet Union) Congress of 1956. This was a cataclysmic shock for the Soviet people. They had been told all their lives that Stalin was virtually a god, and then overnight they were told that this was untrue. This turnabout bred a generation of people who would be unlikely ever again to take any official statement on trust. If they had been lied to once, they could be lied to again. People now wanted to think things through for themselves and work out their own values upon which to base their lives. For many, this path led to the Church.

The Ukrainian Orthodox Church

The Ukrainian Autocephalous Orthodox Church (UAOC) considers itself the successor of the Church of Kievan Rus, established in 988 and subsequently split into Russian and Ukrainian components, the former absorbing the latter after the seventeenth century.[5] In 1918, the All-Ukrainian Church *Sobor* (Congress) demanded autocephaly from the Russian Orthodox Church. On 1st January 1919 the independent Ukrainian government legalised an independent Ukrainian Orthodox Church. On 5th May 1920 the Ukrainian Orthodox Church *Rada* (Permanent Council) proclaimed the church's autocephaly. In October 1921 a UAOC *Sobor* elected Archpriest Vasyl Lypkivsky as Metropolitan of Kiev and All Ukraine. He was consecrated on 23rd October 1921—by laying-on of hands by laity and lower clergy since no Ukrainian bishop had agreed to join the schism.

The Soviet authorities actively supported the UAOC until 1928, taking churches from the Patriarchal Church and handing them over to the UAOC. By early 1924, the UAOC had 30 bishops, some 1,500 priests and deacons, and nearly 1,100 parishes. At its peak it may have had between three and six million followers. Fewer than 10% of Ukrainian laity and clergy then joined the UAOC. At the end of the 1920s, the Bolshevik authorities began to persecute the Church, and in January 1930 compelled an Extraordinary *Sobor* to announce the dissolution of the UAOC. Metropolitans Boretsky and Lypkivsky, most of the bishops, and thousands of clergy and laity were exiled, imprisoned or killed.

The UAOC was formally reconstituted in February 1942 after Ukrainian territory was occupied by the Nazis. Headed by Archbishop Polikarp of Lutsk, it had 15 bishops and approximately 1,500 clergy. At the end of the war its remaining members were absorbed by the Russian Orthodox Church. Although the UAOC has no known organised existence in the USSR, its idea remains alive, as indicated by the fact that individuals like Fr Vasyl Romanyuk and Lev Lukyanenko have expressed allegiance to it, while members of unofficial Ukrainian clubs and independent publications have called for its restoration.

The Georgian Orthodox Church

History

The Georgian Orthodox Church is one of the oldest national churches in the world. There is a legend that the apostle Andrew was a missionary in Georgia, and other missionaries from Asia Minor were also active. The most prominent was St Nino, now the national saint, who baptised converts, built churches and, in 326, converted King Mirian. The Georgian Church achieved autonomy in 553 and autocephaly in the eighth century. Since then the Church has fought to maintain the Christian faith and culture of Georgia amid political turmoil, including occupation by Persians, Byzantines, Arabs, Turks and Mongols. Georgia was taken into the Russian Empire in 1801, and in 1811 the Russian Orthodox Church removed its autocephaly and substituted a Russian Exarch[6] for the deposed Georgian Catholicos-Patriarch.[7] In 1917 the Georgian Orthodox Church regained its autocephaly and benefited from the brief period of Georgian political independence (1918–21). In the mid-1920s there was intense destruction of Georgian religious life (the Church had been prominent in resisting the Bolsheviks). Persecution apparently continued throughout the 1930s, but there is little documentation of this. It is reasonable to suppose that Stalin's policy of toleration towards religion after the Nazi invasion of the USSR extended to the Georgian Orthodox Church. In 1943 the Russian Orthodox Church finally recognised the autocephaly of the Georgian Church.

The Church then entered a troubled period. Patriarch Efrem, appointed in 1960, at first gained a reputation as an outspoken Georgian patriot, but as he grew older, he came under increased pressure from the KGB, and his sermons had less and less spiritual content. There were reports of homosexuality, debauchery, drunkenness and venality among the clergy. One Bidzina Keratishvili—who had been expelled from the army, university and seminary for drug-pushing and homosexuality—forced Patriarch Efrem to consecrate him a bishop, and eventually attained the rank of Metropolitan, with the ecclesiastical name of Gaioz. Efrem died in 1972, and instead of his named successor, Metropolitan Ilya (Shiolashvili), the Church had a bishop with no theological qualifications foisted upon it as David V. Corruption ran rife: many hierarchs, together with the CRA commissioner, stole valuable church treasures, and Gaioz became increasingly influential. These events reflected widespread corruption in Georgia generally, and from 1972–4 there was a clean-up headed by Eduard Shevardnadze (now the Foreign Minister of the USSR), who, with a KGB background, deposed the corrupt former First Secretary of the Georgian Communist Party. At first the KGB blocked attempts to halt corruption within the Church, but eventually Gaioz was sentenced to fifteen years' imprisonment for embezzlement. Many of the recovered embezzled items, however, were not returned to the Church but given to state museums.

In 1977 David V died and Ilya II was finally elected as his successor. Under his rule church life has been reformed and renewed. He caused three bishops to retire and appointed seven new ones; increased the number of parish priests; founded a church journal; organised a modern translation of the Bible; and encouraged a growing number of seminarians. There continue to be troubles, however: frequent reports of problems at churches and former monasteries; violence in 1982 between former members of the Shio-Mgvime monastery and the staff of the technical college that now occupies its premises; and complaints by some hierarchs of acts of homosexual debauchery by other hierarchs.

Church structure
As is the case with all other religious bodies in the USSR, no central organisation in the Church has any legal basis. The Catholicos-Patriarch has his seat at Mtskheta, thirty-four kilometres north of Tbilisi, with Zion Cathedral as his base in Tbilisi. He is assisted by the Holy Synod of seven bishops. There are fifteen dioceses, many of which had been vacant for some time up to 1980, by which time they had apparently all been filled. Before the Revolution there were about 2,500 churches in Georgia. In 1980 the Patriarch said there were 200 open churches, and this figure has been confirmed from other sources. Ilya II seems to have reopened a number of churches throughout Georgia, although local congregations petitioning for a new church still encounter difficulties. There is one seminary, which opened in 1963 at Mtskheta. The number of seminarians has grown since 1977, and is now said to total over forty. The Church has no publishing department and books are printed on the presses of the Georgian Academy of Sciences. The Church has produced an annual calendar since 1959, and Patriarch Efrem published some New Testaments and prayer-books and a history of the Church up to 1917. Ilya II has widened the Church's publishing activities. There has been a new theological journal *Dzhvari vazisa* ('Vine Cross'); a new

translation of the Bible was begun; and in 1980 the New Testament was finished and the Church received permission to print 40,000 copies, with paper and printing materials paid for by the United Bible Societies.

The Church joined the WCC in 1962. Ilya II's visit to the Vatican in 1980 was the first such visit by a Georgian primate.

Church membership

As far as is known, nearly all members of the Georgian Orthodox Church are Georgians. There is not much data on social groups within the Church, but a list of young people interrogated in 1974 after attending a service in the Zion Cathedral in Tbilisi shows a wide cross-section of social types: a teacher, school and university students, a typist, a shop assistant, factory workers and a number of nominal young communists.

The Georgian Church claims some three million members, although active members probably number between one and two and a half million. The number of clergy is not known, but since Ilya II was elected a number of clergy have been assigned to churches which did not have them before. Four convents in Georgia house ten to twelve nuns each, but there are no monasteries.

Current growth trends

It appears that the Georgian Orthodox Church may be enjoying modest growth after the corruption of the 1970s, which deterred many from attending services and led many to go to evangelical churches instead. There seems to be no reduction in the numbers of young people interested in religion. There are reports of large attendances at religious festivals. In 1982 it was reported that at a recent congress of the Georgian Komsomol (League of Communist Youth) complaints had been made about the numbers of young people wanting to enter the seminary, about young people being married in a civil ceremony and then having a church wedding, and about pacifist tendencies leading some young people to refuse military service.

The Old Believers

The Old Believers came into existence as the result of a schism in the Russian Orthodox Church in the seventeenth century. The Patriarch, Nikon, reformed the prayer-books and liturgical practices to bring them into line with the Greek originals, and the Tsar (eventually) supported him. The reforms were viewed as heresy and betrayal by many believers, led by the Archpriest Avvakum. Many fled the country, and even burned themselves to death, rather than accept the new practices. The extremity and violence of the schism has left the Russian Orthodox with a horror of schism or separation of any kind. Today there are many Old Believers in the USSR, probably one or two million, though no one knows how many. They have recognised hierarchs and churches, though they are given little publicity.

The True Orthodox

The True Orthodox Christians and the True Orthodox Church are groups of believers who opposed the church's accommodation to the Soviet State in the 1920s. They preferred to go underground, and have mostly remained there since, so that little is known of them. Opposition to the Moscow Patriarchate began in the early 1920s, and intensified after Metropolitan Sergi's declaration of loyalty in 1927. Some—perhaps most—of them rejoined the patriarchal church after the election of Patriarch Aleksi in 1945. However, many remain 'underground' to this day, in various groups with different names. No one knows how many there are: a monk who emigrated to Britain recently suggested that there were millions, but could not be sure, since they have a 'cell' structure, and each knows only the members of his own cell.

The Roman Catholic Church

History

The Roman Catholic Church has never been a Russian church: historically it has been strongly identified with Russia's western neighbour, Poland. The present-day concentration of Roman Catholics in Lithuania, Latvia and Belorussia is the result of the four centuries (1387–1794) when Poland was united with Lithuania under a Catholic monarchy whose territories stretched at one time from the Baltic to the Black Sea. During this period of Polish-Lithuanian ascendancy, the Catholic Church also established itself firmly in south-east Latvia, in the region of Latgale, and in the western part of Belorussia. In the rest of Belorussia and western Ukraine, the Catholic Church absorbed a large part of the local Orthodox Church as a result of the creation of the Eastern-rite Catholic or 'Uniate' Church. From the fourteenth to the eighteenth centuries, the Catholics were the rivals of the Russian Orthodox Church in an area where the Russian Empire and the kingdom of Poland-Lithuania were also military and political rivals. Lithuania, whose rulers adopted Catholicism as the state religion in the fourteenth century, became a country as firmly Catholic as its ally Poland and remained so even after its absorption into the Russian Empire in 1795.

Under the rule of the Russian tsars, the Catholic Church maintained its strong ties with the Lithuanian peasantry and also became linked with the growth of Lithuanian nationalism in the nineteenth century. After the establishment of Lithuanian independence in 1920, the Catholic Church became the state church, claiming 85% of the population as members. In 1939 it had 1,450 priests, 1,180 churches, 4 seminaries and 158 monasteries and convents.

The Catholic Church in the USSR was greatly reduced in numbers in the 1920s and 1930s. Many high-ranking Catholic clergymen from Belorussia and Ukraine were imprisoned or even executed in the 1920s for 'counter-revolution'. The overwhelming majority of Catholic clergy was imprisoned or exiled in the 1930s.

When the Soviet Union annexed Lithuania and the other Baltic states in 1940, the Catholic hierarchy and clergy were among the Soviet régime's first victims. During the 1940s, four out of ten Lithuanian bishops were sent to labour camps, together with hundreds of priests. Bishop Borisevičius of Telšiai was shot in 1947. In Latvia a third of the priests were shot, exiled or sent to labour camps.

After Stalin's death in 1953, a thaw in anti-religious policy allowed survivors of the camps to return to Lithuania and Latvia, but the number of churches had been almost halved and all monasteries and convents abolished. Only two seminaries remained, in Kaunas and Riga. A further anti-religious campaign by Khrushchev in 1960–64 meant that only 628 churches were allowed to remain open in Lithuania and 178 in Latvia.

Nevertheless the Catholic Church retained the loyalty of a remarkably high proportion of Lithuanians. This is shown by the support given to the Catholic movement for religious rights since 1970. In 1972, for example, a memorandum protesting against Soviet anti-religious laws was signed by over 17,000 people, while in 1979 a petition calling for the return of the state-confiscated church in Klaipeda was supported by 148,149 signatures—an almost unbelievable number in Soviet circumstances. Among the Catholic clergy, a majority—522 out of 711—have protested in writing against state interference in religious activities.

Protests, petitions and reports on violations of religious rights have appeared since 1971 in an unofficial publication, *Lietuvos Katalikų Bažnyčios Kronika* ('The Chronicle of the Lithuanian Catholic Church'). 'The Chronicle' reports on relations between the Catholic hierarchy and the Council for Religious Affairs, and has even published a statement by the hierarchy criticising the 1978 Soviet draft Constitution. The journal has survived despite the heavy prison sentences imposed by Soviet courts on many of those who produce and distribute it.

In 1978 the Catholic Committee for the Defence of Believers' Rights was founded by five Lithuanian priests. Working in co-operation with the Russian Christian Committee for the

Defence of Believers' Rights, it issued over sixty documents, but was forced by state pressure to go underground in 1983. Two of the founders, Frs Alfonsas Svarinskas and Sigitas Tamkevičius, were each sentenced to a total of ten years' imprisonment and exile in 1983. Another Catholic Committee member, Fr Juozas Zdebskis, met an 'accidental death' in suspicious circumstances in February 1986.

The Catholic Church in Latvia has maintained its numbers well, although Latvian Catholics are not as vocal in protest as their Lithuanian neighbours. In 1975 a petition to the Soviet government, asking for greater religious freedom, was signed by over 5,000 Latvian Catholics from the Daugavpils area, but this is the only document of its kind. The Latvian Marian shrine at Aglona has retained its popularity, and the number of pilgrims has even increased in recent years.

In 1983 Pope John Paul II created the aged Latvian Archbishop Vaivods a cardinal; it is rumoured that the secret cardinal created at the same time is the exiled Lithuanian Bishop Steponavičius, who has been barred from administering his diocese of Vilnius since 1961.

Church structure and associated institutions

The Roman Catholic Church in the USSR has the usual diocesan and episcopal structure. However, although bishops exist in the republics of Latvia and Lithuania, they have the rank only of 'apostolic administrator' and can thus be replaced if necessary. In other republics Catholic congregations are too few or too scattered to be administered by bishops and are usually run by local priests. There are two dioceses in Latvia, one bishop, Vaivods, and two auxiliary bishops, Dulbinskis and Cakuls.

In Lithuania there are six dioceses, but only four have officially recognised incumbent bishops. The archdiocese of Vilnius has a senior priest as administrator, since Archbishop Steponavičius has been officially exiled to a small village since 1961. Between 1975 and 1982, only two of the dioceses had incumbent bishops—Bishop Povilonis in Kaunas and Bishop Krikščiunas in Panevežys—but the situation improved in 1982: Bishop Sladkevičius of Kaišiadorys who had been in exile since

1958, was allowed to return to his diocese, possibly because of a sustained popular campaign for the release of the exiled bishops; and a new bishop, Vaičius, was appointed to the diocese of Telšiai. In 1984, Bishop Povilonis was given the title of Archbishop and an auxiliary bishop, Preikša, was appointed as his deputy.

There are two Catholic seminaries in the USSR: one in Kaunas, Lithuania, the other in Riga, Latvia with eighty students each. The Riga seminary takes a number of students from other parts of the Soviet Union, thus making it more difficult for local applicants to be accepted. The number of students permitted by the authorities is not enough to replace the ageing priests who die every year. In Lithuania the situation has grown so desperate that unofficial theological courses (a 'secret seminary') have been organised, with the tacit approval of members of the hierarchy. Priests ordained after graduating from this 'secret seminary' have been accepted by congregations, although the state has refused them recognition. In 1985 Fr Jonas Matulionis was sentenced to three years' imprisonment for 'impersonating a priest'.

Church membership
The centre of Catholicism in the USSR is Lithuania. Although the Church's position is certainly not as strong as it is in Poland, the strength of grass-roots support for Catholicism in Lithuania resembles the Polish Church situation much more than that of the Orthodox Church in Russia. As in Poland, the Catholic Church in Lithuania is still closely linked with national identity.

The Catholic Church in the neighbouring republic of Latvia has not fallen in numbers since the war as much as the former largest denomination, the Lutheran Church. The 300,000 Latvian Catholics now almost equal the number of Lutherans. Most are still concentrated in the rural area of Latgale, but many more Catholics now live in the cities than before the war. In Estonia there are about 3,000 Catholics served by one priest, a Latvian.

There are 65 Catholic parishes in Belorussia, with their own priests, but the state authorities will not permit 30,000 Lithuanian

Catholics in Belorussia to have their own churches or services in their own language. In the Moldavian SSR, there are about 15,000 Catholics but only two legally registered churches and only one recognised priest. In 1978 Moldavian Catholics appealed to the Pope because of harassment by the state authorities. In 1979, Fr V Zavalnyuk had his state licence withdrawn and was replaced by another priest because he had attracted too many young people to his services.

There are only a few Catholic churches open in Russia and Ukraine. In Leningrad and Moscow most of the church services are in Lithuanian or Polish. Poles are still a sizeable minority of Catholic communities in Latvia, Lithuania and Ukraine, as well as in churches formed by exiles in Central Asia and Siberia. These churches consist of many different nationalities deported in the 1930s and 1940s: Germans, Latvians, Lithuanians, Poles. Ukrainian Uniates prefer some Latin-rite churches registered in recent years to Orthodox churches.

In Lithuania and Latvia the clergy, although greatly reduced in numbers by deportation and emigration in the 1940s, are still sufficient in numbers to serve the available parishes. Many, however, are very elderly, and some have to take charge of more than one parish. In Lithuania there are 711 priests to about 628 parishes, but many of the parishes are very large and need more than one priest. In Latvia 178 churches are served by 150 priests.

Legally, there are no Catholic monasteries, convents or religious orders. All these were abolished in the 1940s. It is clear, however, that religious orders, especially nuns, still exist. About 1,500 nuns are reported in Lithuania. They are known to teach children the catechism, act as house-keepers to priests and help to produce *samizdat* religious literature. A number of nuns are known to be active in the Lithuanian movement for religious rights.

Current growth trends
The number of Catholic Church members and sympathisers in Lithuania is probably still very high (about two million—70% of the Lithuanian-Polish population) and reportedly includes

even Party members. The Church is much admired because of its involvement in the human-rights movement. In Latvia, the Catholic Church has undoubtedly attracted new members in urban areas, including a number of disaffected Lutherans.

The Eastern-rite Catholic Church (Ukrainian Catholic Church)

History
Eastern-rite Catholics in the Soviet Union are sometimes known as Uniates because their Church was formed by the union of Orthodox and Catholic Churches. At the time of the union the territory in question formed part of the Polish-Lithuanian Commonwealth. From the later part of the fifteenth century the Patriarch of Constantinople was increasingly unable to assert authority against the advances of Latin-rite Catholicism in the Polish-Lithuanian Commonwealth, and under these circumstances the proponents of union sought to preserve the Ruthenian (*Rus*) Orthodox Church with its Byzantine rite as co-equal with the Latin-rite Church by including it in the overall structure of the Catholic Church. Accordingly, the Union of Brest was concluded with the Holy See by the Orthodox Metropolitan of Kiev and a majority of the Ruthenian bishops in 1595–6. By the terms of this Union, the Orthodox Ruthenians accepted papal supremacy on condition that they be allowed to retain their traditional Byzantine rite, laws and customs, such as a married clergy.

A similar union was concluded in Uzhhorod (Uzhgorod) by the Transcarpathian Ruthenians in 1646. Despite considerable opposition by both nobility and peasantry, Poles and Ruthenians, all the Belorussian and Ukrainian dioceses had accepted the Union of Brest by 1702; the Pochaiv (Pochayev) Monastery joined it in 1712. The 1720 Synod of Zamość affirmed the Uniate Church's status as an independent ecclesiastical unit within the Roman Catholic Church, but introduced various latinising reforms. During the eighteenth century, the Church reached a membership of several million. It should be noted, however, that large numbers of Orthodox churches remained on Polish-Lithuanian territory throughout the eighteenth century, and their clergy sent delegates to the Empress Catherine II and the Russian bishops, asking for protection against persecution by Roman Catholics and Uniates.

With the partitions of the Polish-Lithuanian Commonwealth by Austria, Russia and Prussia in 1772, 1793 and 1795, the Uniates of what is now Belorussia came under Russian rule, while those of Ukraine were divided between Russia and Austria. In the Russian-held territories, four Uniate dioceses had been abolished by 1795. Three years later, however, part of the Uniate hierarchy was restored, and in 1806 a metropolitanate was erected for the 'Uniate Church in Russia'. In 1815 the Kholm diocese came under Russian rule as part of the kingdom of Poland. The dioceses of Lutsk and Brest were dissolved in 1828, and seven years later a committee was formed for the conversion of the Uniates to Orthodoxy. In 1839 at Polotsk the Union was declared abolished, and the Uniates were compelled to join either the Russian Orthodox or the Roman Catholic Church. Kholm, the only remaining Uniate diocese in the Russian Empire, was made subject to the Orthodox Metropolitan of Russian-ruled Warsaw in 1875. The 1905 Act of Toleration permitted returns to the Latin-rite Catholic Church but not to the Uniate Church.

The Uniates fared better under Catholic Austria. In 1771 a Uniate diocese was formed at Mukachiv (Mukachevo); predominantly Uniate eastern Galicia passed to Austria the following year. By an imperial decree of July 1774, the Uniate Church was renamed the Greek-Catholic Church in order to signify its distinctiveness from, and equality with, the Latin-rite Catholic Church. From 1795 to 1809 Austria also ruled the Kholm diocese, which then passed to the Duchy of Warsaw. The Galician metropolitanate (1302 or 1303–47, 1371–1401) was restored in 1807 as a Catholic institution, and Pope Pius VII vested the Metropolitan of Galicia with the powers of the Metropolitan of Kiev. In 1818 the Greek-Catholic diocese of Pryashiv (Prešov), Transcarpathia, was created. In the 1830s and 1840s, the Greek-Catholic Church in Austria came to be associated with the Ruthenian (later Ukrainian) national revival and the movement for cultural, socio-economic and political autonomy. Although in the latter half of the century this movement lost its close clerical associations, under the leadership of Metropolitan Andrei Sheptytsky (Galician Metropolitan 1900–44) the Church became the prime institution supporting Ukrainian national aspirations. (Metropolitan Sheptytsky also sponsored the creation of a Russian Catholic exarchate in 1917; revival of the Belorussian Uniate Church was also [unsuccessfully] attempted.)

After the First World War, most Greek-Catholics found themselves within the borders of Poland and Czechoslovakia. After Soviet annexation of western Ukraine in the Second World War, the Ukrainian Greek-Catholic Church was liquidated in eastern Galicia in 1945–6 and in Soviet Transcarpathia in 1947–9. Ukrainian Greek-Catholics were forcibly united with the Russian Orthodox Church. Nevertheless, the Church survived underground, and after Stalin's death in 1953 was replenished by priests returning from labour camps and exile. In 1954 an apparition of the Virgin gave rise to the sect of *pokutnyky* ('penitents'), which rejected all contact with the state. Lately, the activity of this sect appears to have subsided.

Since the Second World War, the Church has come to be known as the Ukrainian Catholic Church.

Church structure and associated institutions

The Ukrainian Catholic Church is a part of the Roman Catholic Church and is subject to the authority of the Pope. It has no legal existence in the USSR, but survives as an underground church. Its head, Cardinal Myroslav I Lubachivsky, resides in Rome. He holds the titles of Archbishop Major and Metropolitan of Lviv (Lvov) and Galicia.

The Archbishop Major may appoint bishops and even metropolitans for his province, from among both secular and religious clergy. Distinguished bishops receive the title of Archbishop. Many Ukrainian Catholics consider him also to be a patriarch, the traditional head of an Eastern Catholic Church, but this status has not been confirmed by the Holy See. The major reason given for denial of a Ukrainian Catholic patriarchate has been the Metropolitan's lack of actual power over his territory. Formally, however, his jurisdiction extends both to the Archeparchy of Lviv and to the eparchies (dioceses) of Peremyshl (Przemyśl, now partly in Poland) and Ivano-Frankivske (Ivano-Frankovsk, formerly Stanyslaviv). Current Soviet borders also include the Greek-Catholic eparchy of Mukachiv (Mukachevo, Munkacs).

The Ukrainian Catholic eparchies now in the USSR formerly had bishops and auxiliary bishops; there are several clandestine Ukrainian Catholic bishops at present in the USSR. Traditionally, each eparchy is administered by a *krylos* or *kapitula*, a capitular chapter consisting of priests with the title of *kryloshany*. Eparchies are divided into parishes.

The Ukrainian Catholic Church is served by both religious (monastic) and secular priests. Until recently, the latter were allowed to marry before ordination.

The most important men's religious order is the Order of St Basil the Great. More recent orders in the Ukrainian Catholic Church are the Studites, Redemptorists and Salesians. The principal women's orders are the Basilian and the Studite Sisters, the Sisters Servants of Mary Immaculate, and the Sisters of St Joseph. In 1939 there were 195 Ukrainian Catholic convents and monasteries. In 1943–4, the number of Ukrainian Catholic monastic institutions in the eparchies now within Soviet borders was as follows: Lviv, 53; Peremyshl, 66 (8 men's and 58 women's); Stanyslaviv, 68 (9 men's and 59 women's); Mukachiv, 8 (5 men's and 3 women's), but all such institutions were dissolved by the Soviet authorities after the Second World War. Several, however, continue to exist in the underground.

Although all Ukrainian Catholic charitable, educational, social and cultural institutions were closed after Soviet annexation of western Ukraine in 1945, two organisations associated with the Church have been formed clandestinely in recent years. The Central Committee of Ukrainian Catholics in the Catacombs publishes the underground *Ukrainsky katolytsky vistnyk* ('Ukrainian Catholic Herald'), which reports on religious persecution. The Initiative or Action Group for the Defence of the Rights of Believers and the Church, founded on 9th September 1982, (renamed the Committee in Defence of the Ukrainian Catholic Church in 1987), strives for the legalisation of the

Ukrainian Catholic Church and publishes the *Khronika Katolytskoyi Tserkvy na Ukrayini* ('Chronicle of the Catholic Church in Ukraine'). A new publication entitled *Khrystianskiy holos* ('Christian Voice') appeared in Lviv in January 1988, its first issue being simultaneously the thirty-second issue of the 'Chronicle of the Catholic Church in Ukraine'.

Church membership
Catholics form a small minority among Ukrainians. Even in Polish-controlled Belorussia and Ukraine (1921–39) the Orthodox outnumbered the Uniates by two to one; and before the Second World War, Uniates totalled some four million out of a population of 40 million Ukrainians. Nevertheless, the Ukrainian Catholic Church is a national church. Virtually all its members are Ukrainian by nationality. Concentrated in western Ukraine, the Church includes Ukrainian ethnic groups like the *Boiky,* the *Lemky,* and the *Hutsuly.* The Church includes all major Ukrainian social groups. Because of the sovietisation of the cities since the annexation of western Ukraine to the USSR in 1945, however, the Church is probably stronger in the countryside, where its activities are harder to detect and control. Thus, many reports of clandestine worship mention villagers gathering at closed or abandoned churches.

The current number of Ukrainian Catholic laity, priests and religious is impossible to determine because of the Church's illegal status in the USSR, in fact, the latest statistics available date from the Second World War. In 1939 there were 4,283,000 faithful on Ukrainian ethnic territory, which extends somewhat beyond the Soviet borders. In the four eparchies on what is now Soviet Ukrainian territory the number of priests (secular and religious) in 1943 was (according to the *Annuario Pontificio*) 2,595. According to underground sources, there are between 800 and 1,000 clandestine priests in western Ukraine today. In 1939 the Church's overall monastic population on Ukrainian ethnic territory was 520 monks and 1,090 sisters. The number of monastics in the Peremyshl, Stanyslaviv and Mukachiv eparchies in 1944 was (according to the *Annuario Pontificio*) as follows: Peremyshl, 101 monks and 246 sisters; Stanyslaviv, 57 and 288; Mukachiv, 35 and 50; in total 777.

According to underground sources, there are a few hundred monks and over a thousand sisters in secret convents in western Ukraine today.

Current growth trends
Current growth trends in the Ukrainian Catholic Church can only be guessed, since the indications are fragmentary. There are reports of underground seminaries and monastic institutions. It is known that many believers who attend Russian Orthodox churches or the few Latin-rite churches remain Ukrainian Catholics at heart. Indeed, entire Orthodox parishes in Ukraine, including the priests, are said to be, in fact, Ukrainian Catholic. The clandestinely published *Chronicle of the Catholic Church in Ukraine* reported in 1984 that in the Transcarpathian region alone, 81 secret Ukrainian Catholic priests had been ordained over a period of three years. It also reported that a three-year monastery school was educating youth in Transcarpathia. In addition, the Church has apparently been able to send missionary priests to eastern Ukraine and to Belorussia. In western Ukraine, many underground priests work as ordinary labourers and wander from town to town, celebrating mass and administering the sacraments in private dwellings and isolated localities.

Growth of the Church is limited, however, by government policy. For example, the *Chronicle of the Catholic Church in Ukraine* lists various villages where the churches have been closed or destroyed by the authorities because the inhabitants refused to accept Orthodox priests. The authorities harass believers and priests in various ways, including physical assault and, in a few cases, murder. Mass opposition by believers to such measures gives some indication of the growth of the Church. According to the *Chronicle*, 520 Ukrainian Catholics burned their passports in protest against religious persecution. The Catholic activist Iosyp Terelya is reported to have predicted that as many as 3,000 might do likewise. Finally, the fact that the Soviet authorities expend considerable energy on attacking the Church through propaganda, intimidation or physical force indicates that it is a major factor in Soviet Ukrainian society.

In August 1987 the Ukrainian Catholic Church issued a statement to Pope John Paul II and the Soviet government, declaring its intention to emerge from clandestinity and seek full legal rights. Within a few months more than 10,000 people had signed the statement, and numerous delegations from Western Ukrainian towns and villages were delivering petitions to the USSR Supreme Soviet, General Secretary Mikhail Gorbachev and President Andrei Gromyko in which they requested the return of their confiscated or padlocked churches and the freedom to worship in them in their own rite. The campaign was considered so serious a challenge to the government that negotiations between the Ukrainian Supreme Soviet and bishops of the Church were initiated. The negotiations stalled because the bishops refused to accept registration of individual parishes, submission of parish membership lists, or any control by the authorities in its affairs, but demanded instead legalisation as a self-governing social organisation.

The Baptist Church

History

The Russian Baptist movement emerged out of the growing together of three quite distinct groups: the so-called Stundists, the Baptists and the Evangelical Christians.

The Stundists were the first Russian Christians to come under the influence of Western European Protestantism. Their movement began in the 1850s and 1860s, when German farmers who had settled in the southern part of the Russian Empire (present-day Ukraine) in the later part of the eighteenth century started to hold Bible studies and invited the Russian labourers, whom they hired, to join them. The Germans called their studies *Bibelstunden* ('Bible hours') and the Russians who attended were soon nicknamed Stundists. As the recently-translated New Testament in Russian became available, the Stundists took the idea of Bible studies back to their own villages and the movement spread rapidly. The movement was the result of a natural sharing of faith, rather than of a deliberate mission strategy.

The Baptist churches, on the other hand, were the fruits of missionary endeavour, though there was also building on existing developments. German Baptists began working among the German farmers, and through them also had contact with the Stundists. A most significant contact was with a congregation in Tbilisi (the capital of Georgia) belonging to the Molokan movement.[8] The Molokans had rejected the ritualism of the Russian Orthodox Church and (with the increasing availability of the Scriptures) developed doctrines according to their own understanding of the Bible. At first they were very suspicious of Baptist teaching—regarding baptism as nothing more than empty ritual—but the first Molokan accepted baptism in 1867. Baptist influence grew steadily among the Molokans and after the formation of a Baptist Union in 1884, many of the most prominent leaders were from a Molokan background.

The Evangelical Christians began in yet another way. A Russian princess heard an English Brethren preacher named Lord Radstock in a salon in Paris. Her curiosity aroused, she invited him to St Petersburg (present day Leningrad), then the capital of the Russian Empire, to speak in her salon. Radstock's two visits had a far-reaching effect. Several well-placed converts took up his simple gospel message and soon meetings were being held regularly not only in the capital but also in other cities and on the country estates of these new aristocratic Christians.

Despite the outside stimulus which began each of these movements, they were never dependent on missionary activity. Outside contacts were maintained, though sometimes with considerable difficulty because of harassment and persecution by the tsarist authorities. Another English Brethren preacher, Dr Baedeker, travelled extensively and gained access to prisons and Siberian convict colonies. In 1884, despite growing hostility from the authorities, the Baptists held an inaugural congress and established a Baptist Union. In the same year the St Petersburg Christians invited representatives of all the evangelical movements to a conference to discuss the possibility of unity or co-operation, but the authorities intervened and sent all the participants home after one day. The Stundists gravitated towards the Baptists, and both Baptist and Evangelical Christian churches spread and grew despite persecution. It was not until 1905, when the Edict of Toleration was passed, that the Evangelical Christian Union was formed alongside the Baptist Union. The Stundist movement had by now merged with the two other branches. Both Unions joined the newly-formed Baptist World Alliance and sent representatives to its first congress in London in 1906. There was, however, a distinct difference in emphasis between the two Unions: the Baptists were close to the Strict Baptist tradition, while the Evangelical Christians were influenced by their Brethren roots.

The 1917 Bolshevik Revolution at first brought new opportunities for the Evangelicals. As former persecuted minorities, they were regarded by the Bolsheviks for a while as natural allies. While the anti-religious campaign centred on the Orthodox Church, the Evangelicals on the whole enjoyed a greater measure of freedom than before the Revolution. This led to a great expansion in the number of congregations and a massive increase in membership in the course of the 1920s.

This revival, however, was cut short. The repressive legislation of April 1929 led to a clampdown on all activity other than the conduct of worship services, and was followed by mass arrests and closure of churches throughout the 1930s. In 1935 the Baptist Union was disbanded by the authorities, though the Evangelical Christian Union survived, on paper, at least.

The Second World War reversed the fortunes of the Evangelicals, though not as dramatically as it did those of the Orthodox. In 1944 evangelical leaders were allowed to gather in Moscow and encouraged to form a united organisation to which all evangelicals could affiliate. Thus the Union of Evangelical Christians-Baptists (ECB Union) was born. Thousands of congregations were re-formed. Pentecostals and congregations in the formerly independent Baltic republics and the western parts of Belorussia and Ukraine which had been annexed from Poland, Czechoslovakia and Romania joined the Union in 1945.

In the late 1940s the tide turned again, however. The Union's journal ceased publication in 1949 and there were once more many arrests, though the Union leadership in Moscow remained intact. Only the death of Stalin in 1953 stopped the wave of arrests. The journal resumed and prisoners were gradually amnestied and rehabilitated. Something of a revival broke out again, with many local churches witnessing boldly in the knowledge that the gates of hell had not prevailed. Many German Baptist and Mennonite congregations joined the Union when restrictions on the German population were lifted at the end of 1955. The Mennonite Brethren formally joined the Union in 1963.

Khrushchev, in most respects regarded as a liberal, launched a brutal attack on the churches in 1959. In 1960 the ECB Union leadership, anxious to preserve what had been gained, issued instructions to the regional superintendents to persuade the local churches to adopt a low profile, and in particular to restrict evangelism and discourage baptism of young adults under the age of thirty. These instructions, and a draft new constitution for the Union, disturbed many of the bolder pastors and preachers. In the summer of 1961, a group was formed to press for the holding of a Union congress to discuss these issues. They met hostility from the authorities and little understanding from their leadership. Although a congress was called in 1963 and some of their criticism of the draft constitution was heeded, they were excluded from participating. Losing hope of reforming the Union, they organised themselves into a second union, the Council of Churches of Evangelical Christians-Baptists (CCECB) in 1965.

Since then the two bodies, one official and the other unofficial and at times severely persecuted, have existed side by side. The CCECB has been consistent in its uncompromising stand, while the ECB Union has continued to operate within the limitations laid down by Soviet law. Nevertheless, the authorities have also been more willing to compromise with the ECB Union in order to diminish the influence of the CCECB, and the Union has made a number of gains. They obtained permission to print or import Bibles and other items of basic religious literature in increasing quantities; they have held and established regular congresses; they have introduced a Bible correspondence course; more democratic procedures for the appointment of regional superintendents; registration of new congregations has become somewhat easier; and the authorities have shown greater toleration of youth work and even Sunday schools, both of which are areas of activity that are specifically excluded by Soviet legislation on religion. The CCECB has engaged in youth and Sunday school work, evangelism and printing, regardless of the penalties.

During the 1970s the Soviet authorities attempted to persuade CCECB congregations to work within the law, but there was never any suggestion of registering the CCECB as an independent union. The conditions attached to registration (limitations on activity and state control over church appointments) were the basic stumbling-block and not more than 100 congregations are believed to have registered as autonomous churches. Although some have maintained links with the CCECB, they are on the whole regarded with suspicion by CCECB leaders. The early 1980s brought increased persecution, with an increase in the number of prisoners and most of the top leadership of the CCECB under arrest. However, these trends have been reversed under the leadership of Mikhail Gorbachev, and by the spring of 1988 the number of CCECB prisoners was the lowest ever.

During the 1970s emigration of Soviet citizens of German origin was allowed to rise, as a result of which a significant number of German Baptists from both registered and unregistered churches moved to West Germany. Those from unregistered churches have set up an organisation to channel support to the unregistered churches in the Soviet Union, concentrating on aid for prisoners' families, Christian literature and supplies for the secret printing presses. This has been an important factor in maintaining the high output of the presses.

Church structure and associated institutions

As far as Soviet law is concerned, the only recognised religious institution is the local religious association. Nevertheless, since the Second World War, the major denominations have succeeded in setting up various central administrative bodies and institutions, though only the Baptists and the Orthodox have central bodies covering the whole of the USSR. The Baptist Church consists basically of the two parallel unions, the registered ECB Union and the unregistered CCECB. However, there is also a certain number of congregations, some registered and others unregistered, which are independent of both unions.

The ECB Union has a highly formalised structure closely resembling the Soviet secular state structure. The supreme legislative body of the Union is the delegates' congress called every three to five years, and held regularly since 1963 after a gap of nineteen years since the inaugural congress of 1944. Local churches, of which there are between 3,000 and 5,000 in the Soviet Union, send representatives to conferences at regional and republic level which elect delegates to the congress. Only the congress has the authority to amend the constitution and the Union's doctrinal statement. It elects from its participants a council, which in turn elects a presidium (executive committee) which is responsible for the day-to-day running of the Union. The full council meets twice a year and the full presidium more frequently. All of the key officers of the Union (President, General Secretary, Assistant General Secretary and Treasurer) have offices in the Union headquarters in Moscow and in effect form an inner presidium. The Union has a number of central departments under the presidium, including: one responsible for theological training, which runs the Bible Correspondence Course; one responsible for evangelism and Christian unity, which seeks to foster harmony between Christians of different backgrounds within the Union and better relations with evangelicals outside the Union; and the International Department, which arranges foreign travel for Union representatives, and invitations and itineraries for foreign guests. The Union appoints superintendents at regional and republic level, whose nominations are now ratified by conferences of the churches for which they have responsibility. The regional and republic conferences also elect advisory councils to assist the superintendents. Local churches elect their own pastor and deacons, and request the superintendents to ordain them. Each church also elects a panel of preachers, and a three-member executive committee responsible for the administrative side of church business. It is a state requirement that such a committee should exist and the local authorities have a veto over its membership. The Union publishes a journal which is distributed to pastors and to foreign subscribers, and which is printed on a state press, as are the publications of all religious bodies allowed to publish literature in the Soviet Union (except the Armenian Apostolic Church).

The CCECB is unable to maintain such a detailed structure. The only full conference was held in 1969, with permission from the authorities, though after the conference had taken place the permission was revoked! Since then, conferences have had to be held in conditions of secrecy and have therefore not been fully representative. At the last known major conference, in 1976, the chairman of the CCECB, Gennadi Kryuchkov, who has lived in hiding since 1970, felt unable to be present for security reasons and delivered his report on tape. The main aim of the CCECB leaders is to give direction to the unregistered churches, of which there are probably about 1,000 in the Soviet Union, and to encourage them in their uncompromising stand. One of their major accomplishments is the creation and maintenance of a network of underground printing presses, which, since the early 1970s, claim to have produced 1 million items of literature—ranging from whole Bibles, New Testaments, hymn books, and Bible study aids to devotional magazines and newsletters. Despite the discovery of six presses and the loss of tens of thousands of copies of books confiscated with the presses, the work continues and has made a significant contribution to the availability of Christian literature, not only in CCECB congregations, but also in ECB Union congregations and those of other denominations.

A largely autonomous group attached to the CCECB is the Council of Prisoners' Relatives, which was established in 1964. It publishes regular bulletins with details of arrests, trials and other repressive measures and reports on the condition of individual prisoners. The Council also organises the distribution of aid to prisoners' families, who receive no state benefits. With the reduction of the number of prisoners in 1987–8, the Council has begun more general relief work for low-income Baptist families.

Some churches are independent of both unions. There are both unregistered churches, and a number with 'autonomous' registration, which means that they do not accept the authority of the ECB Union, but may not form any other association of churches. Nevertheless, many of them do have informal relations with each other and with churches in the ECB Union. A group of the leaders of autonomous churches have had three meetings with the ECB Union leadership, and some of their preachers have completed the Union's Bible Correspondence Course.

Church membership

The ECB Union has between 300,000 and 500,000 members, and up to 2½ million adherents. The CCECB has between 50,000 and 100,000 members, and perhaps another 100,000 adherents. All the major European nationalities living in the USSR are represented in Baptist churches. About 50% are Ukrainians, 33% Russians and 10% Germans. In western Ukraine there are gypsy churches. There are very small numbers from non-European nations, for example a few Uzbek converts.

Most of the churches are located in urban areas, with a small number of rural churches closing each year, thus increasing the urbanisation. Baptists are predominantly working class. Their further education is mostly technical, and there are few university graduates, partly because it is difficult for any religious believer to be accepted into higher education. Geographically, the Baptist churches are most strongly represented in Ukraine, the western regions of the European part of the Soviet Union and Central Asia.

There are probably no more than a few hundred full-time paid members of staff of the registered churches: these include office staff in Moscow and Kiev, the members of the presidium, the republic and regional superintendents (some of whom have assistants), and pastors and assistants in major churches. Unregistered church leaders may not legally be employed by their congregations, though in practice some are. However, the backbone of local leadership in both registered and unregistered churches is made up of retired people and working people offering their services in their spare time. These form a large body of voluntary pastors, preachers and deacons.

Current growth trends

The ECB Union officially states that it is receiving an average of 8,000 new members per year. This compares with a figure of about 6,000 per year during the 1970s. The net increase, taking into account deaths and excommunications, is about 2,000 per year. However, it is widely believed that these figures do not reflect the true growth rate accurately. Many, if not most, congregations are thought to have as part of their community Christians who have been baptised on profession of faith, but who do not appear on the official membership lists in order to minimise the likelihood of their being discriminated against.

Since the mid 1970s an average of 50 new congregations have been registered by the authorities as members of the Union each year. These new congregations do not necessarily all represent church growth: some of them are formerly unregistered congregations which have decided to join the Union. However, others represent small groups that have grown sufficiently to form viable congregations (and to meet the legal requirement of twenty adults who will agree to be responsible for any property held by the congregation and who sign the application for registration), while others are daughter congregations which split off from larger congregations to meet the needs of members in a particular district. The need for such daughter congregations is in itself evidence of church growth.

No overall figures for new baptisms or the formation of new congregations are available for the CCECB. Nevertheless, it is clear that in addition to individual witness there is also organised evangelistic activity which is bearing fruit. Some individual congregations show dramatic growth from a few dozen members to several hundred over periods ranging from over twenty years in the case of groups of the earliest supporters of the CCECB to just a few years in some other cases.

Many autonomously registered churches also show steady growth.

The Pentecostal Church

History

The worldwide Pentecostal movement is a twentieth-century phenomenon, and the Russian and Soviet movement is no exception. The first Russian Pentecostal groups were formed under the influence of visiting Pentecostal preachers in 1911–13. Two Russian Evangelical Christians, Ivanov and Smorodin, took up the Pentecostal message and travelled widely in Russia in the two years before the outbreak of the First World War, preaching mainly in Baptist and Evangelical Christian churches and founding small Pentecostal groups wherever they went.

A far greater impetus came in 1921 with the arrival in Odessa of Ivan Voronayev, who had left Russia a decade earlier as a Baptist preacher and had become a Pentecostal pastor in New York. He was a gifted preacher and able organiser, and within six years had established 350 congregations throughout Ukraine; these congregations formed the Union of Christians of Evangelical Faith in 1926. At this time Voronayev and a few of his co-workers were sponsored as missionaries by the Assemblies of God in the USA and received some financial support; however, it appears that there was no other form of assistance. Voronayev also travelled beyond Ukraine, for example, winning over a 500-member temperance congregation in Moscow. Although some of Voronayev's success was at the expense of existing evangelical churches, the new congregations were successful in evangelising those who did not normally go to church.

In 1927 a conference with representatives from all over the USSR was held and a nationwide union established. In 1928 Voronayev began publishing a magazine *Yevangelist* ('The Evangelist'). At this time there were believed to be 80,000 members, but Stalin's clampdown on the minority churches brought further development to a halt. Voronayev and other leaders were arrested in 1930 and decades of outlaw existence and persecution began. During the 1930s all churches were closed and many leading members were arrested. Voronayev himself is thought to have died in a remote labour camp in 1938 and many others also perished.

The Second World War brought radical changes. In German-occupied territory churches were reopened and within two years there were 350 Pentecostal churches in central Ukraine alone. On the Soviet side of the front, religious activity was once more tolerated in order to rally the whole population to the war effort. The Soviet Union's territorial gains during the war also added hundreds of Pentecostal churches from the Baltic republics and what had been Eastern Poland. (Before 1918 in these Eastern territories of Poland there had been virtually no evangelical churches, until American and West European Pentecostals became active in support of local converts as missionaries).

In 1944 the Soviet authorities allowed the establishment of the Union of Evangelical Christians and Baptists. It was made clear that no evangelicals would be allowed to operate legally independently of this Union. Four Pentecostal leaders, two each from Ukraine and Belorussia, came to Moscow in August 1945 and signed an agreement by which Pentecostals could be received into the Union. The Baptists and Evangelical Christians, remembering all too well the way Pentecostals had divided many of their congregations in the 1920s, imposed very strict terms to try to minimise the influence of Pentecostals in united congregations. The Pentecostals had to agree to refrain from speaking in tongues and other Pentecostal practices, and even from discussing their beliefs with non-Pentecostals. There are thought to have been about 1,000 congregations at this time, of whom probably less than half (mostly in regions annexed from Poland where Pentecostal relations with other evangelicals had been better) actually came into the Union. By 1947, some of the Pentecostals, including Afanasi Bidash, one of the signatories of the August 1945 agreement, had become dissatisfied with the arrangement and began withdrawing. Soon Pentecostal leaders, both within and outside the Union, were arrested. Others took the opportunity to emigrate to Poland before their turn came.

The death of Stalin in 1953 once more brought a change. By

1956, most surviving prisoners had been released and there was an upsurge in independent Pentecostal activity. The leaders petitioned the authorities for the registration of a separate Pentecostal union, but the response was a new wave of arrests. Nevertheless, an independent leadership has remained in existence since then, though its ability to lead and exert authority probably fluctuates.

After forty years of resolute refusal to permit Pentecostal activity, the authorities began in about 1970 to experiment with the registration of individual Pentecostal congregations independently of the ECB Union. Although the usual requirements for registration were imposed, including the normal limitations on the activities of the church, Pentecostals were allowed the freedom to be themselves—hard to achieve in united congregations. For some this arrangement had a certain appeal, and after 1975 the authorities also apparently felt it was a successful experiment and made autonomous registration more widely available. Since then, at least 200 Pentecostal churches have become legally registered in this way. Nevertheless, many Pentecostals who had suffered hardship and imprisonment for the right to be independent of both Baptist and state control rejected registration because of the unacceptable limitations on church life which accompanied it. These unregistered Pentecostals came under increasing pressure and the response of many was to seek emigration to any country where there was freedom to practise their faith without interference. In the late 1970s lists of would-be emigrants, totalling up to 30,000 men, women and children, were compiled and submitted to the authorities. Only a small number received permission and many of the chief organisers were arrested. The movement subsided, but did not disappear altogether. Two families who finally did emigrate were the Vashchenkos and Chmykhalovs, seven of whose members took refuge in the US Embassy in Moscow in 1978 and became famous as the 'Siberian Seven'. In the mid-1980s the emigration movement regained some of its momentum, and some families were permitted to leave.

Church structure and associated institutions
Soviet Pentecostals do not form a united movement. They are

fragmented in three different ways: by denominational differences, by attitudes to participation in the ECB Union and by attitudes to registration.

The majority of Pentecostals, using the name Christians of Evangelical Faith, are close to the mainstream Pentecostalism of the Assemblies of God, with whom Voronayev and many of the pioneers in Eastern Poland in the 1920s and 1930s had strong links. A minority of the Christians of Evangelical Faith are in the ECB Union.

There are many other groups of Pentecostals. The main ones are the Christians in the Apostolic Spirit, who grew from the work begun by Ivanov and Smorodin, and the Pentecostal Zionists, founded by one of Voronayev's early converts. The former are often called unitarians because of their emphasis on the person of Jesus, similar to 'Jesus Only' Pentecostals in the USA. Some are undoubtedly Unitarian in theology, but it is not clear if all go as far as denying the Trinity. They are strongest in and around Leningrad and in Estonia, Latvia and western Belorussia and Ukraine (Smorodin lived in Poland in the 1920s and 1930s), but are also to be found in many places in Siberia and the North, where people from the western part of the Soviet Union were deported. Smorodin signed an agreement with the ECB Union in 1947 and since then, his followers have been present in the Leningrad congregation and elsewhere. The Zionists place a strong emphasis on the Second Coming, hoping to meet Christ on Mount Zion. Apart from Ukraine they are also to be found in Siberia and the North. Other groups have only local significance.

Pentecostals have nearly always been represented in the leadership of the Union. One of the signatories of the 1947 agreement, Dmitri Ponomarchuk, was a member of the Union's Council from 1945 until he retired in 1966. From 1966 to 1969 there was no Pentecostal on the new executive body, the Presidium, but from 1969 to 1979 there was one and since 1979, there have been two Pentecostal representatives at this level. Where there are large numbers of Pentecostals in a region, the superintendent, or more often his deputy, may be a Pentecostal.

Outside the Union unregistered Christians of Evangelical Faith are led by bishops, who may be pastors of a large congregation, which will often have to meet in small groups led by assistant pastors, deacons or preachers. Some bishops are recognised leaders of congregations spread over a much wider area. Any meetings they have together must be organised in secret, but they undoubtedly maintain fellowship among themselves. It is known that bishops and other pastors attempted to meet in Moscow in December 1985, but were prevented from doing so by the authorities.

Independently registered congregations are required to exist totally autonomously. They are regarded with suspicion by leaders of the unregistered churches, but often have good relations with leaders of the ECB Union, from whom they have received officially produced or imported Bibles. A number of Pentecostals from autonomous registered churches have studied on the Union's Bible Correspondence Course.

There are probably something over 1,500 Pentecostal churches in the USSR, belonging to both registered and unregistered congregations.

Church membership

Pentecostal membership numbers around 150,000, with possibly a further 150,000 adherents. The ethnic composition and geographical distribution of the Pentecostals is very similar to that of the Baptists, with Ukrainians being the largest group. Most of the other European nationalities are represented, including the Germans, and also some Hebrew Christians.

Socially Pentecostals are predominantly urban working class, especially since the 1960s. Of course, this reflects the increasing urbanisation of the Soviet Union: while surviving rural communities are often elderly, the urban congregations have all age groups present. Pentecostals are often discriminated against in education, but adult converts include graduates from many professions.

Even in registered congregations much of the leadership is exercised by laypeople in other full-time employment, unless they are retired. There are some full-time church workers within the ECB Union. In unregistered churches there are no opportunities for legal full-time church work, and usually only the retired can devote themselves fully to church work. Some

unregistered congregations have deaconesses with responsibilities for pastoral and social care. Even ordained pastors
and bishops are usually in full-time secular employment. In all
congregations, therefore, leadership is widely shared among
pastors, deacons and preachers.

Current growth trends

Claims of dramatic growth of Pentecostal Churches over the
past twenty or twenty-five years can be neither discounted nor
substantiated. However, individual congregations are known
to have experienced steady growth from small beginnings to
considerable membership. In Moscow, for example, there was
only a small Pentecostal group in 1959, as well as other small
groups in the Moscow region. Today there are reported to be
30 worship groups with up to 200 members in each—a total of
over 2,000—as well as two small registered congregations.
Reports from a number of places indicate that new converts
are being made, sometimes in large numbers. For example, in
Lithuania, where Pentecostals have been a tiny minority
among the non-Lithuanian immigrant population, secularised
ex-Catholic young Lithuanians have recently been becoming
Pentecostal Christians. However, since there is no reliable (or
even unreliable!) information available about the total number
of churches or total membership, there cannot even be an estimate of growth rates. Nevertheless, Pentecostal churches certainly have a warmth of fellowship and a depth of faith that are
highly attractive in the alienated conditions and ideological disillusionment that mark Soviet society.

The Adventist Church

History

The Seventh-day Adventist Church, founded in the USA in
1861, first found converts in the Russian Empire in the 1880s,
among the German communities on the Volga river and in
Ukraine. Adventist literature was sent to relatives and friends
by German immigrants in the USA, as well as by missions in

Switzerland. The first Adventist church in the Russian Empire was founded in Berdebulat in 1886.

Tolerated by the tsarist authorities as long as the Church membership consisted of Germans, the Adventists began to be harassed and persecuted when they converted Russians. The first congregation of Russian Adventists was founded in 1889 in Stavropol', and by 1912, 64% of the Adventists in the Russian Empire were former members of the Russian Orthodox Church. Such evangelisation often resulted in the arrest of both converts and preachers and led to exile to Siberia or Central Asia. Adventist meeting houses were boarded up, and before 1905 most Adventists met in private houses. The production of Adventist literature was severely restricted and until 1905 most of it was imported from Switzerland, Germany and the USA.

The 1905 Constitution, by which Tsar Nicholas II granted freedom of conscience, made the Adventist Church legal. By 1914 it had 240 churches and 5,880 members. Three Adventist publishing houses were established, in Kiev, Saratov and Riga, and a monthly journal began publication in 1914. There were few clergymen in relation to the number of churches—only 40 in 1914—and these were all trained at the Friedensau Mission School in Germany. The first minister of Russian descent, E Gnedin, was ordained in 1908.

The Adventists still suffered discrimination and persecution because of their pacifism and observance of the Sabbath. They were disqualified from employment by the state, and during the wars of 1904 and 1914–17 many were imprisoned for refusing to bear arms. In 1914 they were also disliked because of their German links.

During the early years of Soviet power, non-Orthodox 'sects' were tolerated by the Bolsheviks—despite their militant atheist ideology. They were seen as potential socialists and allies against the Russian Orthodox Church. In the 10 years after the 1917 Revolution, the Adventists greatly expanded their activity. Although the Baltic communities of Adventists were no longer part of the USSR, the Adventist Church doubled its membership to 12,697 by 1926 and by 1928 had 600 congregations. The Church was allowed to print three periodicals, organise its own collective farms, and hold theology courses and religious classes. In 1919, the Soviet government also permitted exemption from military service on religious grounds, allowing Adventists and other 'sectarians' to serve in medical or construction units instead. In return, the Adventist Church leadership declared its loyalty to the Soviet government in 1924.

After the abolition in 1926 of the 1919 decree on exemption from military service, a split occured in the Adventist Church. In 1928 a group of 'Reform Adventists' (later known as the 'True and Free' Adventists), led by P Manzhura and G Ostvald, broke away from the main Church body: they rejected active army service, while the official Church leadership under H J Loebsack was prepared to accept it, and also opposed state registration of churches, which was legalised in 1929 as part of the new Law on Religious Associations. As a result of this law, which forbade all forms of religious evangelism, the Adventist publications, theological courses and collective farms were abolished. In the 1930s, almost all Adventist churches were closed and almost all Adventist clergy imprisoned.

The official Adventists revived only in the 1950s and by 1964 again had 21,500 members; but during Khrushchev's anti-religious campaign in the 1960s, the membership and the number of churches were again reduced by half. Only in the 1970s did the official Adventist Church begin to grow again.

The True and Free Adventists survived as an underground organisation, despite savage repression. Their original leaders died in labour camps in the 1930s and 1940s, but Vladimir Shelkov, elected as leader in 1954, united the unofficial churches and established an illegal printing press '*Vernyi svidetel*' ('True Witness') which 'published' at least 110 *samizdat* works. In the 1970s, Shelkov—though now an old man—led the True and Free Adventists in co-operation with Russian intellectual 'dissidents' in an open campaign for human and religious rights. The True and Free Adventists sent documents to the West, publicising individual cases of religious persecution and stressing their own commitment to non-violence. The Group for Legal Struggle, supporting implementation of the human rights promised in the 1975 Helsinki Agreement, was founded by

Rostislav Galetsky in 1978.

In 1978 Shelkov was arrested and in March 1979 was tried for 'slandering the Soviet state' and sentenced, at the age of 84, to five years in a strict-régime camp. He died there on 27th January 1980. Rostislav Galetsky was also sentenced in 1980 to five years' imprisonment. Disappointed with the lack of support from the West, despite an 800-page collection of documents sent to the Madrid Conference reviewing observance of the Helsinki Agreement, and weakened by the imprisonment of many of their leaders, the True and Free Adventists have returned to an underground existence.

The official Adventists, now led by M P Kulakov, benefited from the True and Free Adventist activity by stressing their own loyalty to state laws. To offset the publicity gained by the True and Free Adventists, they have gained certain concessions in the last ten years: more links with the Adventist leadership abroad, permission for more churches to register, permission to send some students abroad to study theology, and some publications, including a yearbook issued since 1979.

Church structure and membership; current growth trends
Before 1905 the Adventist Church in the Russian Empire was organised on a regional basis. In 1907 it first elected its own central ruling body—the Union Conference—headed by its first president, J T Boettcher. According to Adventist tradition, a Union Conference consists of delegates elected by regional conferences, whose members are themselves elected by local congregations. The president is automatically a member of the General Conference of the World Adventist Church, based in Battle Creek, Michigan, in the USA.

After the Revolution in October 1917, the Adventist Church in the USSR was reorganised into five Union Conferences united under an All-Union Council, headed by the president, and maintained links with the General Conference. By 1937, because of mass arrests of Adventist leaders, including the All-Union Council, the Adventist Church had almost ceased to exist as an organisation, except for a nominal president. Meetings were held only in private houses.

In the 1950s Adventist congregations were permitted to

register once again, but the All-Union Council was formally abolished in 1960 and regional meetings of Adventist representatives were not permitted officially until 1967. It was only in 1971 that an All-Union 'meeting' of Adventist representatives was allowed. Since 1978, the Council for Religious Affairs has allowed Adventist congregational leaders to hold regular meetings in most republics, as well as 'inter-republic meetings'. The RSFSR Council of Seventh-day Adventists, headed by its chairman, Kulakov, is now recognised by the Soviet state as the only body representing all Adventists in the USSR. Since the 1970s, delegates from the officially recognised Adventist Church in the USSR have been permitted to visit the General Conference in the USA.

The True and Free Adventists have maintained a parallel network of underground congregations, headed by an All-Union Council, but few details are known concerning their church organisation.

Adventists are largely members of the working class or the children of peasants deported from the Volga or Ukraine. Nowadays a majority of Adventists are Russians or Ukrainians, although a sizeable group are from German families, and there are quite large communities in the Baltic republics. Because of deportations in the 1930s and 1940s, there are many Adventist congregations, official and unofficial, in Central Asia, particularly in Kazakhstan.

Adventists in the USSR have very few trained clergy, although official Church membership is 40,000; and the True and Free Adventists may well be equal in numbers. Instead, congregations are often headed by elders.

When permitted to do so, the Adventist Church has always grown in numbers during the Soviet period and seems to be doing so still. The official Adventist Church has benefited since the 1970s from the state's hostility to the True and Free Adventists in that it has obtained permission for more churches to be opened, though it often has to share buildings with Baptist congregations.

The Lutheran Church

History

Apart from a small number of Finns, the Lutheran Church in the USSR is the result of German conquest or settlement. It is wholly non-Russian, though by no means wholly German. Historically, the Lutheran Church developed in two areas: the Baltic, and south Russia mainly along the Volga River.

In the Baltic territories now known as Latvia and Estonia, incorporated into the Russian Empire only in 1710, the Lutheran Church became the dominant religious denomination in the sixteenth century, soon after the Reformation. Lutheranism was the religion of the Baltic German ruling class, descendants of two crusading orders of knights who had conquered the pagan Latvians and Estonians in the twelfth century, and was imposed on the native population as Catholicism had been earlier. The majority of the clergy were Germans until the second half of the nineteenth century. Under the Russian tsars, the Lutheran Church in the Baltic was treated with tolerance, because of its non-Russian membership and the strict control exercised over the clergy and peasantry by the Baltic German nobility.

On the Volga, in south Russia, and in Ukraine, the Lutheran Church grew up among the communities of German farmers invited to settle there by the Russian government in the sixteenth to eighteenth centuries. They were numerous only on the Volga and remained scattered congregations with no central organisation until 1832. The Lutheran congregations often worshipped with Calvinists, and in 1820 the Calvinists on the Volga were absorbed into the Lutheran Church. Individual congregations summoned clergymen from Germany or sent selected individuals to study theology in Germany. In 1832 the Lutheran Church in the Russian Empire was formally united under an Imperial General Consistory, but in practice the Baltic Church looked after its own affairs.

Before the Revolution there were also Lutheran churches in

most large towns throughout the Russian Empire, as many Germans and Balts were employed as state officials.

After the Revolution of October 1917, the Lutheran Church became the majority denomination in the newly-independent states of Latvia and Estonia, acquiring almost the position of a state church. This situation came to an end in 1940, when the USSR annexed the Baltic states. Most of the Lutheran hierarchy and many of the clergy were deported to labour camps by the Soviet authorities or else emigrated westwards during the Second World War.

The German Lutherans on the Volga were decimated by the deportation of *kulaks* (independent peasant farmers) in the 1930s and the Lutheran community in European Russia and Ukraine was completely liquidated as an organisation at the beginning of the Second World War, when all Germans were deported to Central Asia or Siberia.

Church structure and membership; current growth trends
There are great differences in the structures of churches of the Baltic Lutherans on the one hand and of the German Lutherans of Russia on the other. The Lutherans of Estonia and Latvia, as well as the small Lutheran Church of Lithuania, retain the national and episcopal structure they inherited from the pre-war period of independence. The parishes (all registered according to Soviet law) are organised in dioceses, headed by provosts (or deans). The highest Church authority is the Consistory, headed by the Archbishop.

The German Lutherans who formerly lived on the Volga are now scattered all over Central Asia and Siberia, where they were exiled. They were first permitted to register churches again in 1955, but the Lutheran congregations in Central Asia and Siberia were united as an organisation only in the 1970s, owing to the work of Pastor Haralds Kalninš, a Latvian who now acts as superintendent of these churches.

The main centres of the Lutheran Church in the USSR today are in Latvia and Estonia, though some Lithuanian Lutheran parishes also exist. Nowadays there are hardly any Germans among the Baltic Lutherans, as they either emigrated or were deported by the Soviet authorities. Most Lutherans of German descent are now living in Central Asia and Siberia. Lutheran congregations in these areas also include some Estonians and Latvians. Finns to the north of Leningrad have only one registered Lutheran church, while the church in Leningrad itself is mainly attended by Finns and Estonians.

The Estonian Lutheran Church has a lay membership of 250,000, while the Latvian Lutheran Church has 350,000 members. In Lithuania there are 20,000 Lutherans. The number of Lutherans in Central Asia and Siberia is difficult to estimate, but may well be over half a million. East of the Urals, 490 congregations are known to exist. The number of Lutheran clergy is quite inadequate even in the Baltic republics, where 100 pastors in Latvia, 80 in Estonia and 7 in Lithuania are far fewer than the number of congregations. The theological correspondence courses, mainly based in Riga, do not provide enough candidates for replacement, especially as candidates from Asia and Siberia are now competing for student places.

The Lutheran Church in the Baltic republics has fallen greatly in numbers since the war, partly as a result of deportation or emigration of clergy and active members. Some Lutherans have joined the Catholic or Baptist churches, as they are considered more active. In Central Asia and Siberia, the Lutheran Church has regained members since 1970 as congregations continue to register and reorganise. They still seem to be growing in numbers.

Other Protestant Denominations

Mennonites

Mennonites were religious refugees from Germany and Holland who were invited by Russian Empress Catherine the Great to colonise the frontier regions of Russia in the late eighteenth century. Mennonites are pacifists and believe in complete independence from the state. Catherine offered many privileges, including exemption from military service, and thousands of Mennonite families settled in what is now southern Ukraine, recently taken by conquest from Turkey, and in the Urals and Siberia. In the nineteenth century there was a split between the more traditional, who began to be called Church Mennonites, and those more closely oriented to the Baptists, who became known as Mennonite Brethren. In the 1870s and again in 1923–6 many Mennonites emigrated to North America. Of those who remained, the Ukrainian colonists were deported during the Second World War to Siberia for fear they would collaborate with the German invaders. Their church life, severely affected by the persecution of the 1930s, was completely destroyed. After the war, however, and especially after the rehabilitation of Soviet Germans in 1955, Mennonite religious life was gradually restored. Some Mennonite Brethren found a welcome in ECB churches, while others, as well as the Church Mennonites, remained independent and unregistered. In the 1970s emigration resumed and many congregations were considerably weakened. Since the late 1960s, autonomous registration has been a possibility which some have taken up. The strength of the Mennonites has been the combination of ethnic and religious identity; increasing Russification of the younger generation brings not only the danger of losing the young people but also the possibility of a multilingual church that will reach out to the people around it.

Reformed Churches

Reformed churches survive in two parts of the USSR: Lithuania and Transcarpathian Ukraine. Both churches have a bishop, and active pastors and parishes. The Transcarpathian church is mostly Hungarian and maintains links with the Reformed Church in neighbouring Hungary. The Lithuanian Reformed Church is weaker and more isolated. Until after the Second World War there was a Ukrainian Evangelical Reformed Church also in Transcarpathia (the territory annexed from Czechoslovakia in 1945), but it is not known if it has survived.

The Methodist Church

This Church in the Soviet Union is a result of twentieth-century mission work. Before the Revolution there was an

American Methodist pastor working in St Petersburg, but nothing has survived of his work in the city. He did play some part, however, in helping to establish Methodism in Estonia, where it took root firmly. During the 1920s and 1930s Methodist churches were begun also in Latvia, Poland and Czechoslovakia. However, in Latvia and the territories annexed from Poland, Methodism did not survive the disruption of war and Soviet occupation. Only in Estonia did the Methodist Church continue in any strength, more than doubling its membership since 1945. At the present time this growth has not been maintained, but it remains, in proportion to the population of Estonia, the strongest Methodist Church in mainland Europe. It is still a very lively, caring church, with both Estonians and Russians among its members. In Transcarpathia one small Ukrainian congregation survives. After facing near extinction some years ago it is now legally registered and growing.

In conclusion, it should be borne in mind that there has been a general tendency for smaller Protestant groups of 'free-church' tradition to be absorbed into the Union of Evangelical Christians and Baptists, either formally or informally. A formal, though local, arrangement was made in 1946 between the Union and the congregations of Free Christians in Transcarpathian Ukraine. The Free Christians had autonomous congregations with lay leadership. In the case of the Mennonite Brethren actual unity preceded the formal arrangement, which was approved by the 1963 Union congress. In Latvia and western Ukraine, though there was never any formal agreement, many Methodists joined Baptist churches when their own churches failed to reopen after the Second World War or were closed by the Soviet authorities, as Methodists in these areas had ceased to have any formal existence. However, as we have seen above, not all Protestant minorities have been brought into the ECB Union.

The Armenian Apostolic Church

History

Armenia became the first Christian nation in the world, 79 years earlier than the Roman Empire, when the court was converted by Gregory the Illuminator in 301. The name Armenian 'Apostolic' Church refers to the tradition that the Church was first established in Armenia by St Bartholomew and St Thaddaeus. The Armenians did not participate in the Fourth Ecumenical Council at Chalcedon in 451 at which the Monophysite[8] heresy was rejected. They now keep to an essentially Monophysite doctrine, though maintaining that they are not technically Monophysite and that their church preserves the essential elements of the faith of the earliest Christians.[9] Recently, however, the head of the Church has admitted that they do differ from other churches over their interpretation of the nature of Christ, and that this constitutes the main block to ecumenical union with other churches. (The Armenians hold that Christ's human and divine natures are undivided).

Throughout history the Armenians, like the Jews, have suffered frequent persecution and have been without an independent homeland for long periods, but their church has endured and has been the focus for cultural, national, artistic and religious identity.

Armenia was taken into the USSR in 1922, and persecution of the Church began soon afterwards. Its fate from then until 1964 was not substantially different from that of other churches. Since the fall of Khrushchev, the Armenian Church has become one of the freest in the Soviet Union. Catholicos Vazgen I was elected in 1955 and has pursued a diplomatic policy.[10] Visitors speak of a thriving church life and a relaxed atmosphere at church services. One foreign visitor reported that Armenia was the only place in the USSR where he had seen Bibles openly on sale. One reason for the vitality of the Church is that there are very large numbers of Armenians living abroad, many of whom are prosperous: the Soviet government encourages the Armenian Church to call upon them for financial support or even to repatriate; and there is thus continual contact with the outside world.

Church structure

Although, as with other churches in the Soviet Union, no central church organisation has any legal basis, the Catholicosate is well established at Echmiadzin, twenty kilometres west of Yerevan. It has a staff of about 160, and has jurisdiction over the Armenian diaspora as well as Armenians in the USSR. There are twenty-six dioceses, of which six are in the USSR. Three of these are within Armenia; the other three are the dioceses of Georgia and Azerbaidzhan, and the 'Anti-Caucasian' diocese which covers the rest of the Soviet Union. In 1969 the central administration of the three dioceses outside Armenia but within the Soviet Union was dissolved, the three bishops were subsequently relieved of their duties and each parish was forced by the state to appoint a head of its own, supervised by local Party officials.

The Church is supported by the donations of the faithful and by substantial contributions from the diaspora. The latter have supplied a major share of the budget until recently and have financed the Church's printing press (it is the only church in the USSR to have its own), its international activities and the restoration of churchcs and a monastery. However, in 1975 Vazgen reported an 11-fold increase in giving over the previous twenty years by the faithful in Armenia, and said that while finance from abroad was still welcome for special projects, it was no longer essential to subsidise the Church's budget.

Before the Revolution there were about 1,500 open churches in Armenia. The figure normally given nowadays, by Vazgen among others, is about forty, but other sources have given lower figures, the lowest being fifteen. Armenians make a practice of visiting closed churches to carry on religious rites, which include the sacrifice of animals and the tying of votive ribbons on bushes. There are only a handful of churches in the three Soviet dioceses outside Armenia. There is a seminary at Echmiadzin, which has about 100 students. On its printing press the Church produces the monthly newspaper (*Echmiad-zin*) with a circulation—according to Vazgen in 1975—of 5,000 copies. He also stated that the Church produced, annually, a church calendar in an edition of 20,000 and a wall calendar in an edition of 10,000. Again, in 1981 he reported that the New Testament was being printed for the third time in modern Armenian in an edition of 20,000 copies, but added that this would be insufficient for demand and that a further printing would be necessary.

The Armenian Apostolic Church joined the World Council of Churches in 1962, and the Conference of European Churches in 1977.

Church membership

As far as is known, all members of the Church are Armenians. There is little data on social composition, but church attendance is reported to be widespread and therefore presumably includes most sectors of the population. A member of the Armenian Supreme Soviet said in 1978 that he attends church services, and in the same year Vazgen stated that practising members of the Church include some Party functionaries and members of the military. He added that atheist propaganda had not penetrated the masses and was limited to the intelligentsia. Elsewhere he said that there is a revival of interest in religion among young poeple, students, Party members and soldiers.

In 1975 there were estimated to be 115 priests in Armenia. There are roughly three million members of the Church in Armenia and one and a half million in other parts of the Soviet Union. There are six monasteries in Armenia; four at Echmiadzin, one at Khatch in eastern Armenia and one at Geghard near Yerevan. In 1977 the latter consisted of an abbot, six monks, two archpriests and two deacons. Numbers at the other monasteries are unknown. Armenian families flock to Geghard at weekends to picnic, worship and sacrifice animals. One visitor has said that between 100 and 200 children are baptised at weekends.

Current growth trends

Armenians are proud of their church, and it continues to play a central role in the life of the nation. Even unbelievers feel free to participate in services. Vazgen has reported growth of interest in religion recently, and a fourfold increase in baptisms in recent years. He has stated that 80% of the population consider themselves believers, that some 70% of children are baptised, and that 60% of the population attend church—though it is difficult to see how these levels of baptising and church-going can in fact be achieved, given the very small number of open church buildings in Armenia.

Quasi-Christian groups

Probably since the Middle Ages and certainly since the seventeenth century Russian Christianity had its share of fringe groups. In many pre-revolutionary accounts it is hard to distinguish fact from fiction when it comes to such groups. Certainly as far as the Orthodox Church was concerned, their beliefs and practices were beyond the pale and many of them would be alien to Western Christianity too. Some were bizarre to say the least, such as the *khlysty* ('flagellants') and *skoptsy* ('castrates'), but others, such as the Dukhobors and Molokans, were striving for simplicity of faith, which brought them closer to Western Protestantism. All these groups have declined during the Soviet period and many are virtually extinct; but others may well still have a larger number of adherents than some of the Protestant denominations and other quasi-Christian groups. The main quasi-Christian group in the USSR today is a Western import, the Jehovah's Witnesses. Their congregations were among the gains made by the USSR when they annexed the Baltic republics and eastern Poland during the Second World War. Through deportation by the Soviet authorities and through their own missionary zeal, Jehovah's Witnesses were soon established all over the USSR. Although details of their organisation remain a closely guarded secret, they are evidently able to distribute editions of *Watchtower* in Russian and Ukrainian, presumably reproduced clandestinely in the USSR from texts sent in from abroad. Their traditional door-to-door evangelism is carried out, though it seems that other methods of contacting people are often preferred. Jehovah's Witnesses have been bitterly persecuted by the Soviet authorities, who regard them as implacably anti-Soviet and publish a barrage of propaganda against them. Their young men frequently refuse to serve in the armed forces, and thus face automatic prosecution and usually imprisonment. Congregational leaders are also subject to arrest and imprisonment.

A completely distinct group, with a confusingly similar name, are the Jehovists. They were founded in the middle of the last century by a retired army officer in Siberia. Some of their doctrines are believed to have some resemblance to those of the Jehovah's Witnesses, but they have nevertheless remained quite separate. According to a recent Soviet press report, representatives of the Unification Church, with assistance from a Jehovist couple who emigrated to the USA, have tried to infiltrate the Jehovists in order to establish a base in the USSR. As far as it is known, these plans did not come to fruition.

CHRISTIAN ACTIVITIES

Evangelism and mission

Before the Revolution, the Orthodox Church had a programme of mission to the minority peoples of the Empire and beyond, for example in Japan and China. Some previously pagan peoples were successfully Christianised, such as the Komi in northern Russia. Virtually no impact was made on the Muslim peoples, however, and elsewhere progress was often minimal because of the lack of knowledge of indigenous languages.

There was also some Protestant mission activity at times. In the early nineteenth century a Russian Bible Society was established, with the protection of Tsar Alexander I. It began translation of the Bible into modern Russian and distributed Scripture portions. There was little visible result, and later the Bible translation project was taken over by the Russian Orthodox Church, which insisted that many archaisms common in the Old Church Slavonic liturgical language should continue to be used. Nevertheless the availability of the Bible was crucial to the later rise of evangelical Christianity in Russia. In the same period there was a Scottish mission in the Caucasus, but it is not known to have had any lasting results.

The evangelical churches that arose in the 1860s and 1870s took spreading the gospel seriously, without necessarily having a special mission strategy: they simply wanted to share their faith. The 1920s brought them many opportunities as the Soviet authorities for a time favoured the previously persecuted minorities, and concentrated their attack on the Orthodox and Catholic Churches. Vigorous youth organisations were set up and the extent of the Evangelicals' social and evangelistic activity was reflected in the prohibitions introduced by Stalin's 1929 Law on Religious Associations.

Since 1929, all organised mission and charitable activity has been banned, and evangelism has therefore become the responsibility of the local church, and, above all, of the individual Christian. The witness through word and example of each Christian has assumed the greatest importance. In these circumstances evangelism is generally not targeted at particular groups, but at neighbours and work-mates. Nevertheless, Christians have a particular sensitivity to the lonely and those isolated from society, and Soviet propagandists frequently recognise the Christian churches' effectiveness in this respect. Some have felt a calling to reach the outcasts of society, such as hippies and drop-outs. In the 1970s the youth rallies of the Khar'kov unregistered Baptist church over the Mayday holidays became a fixture in the hippy calendar. The Orthodox Christian Seminar and the inter-denominational ecumenists helped many drop-outs in their spiritual search, and the ecumenists brought faith and regeneration to a number of drug addicts. The well-known Baptist musician Valeri Barinov also evangelised among alcoholics, addicts and prostitutes when he was still living in Leningrad.

Only the unregistered Council of Evangelical Christian-Baptist Churches seems to have a specific policy on evangelism, and appoints evangelists to spearhead the missionary work of the churches. The registered ECB Union has a department of 'Evangelism and Christian Unity', but its reported activity concentrates on relations with evangelicals outside the Union rather than on evangelism.

While some Orthodox think in terms of re-Christianising Russian society, most evangelicals take an individualistic approach, looking no further than their immediate neighbours. However, there are signs of a nascent awareness of the unreached peoples of the USSR. In Central Asia many Baptists have Muslims for neighbours and in recent years a small number of Muslims have been converted. They are hampered by a lack of suitable materials, including the Scriptures, in the Central Asian languages.

Broadcasting

There has never been any Christian broadcasting by believers within the Soviet Union. There is no prospect whatever that it could commence under present conditions. Christian radio broadcasts from the West, therefore, continue to be a life-line, tremendously appreciated by Soviet Christians, and also an effective medium for evangelism. Among the broadcasting companies which devote themselves to religious programmes are Trans World Radio, the Far East Broadcasting Association, IBRA Radio, HCJB ('Voice of the Andes'), the Voice of Orthodoxy, and Vatican Radio. Religious programmes are also broadcast by the BBC, the Voice of America and others.

Literature

All Christian groups in the Soviet Union place a heavy emphasis upon the need to produce Christian literature, in great quantity and of better quality. Because Soviet citizens are starved of any reading matter that is not ideologically biased, they are far more likely than Westerners to read Christian literature if they have the chance to do so.

Official production

Possibilities for the production of Christian literature officially have already been outlined in the sections of the different denominations. Since official religious printing resumed in 1956, a growing amount of literature has been published, but it is still grossly inadequate to meet even the needs of believers, let alone for evangelistic purposes. Official production has consisted mainly of Scriptures, service-books and hymn books, calendars and journals. Though these are doubtless priorities, it means that no Bible study aids, apologetic or devotional works have been published, and nothing for children. There is also a dearth of any books officially produced in any language other than Russian, though in recent years a small amount of literature has been produced in German, Ukrainian, Georgian, Armenian and the Baltic languauges.

A relatively new development has been the granting of official permission for Soviet churches to import Christian literature from the West, principally from the United Bible Societies. Several tens of thousands of Bibles and New Testaments have been imported, and recently a Russian translation of five volumes of the seventeen-volume Bible commentary by William Barclay was added to the list. Early in 1988, permission was given to import 9,000 copies of a three-volume Orthodox Bible commentary, with hopes that a further 150,000 copies would follow.

There can be no doubt that all the churches would like to produce much more literature officially than they do at present, even taking the gains of recent years into account. The only reason they do not is that the state will not permit them to do so. The main way in which this is effected is by restricting the annual paper allocation to the churches. This is sometimes explained as being the result of a paper shortage. However, the Soviet Union, with some of the largest tracts of forest in the world at its disposal, produces millions of tonnes of paper every year. Paper is its twelfth largest export. Furthermore, the Soviet Union claims to produce more books annually than any other country in the world. It is clearly a matter of state policy to restrict production of Christian literature, and to allocate paper instead to Communist-approved works—including an ever-growing annual production of atheist literature.

The Churches permitted to produce the greatest amount of Christian literature are the Russian Orthodox and the Baptists. Smaller groups permitted to increase production slightly in recent years, for use within their communities, are the Georgian Orthodox, the Armenian Church and the Lutherans. The groups most restricted in literature production are the Lithuanian Catholics, the Ukrainians (both Orthodox and Catholics), and the Pentecostals.

Most of the officially produced literature is aimed at members of existing communities. Enterprising individuals can, however, use such materials, especially Scriptures, for drawing unbelievers into the faith. Literature can be produced only by the officially registered churches, with state permission for each new venture. All literature is produced on state printing presses (except for the Armenian Apostolic Church) and subject to state censorship. It seems likely that modest growth will be permitted in both the official printing and the official import of more of the kind of books described above.

Unofficial production

Because of the restrictions on official production of Christian literature, many believers have resorted to producing it unofficially. *Samizdat* ('self-published') literature, as it is known, has now become widespread in the USSR for all kinds of works that would not pass state censorship. They include works of literature, poetry, philosophy and political commentary, as well as documentation of Soviet abuses of human rights and a flood of complaints, protests and appeals about violations of the rights of Soviet citizens. It has been estimated, however, that religious *samizdat* forms about half of all *samizdat* output; and since Muslim and Jewish *samizdat* output has not been extensive, most of this must be Christian.

Most *samizdat* has been typed, but it is also produced by other means: handwriting, duplicating, photocopying and even printing. Photocopying and printing machines are closely guarded, and reproduction by these means can be done only clandestinely and with great danger.

The groups most involved with the unofficial production of Christian literature have been the Baptists, Pentecostals, Adventists, Russian Orthodox and Lithuanian Catholics. Latterly, Ukrainian Catholics have also published *samizdat*. In the case of the Pentecostals and Adventists, all the *samizdat* literature has been produced by unregistered groups. In the cases of the Russian Orthodox, Baptists and Lithuanian Catholics, people who are members of registered churches have decided to act unofficially and on their own initiative to produce Christian literature.

The unregistered Baptists have taken the most determined stand on this matter. As early as the 1960s, after breaking off from the officially recognised All-Union Council, they decided that one of their main tasks would be the provision of Christian literature. They therefore constructed their own printing machines, using parts from old washing-machines, motor cycles and whatever came to hand. These presses could operate only under conditions of strictest secrecy, and so the printers would live literally underground for months at a time. Every now and then the KGB discovers one of these presses and arrests and imprisons the printers. Each time, however, another printing press has emerged elsewhere, so that the work can carry on. The sophistication of the machines has gradually improved: first they were improved to produce double-sided copies (where state machines of comparable size produced only single-sided ones!); later again they were refined to produce Bibles as well as New Testaments.

As well as Scriptures, the Baptists also produce evangelistic materials for unbelievers. The chief item is the magazine *Vestnik istiny* ('Herald of Truth').

The Pentecostals too have placed great emphasis on producing Christian literature, though they have not been well-organised and as technically competent as the Baptists. For a time the unregistered Seventh-day Adventists also produced a remarkable amount of literature, on a secret printing press and by other means. This appears to have been due to one remarkable man, Vladimir Shelkov, the leader of the True and Free Seventh-day Adventists. Shelkov died in a labour camp in 1980 at the age of 84, and production of Adventist literature has not maintained the same level since.

The Russian Orthodox Church has not traditionally been as active in this area as the smaller groups mentioned above. Over the last few years, however, production has increased. A group of Moscow believers was able to obtain access to a disused photocopying machine on which they produced prayerbooks and other Christian literature. This activity came to light on 6th April 1982, when 6 people were arrested after lengthy house searches during which large quantities of Christian literature were confiscated by the authorities. Six thousand prayerbooks were taken from one address alone. All six people were sent to labour camps. Such a remarkably large quantity of books testifies to a well-organised production operation. It is known that the distribution was widespread, as a priest in Novosibirsk, Fr Aleksandr Pivovarov, was sentenced for receiving and distributing some of this literature.

Another example of Orthodox *samizdat* is the journal *Nadezhda* ('Hope'). Its editor was a Soviet writer, who, with her husband was converted in middle age. They began to write about their new-found beliefs and found that there was a tremendous thirst for such writing. Zoya Krakhmalnikova began to assemble collections of Christian readings from a variety of sources: the church fathers, more recent Russian Christian writers, memoirs of those who perished in the 1920s and 1930s, contemporary writing, poetry, translations from Western Christian authors. Readers begged for more of these typewritten works. Then *Nadezhda* began to be published in the West and copies were sent back to Russia in the form of small paperbacks. After a few issues had appeared, Krakhmalnikova was arrested, at the age of fifty-three, and sent thousands of miles away to a Siberian village.

Since 1972, Lithuanian Catholics have produced *samizdat*. The best-known item is the *Chronicle of the Lithuanian Catholic Church*, which reports anti-religious discrimination by the state, but there are also spiritual journals in circulation. Many prayer-books are also produced. In 1974 Povilas Petronis was sentenced to four years' imprisonment for producing the remarkable number of 20,000 unofficial prayer-books.

In 1973, 3,500 Eastern-rite Catholic prayer-books were secretly run off by a priest in the Lvov state printing works. More recently the Ukrainian Catholics have produced a *samizdat Chronicle* similar to the Lithuanian one, but it is not known what, if any, Eastern-rite Catholic spiritual works are circulating in *samizdat* at present.

It seems certain that many Christians will continue to produce literature unofficially, despite the dangers involved. However, the authorities are repressing such activities even more strongly than during the 1970s (as with all unofficial activities), and sentences are longer for those who are caught. Unless the present restrictive atmosphere changes—and there is no sign of that—then the situation will get even more difficult.

One likely future development is that greater use will be made of cassettes and videos. Cassettes are already used widely, for example, for recording sermons for the housebound. Videos are beginning to be used for Christian purposes as the video boom begins to spread in the USSR.

Despite all these efforts, the dearth of Christian literature in the Soviet Union is so great that believers there will have to continue, for the foreseeable future, to be heavily dependent upon those who bring Scriptures and Christian books into the country unofficially from the West.

Bible translation and distribution

The first Russian translation of the Bible was published in 1876 by the Synod of the Russian Orthodox Church. Before that, the books of the Bible were available in a translation in Slavonic: the first Slavonic Bible was published in 1581. The 1876 translation, which is the equivalent of the English Authorised Version, is still in use today. A co-operative venture between the United Bible Societies and the Leningrad Theological Academy of the Russian Orthodox Church to produce a modern Russian translation began at the end of the 1970s, but appears to have petered out. In 1988, the millennium of the Christianisation of Russia, the Russian Orthodox Church plans to publish a 5-volume history and a prayer-book, and has apparently received permission to print 100,000 Bibles.

Other officially published translations of the Bible since 1956 have been: Georgian (1963, 1982); Armenian (1970, 1974–5, 1981); Latvian (1960, 1970s); Estonian (permission given for translation 1971: progress unknown); Lithuanian (1973). Recently the Georgian Orthodox Church has announced plans to print 10,000 Bibles in Georgian, and the Baptist Church in Moldavia has received permission to print 8,000 Bibles and 8,000 hymn books in Moldavian. From 1982 the Baptists have been able, officially, to import Scriptures in Estonian, Latvian, German and Georgian as well as Russian. The Baptist World Alliance plans to import 100,000 Bibles in 1988. In 1977 the Lutherans were able to import German Bibles. It is remarkable that no Scriptures have been officially published or imported in Ukrainian, apart from 300 Bibles sent in 1985 from Canada to Baptists in Kiev.

Distribution is only through registered churches. Scriptures are not on sale anywhere, and may not even be bought by post.

Scriptures in languages of the Soviet Union have been published abroad. These include a Ukrainian Bible and New Testament. The Hundred Languages Project of the Institute for Bible Translation in Stockholm has undertaken the task of producing Scriptures in languages of the Soviet Union into which they have never been translated. These Scriptures may be taken in only unofficially.

Some churches, particularly the unregistered ones, have reasonably efficient distribution channels for Scriptures received unofficially from the West, but these, of course, remain secret. Among other groups, distribution is more haphazard. Foreign visitors to the Soviet Union have often been able informally to give Scriptures to unbelievers, or to enquirers who do not belong to any church.

It seems probable that the Soviet authorities will continue to permit more editions of the Scriptures to be officially published and imported, though not on anything like the scale required. At the same time, they will continue to try to stop the unofficial production, importing, and distribution of Scriptures.

Education

Education is perhaps the most difficult problem confronting the churches in the Soviet Union. All religious education is illegal except for that of children by their own parents. Even so, there have been cases (though not recently) of persecution of families because the parents gave their children a Christian upbringing. No formal education of children by pastors, priests or other adults is permitted, nor education of adult converts. This means that the only legal forums for Christian education are church services and family life.

The churches, therefore, use to the full the opportunities for teaching afforded by church services. This is most obvious in evangelical churches, where preaching has always been a central element. Church members who have no Bible of their own benefit from detailed Bible exposition by a pastor. It is, therefore, important that pastors have access to biblical commentaries and apologetic and other works. These are still in short supply, opportunities for official printing are limited, and gifts from the West are, therefore, of prime importance.

In the Orthodox and Catholic Churches, the teaching element is less obvious to the outsider, but exists nonetheless. A great deal depends upon the priest. A zealous and devout priest will make full use of opportunities afforded by the liturgy or mass; a frightened priest will make a less effective teacher.

The Orthodox liturgy provides many opportunities for both children and adult converts to learn more about their faith.

Most of the chants and hymns which form a major part of the service are repetitions of sentences of Scripture, especially the psalms. The icons and frescoes which customarily adorn all the walls of the church contain scenes from the life of Christ and of other major figures of the Bible, as well as of Russian and other saints. Ritual observances, such as lighting candles and crossing oneself, are meant to be aids to prayer and to concentration, not merely empty gestures. Much depends, of course, upon the extent to which the congregation can be taught the meaning of these practices. There is always a sermon towards the end of the liturgy: it is usually about ten minutes long, nearly always based on the Gospel reading for the day.

A few enterprising priests go further than this and attempt to teach their flock outside services. They need a careful combination of boldness and discretion, since they do not want to risk attracting the attention of the local Council for Religious Affairs (CRA) commissioner. However, the legal position here is not absolutely clear-cut. Although teaching is forbidden, it is permitted for a priest to give advice on personal spiritual life. The dividing line is unclear, and in practice would probably depend upon the CRA commissioner's personal opinion. There is scope, therefore, for variation between one region and another. For example, during a talk in the Russian Orthodox Cathedral in London, Metropolitan Filaret of Minsk stated that he advised the priests in his diocese to gather all the children preparing for confession and communion into one group before the liturgy and to hold a discussion with them. This might be regarded as teaching, or youth work, but apparently the CRA in this instance did not object.

Nonetheless, the framework within which the church has to operate is so restrictive that, with the best will in the world, the priests cannot meet all the teaching needs of their congregations. This appears to apply particularly to young, educated converts. They come to the church with questions about Christianity teeming in their minds that cannot all be answered during a church service. This is the main reason for the growth of study circles, discussion groups and seminars within the Russian Orthodox Church. These began to appear during the early 1960s and spread during the 1970s. Despite the repressive atmosphere of the 1980s, such groups continue to function, though with a much lower profile than formerly. One or two well-known discussion groups, notably the Moscow-based Christian Seminar, suffered severe reprisals from the KGB and this has led other groups to be cautious. There is, therefore, no way of knowing how many of these groups there are, nor where they meet. Fairly frequent reports from unofficial sources, however, suggest that they are still influential, and an important means of supplementing the teaching given in the registered churches. Some of these groups meet around a priest, others have lay leadership. They form an important forum for fellowship as well as teaching. They usually have to meet in farily small groups where all the members are known to one another but to no one else, for fear of informers, since it is known that the KGB is trying to stamp out what it believes to be a subversive network of discussion groups. This cell-type structure can lead to authoritarianism.

The situation in the Catholic Church is analogous in that the extent to which teaching given in church services is supplemented by more detailed, unofficial teaching depends largely upon the priest. The main issue here is that of catechism of young children, which is illegal. Several priests, especially in Lithuania, have been imprisoned for this. However, Catholicism is so strong in Lithuania that many children still benefit from catechism classes. In Lithuania, also, it is difficult for the authorities to enforce atheistic teaching in schools to the same extent as in other republics, since it has not proved possible to exclude all Christian teachers from schools, given the high proportion of Catholics in the population as a whole.

The unregistered Baptists and Pentecostals have probably been the most determined and systematic in their attempts to teach children and young people. They regularly hold unofficial Sunday schools, and also summer holiday camps for Christian children—particularly the children of prisoners, who otherwise could not afford a holiday. A number of adults have been imprisoned for such teaching activities.

The education of children as Christians depends to a very large extent upon their families. In most cases this depends upon the example and teaching of the parents and participation in family prayers and Bible studies, as well as church attendance. Such education through the family is most developed among the evangelicals and Catholics, where it has a strong tradition. Such families are well used to the problems their children encounter in schools, where they are often held up to ridicule by teachers and mocked, bullied and sometimes severely maltreated by their classmates. Traumatic though such experiences are, it seems that these families have sufficient resilience and strength of faith to counter them.

Orthodoxy is also passed on through the family to an important extent. However, generally speaking, Orthodox families do not seem to be as cohesive as evangelical and Catholic ones. It is not uncommon for people who have been baptised into the Orthodox Church as children not to pay much attention to Christianity during their growing and working years, but then to return to it later in life, particularly after retirement. Much depends upon whether there is an open church near enough to their home for them to attend. An exception to this pattern, however, is the conversion of young people and adults, sometimes from nominal Orthodox backgrounds as well as from atheistic ones. In recent years, with the eclipse of the dissent movement, many such young converts have come to believe that their most important role is to bring up a Christian family of their own and in this way help to 'Christianise' their nation. Their vision and devotion are exemplary, but they do encounter practical problems in teaching their children about their faith. Not having had a Christian upbringing themselves, they have no example to fall back upon. There is a great need here for teaching materials for children and for Christian families, a need which the church at present appears unable to meet. There is no doubt that Orthodox, evangelicals and Catholics, would all welcome teaching materials for children from the West.

Social concerns

The churches are legally prevented from becoming involved in charitable or social welfare activity because, in theory, a socialist state is fully competent in these areas. Churches are not even allowed to give charitable help to members of their own congregations who may be in need, through illness or bereavement, for example. This ban particularly affects families of Christian prisoners, who receive no welfare benefits whatever from the state, and are in effect virtually destitute. In practice, however, individual believers or families of believers do help prisoners' families informally, according to their means. The unregistered Baptists have organised a fund to help the families of their members who are imprisoned.

A number of social problems exist, problems that the churches could help the state to tackle effectively, were they permitted to do so. The most obvious is the problem of alcoholism. This is a major social evil, leading to serious labour problems and loss of production—one which the authorities have long shirked tackling, although Mr Gorbachev has now begun to do so. However, the churches' help is rigorously excluded, because the Soviet authorities fear the 'ideological baggage' that they would bring with them in helping to resolve the problem. An unofficial temperance movement begun by some Lithuanian Catholics in the 1970s was suppressed by the KGB. According to an as yet unconfirmed source Mr Gorbachev did ask Orthodox Church leaders to help combat alcoholism during a private meeting towards the end of 1986. If so, this would mark a significant policy change.

There is just one area of social concern in which church involvement is not only possible but obligatory. All the registered churches are required to support the 'peace campaign' as inspired and promoted by the Soviet government. In fact, this means giving undeviating endorsement to Soviet foreign policy. Western observers of the religious scene in the Soviet Union regularly receive the incorrect impression that the Soviet churchmen's concern for 'peace' is spontaneous and voluntary; worse, they then frequently go on to make the assumption that the churches in the Soviet Union are generally free to intervene and comment on matters of social or political concern within their own country.

CHAPTER 2

Poland

POLAND: OVERVIEW

The country; the people; brief history

Poland, a country of 120,725 square miles, lies in the centre of Europe in a zone of moderate climate and mixed forests. The country is made up predominantly of lowlands. Over 90% of the area is less than 300 metres above sea-level, but the countryside is not completely flat, due mainly to the mountains in the south and to glacial formations in the north. Poland's present boundaries were established in 1945. In the south and south-west the Polish frontier is formed by the ranges of the Carpathian and Sudeten Mountains, in the north by the Baltic Sea. The principal rivers of Poland, the Vistula and the Odra, flow to the Baltic. Administratively Poland is divided into forty-nine provinces (voivodeships). The five largest Polish cities (Warsaw, Kraków, Wroclaw, Lódź and Poznań) also have the status of provinces. Poland's most important natural resource is hard coal, mainly located in Upper Silesia. In many areas there is brown coal and also rich deposits of peat and sulphur. Crude oil and natural gas as well as iron-ore exist in relatively small quantities.

Since the redrawing of Poland's borders in 1945, the population of Poland has become largely homogeneous from an ethnic point of view. Over 97% of the population is Polish. National minorities (in descending order of size) include Ukrainians, Kashubians (Pomeranians), Belorussians, Germans, Russians (including Russian troops), gypsies, Slovaks, Lithuanians and Greeks; and 5,000 Jews.

In 1931, 60% of the population worked on the land, and this proportion had virtually halved by 1967. In 1984, out of a population of 37 million, nearly two-thirds lived in towns and cities.

Until the sixteenth century, Poland was a powerful monarchy.

Weakened by wars with Sweden and Turkey, however, Poland declined throughout the seventeenth century just at the time when the Russia of the Romanovs, the Prussia of the Hohenzollerns and the Austria of the Habsburgs were growing in strength. Efforts to regenerate the country (including promulgation in 1791 of a new constitution, which was the second democratic constitution in the world after that of the American states) failed, and by 1795 Polish territory had been completely divided between its three neighbours. Poland regained its independence in 1918 at the end of the First World War and two years later defended itself successfully against a Bolshevik invasion. In September 1939, as a result of the Molotov-Ribbentrop pact, Poland was invaded by Germany and the Soviet Union, and then 'liberated' by the Red Army at the end of the Second World War.

The multi-party elections in 1947, which were to decide the political future of Poland, were rigged, and by 1948 the Polish United Workers Party (PZPR) had established a dictatorship. Poland, now called the Polish People's Republic *(Polska Rzeczpospolita Ludowa)*, has proved the most difficult to control of all the Soviet satellites. In the post-war period the Poles have rebelled five times against communist rule: in 1956, 1968, 1970, 1976, and most recently in 1980, when the 10-million strong Solidarity Free Trade Union was formed, strengthened by the Farmers' Solidarity Union, which claimed over two million members. Martial law, imposed on 13th December 1981, ended the process of political liberalisation which had been forced on the government during the time of Solidarity.

The economy; social conditions; political life

Under the communist post-war government the whole of the Polish economy was nationalised and made the subject of central planning. In the 1970s Poland experienced a period of economic boom after the Party changed its economic policy, emphasising the need to raise the standard of living and modernise the economy, and opening the way to imports and credits from the

West. The boom nevertheless ended in disaster. In 1987 Poland's gross debt was estimated at 39 thousand million dollars.

Despite all attempts to collectivise individual farms, 71% of agricultural land is still privately owned. For ideological reasons, however, state farms receive preferential treatment in investments and in supplies of fodder, fertiliser and machinery. Despite the fact that all state farms are heavily subsidised by the government, in 1980 Poland had to import some nine million tons of grain (40% of its own harvest) to meet domestic demand.

The 1980s have been marked by rapidly increasing pauperisation of society, caused by 3 factors: economic bankruptcy; the sudden withdrawal of Western credits; and the passive resistance of the population to the present régime, which affects productivity. In 1980, 20% of the population were living below the poverty line; in 1984 the proportion had risen to one Pole in three. Infant mortality in 1985 reached 20% and there has been a dramatic increase of tuberculosis cases among young people between the ages of 15 and 35. Life expectancy has also decreased, especially for men. Young married couples have to wait for years to get a flat—up to twenty-six years in some cities. Poverty and the lack of any prospects for political change are blamed for the increase in social diseases such as drug addiction and alcoholism. In 1982 the average consumption of alcohol per individual was ten litres; by 1984 it had increased by 6%. The number of drug addicts (mainly heroin) is officially estimated at 300,000. The lack of prospects for young people even with university degrees has resulted in an increasing brain drain through emigration to the West.

Since 1948, Poland has been a one-party state. According to the constitution of 1952, as amended in 1976, the guardianship of the Party over the state and Poland's alliance with the USSR are the cardinal principles of the government. Although the organs of the Party are quite different from those of the state, all policies of the government and administration are determined by the Political Bureau of the Party.

In comparison with the other Eastern European countries, the Stalinist period in Poland (1948–56) took a relatively mild form. Since then, Poland has been ruled by a native 'national communist' government. After 1956, for a short period of time, a Catholic group called ZNAK was allowed in Parliament as an 'opposition' group with an independent voice, but later all members were replaced by Catholics subservient to the régime.

After 1970 the ideological aim of achieving communism in Poland was replaced by plans for rapid economic growth. The 1970s were also noted for growing liberalisation in society, and, since 1976, a rapidly growing dissent movement. In 1980 the Party's monopoly of power was challenged by the Solidarity Free Trade Union which, together with Farmers' Solidarity, claimed some 12 million members. Solidarity was in fact a form of popular opposition which, even if it was not seeking direct political change, was certainly attempting to curb the Party's unlimited power and make it answerable to the population at large. Its leader, Lech Walesa, won the Nobel Peace Prize.

Since martial law was introduced in December 1981, Poland has returned to strict Party dictatorship. The Party is, however, unrepresentative of the population. In 1985 it claimed only 1,800,000 members—mostly Party bureaucrats. The percentage of workers is minimal: in the Lenin shipyard in Gdańsk only 69 workers out of 1,000 are members of the Party. The percentage of peasant Party members is even lower. Passive resistance to the régime is strong and the Solidarity Free Trade Union as well as several opposition groups have gone underground, resulting in a political impasse.

THE STATUS OF CHRISTIANITY

The religious complexion of the country

It is believed by historians that the lands which were later to form Poland were visited quite early by Christian missionaries: certainly the missionaries of St Methodius were operating there. In 961 the German missionary Adalbert passed through

Poland. Under the terms of an agreement reached between Prince Mieszko I of the Piast dynasty and the German Emperor Otto I, Mieszko pledged to marry a Christian Czech princess, Dąbrówka. In 966, a year after the wedding, Mieszko I and his court were baptised and in 968 the first bishopric was established in Poznań.

Since the redrawing of Poland's borders at the end of the Second World War, Poland has been an almost homogeneously Catholic country with over 90% of the population pledging allegiance to the Catholic Church. Over 95% of Polish children are baptised into the Catholic Church and Catholicism forms almost a 'national ideology' at variance with the ruling Marxist ideology.

Apart from the Roman Catholic Church, there are over thirty Churches and denominations which are recognised by the Polish authorities. Non-Catholic Christian Churches currently represent less than 3% of the population; among them the largest is the Polish Autocephalous Orthodox Church with over 800,000 members. Protestants constitute a minority of about 100,000, with the 80,000 Lutherans constituting the largest group. The Polish Ecumenical Council (PEC), created in 1945, co-ordinates the activities of the country's non-Roman Catholic Christians. The only significant Christian minority which, for political reasons, has been denied official recognition is the Eastern-rite Catholic Church, embracing some 250,000 to 500,000 Ukrainians living in Poland (for further details, see p 127).

There is a small number of non-Christian people in Poland. Out of the 3.3 million Jews living in Poland in 1939, 2.9 million were killed by the Nazis. Since 1945, a large proportion of the survivors have emigrated to Israel. In 1980 there were only 5,000 Jews, 1,739 of whom were regarded as members of Jewish religious communities. There are about 2,300 Muslims living in six communities in Poland. They are descendants of the Tartars who settled in the lands of the grand duchy of Lithuania at the end of the fourteenth century. Adherents to other religions include Buddhists, Yogists, Occultists of various kinds and several thousand non-Christian gypsies. It is difficult to estimate the number of atheists within the Party;

but it is relatively small: for example, in 1971 the Society for the Propagation of Secular Culture had only 316,000 members.

The state's attitude to religion

The Constitution of 22nd July 1952 guarantees 'freedom of conscience and religion to all citizens' and proclaims the separation of church and state; but also declares that it is punishable by law to abuse freedom of conscience and religion for ends contrary to the interests of the Polish People's Republic. In 1975 the government tried to introduce constitutional amendments which, among other things, were to make a citizen's rights dependent upon his fulfilment of his duties towards the communist state. After strong protests from the church and public opinion, the explicit connection between rights and duties was replaced by an admonition to citizens to fulfil their duties conscientiously.

Over thirty Churches and denominations are recognised by the state. The only major denomination not so recognised is the Eastern-rite Catholic Church. Officially, all denominations are equal. Since, according to the Constitution of March 1921, the Roman Catholic Church was granted 'the leading position among the equal Churches' and only 7 denominations had their status officially recognised, the Polish communist authorities claim to be more tolerant than the pre-war 'Christian Polish government'.

In fact it was only during the period from 1945 to 1947, while the Communists were trying to gain public support, that religion enjoyed relative toleration. From 1947, when the Marxist-Leninist Polish United Workers Party (PZPR) established its dictatorship, eradication of religion became one of the main aims of the state. However, the moral prestige and organisational strength of the Roman Catholic Church have meant that the struggle against religion, in fact, takes a milder form than in many other communist countries.

Since 1950, the activities of the Churches have been controlled by the Office for Religious Affairs and supervised by one member of the Central Committee of the Communist Party. There is also a special 'Church' department within the Ministry of the Interior. Throughout the post-war period the state authorities have attempted to confine the activities of the Churches within the four walls of the building. No religious associations have been allowed (with the exception of the few Catholic Intellectuals Clubs [KIKs] first allowed in 1956). Christian culture has been excluded from the state-controlled mass media and Christian elements removed from the history text-books. Since 1960, religious instruction has been forbidden in schools. The Churches have no legal status.

Before 1956 state pressure was directed against all religious denominations indiscriminately. Since then, however, different tactics have been used towards the Roman Catholic Church on the one hand and the religious minorities on the other. For the last thirty years the non-Catholic Christian Churches, representing a small percentage of the population, have been enjoying relative tolerance and state support in order to offset the power of the Catholic Church, which has been singled out as the main enemy. This dual policy has incidentally helped to create the impression among some Western Protestant communities that the Polish government is tolerant towards all religions.

THE VARIOUS CHURCHES

The Roman Catholic Church

History

In 966 Poland's first ruler Mieszko I became a Christian and, following the custom of that time, the rest of the new nation was baptised soon afterwards. This development brought Poland into a close relationship with the other countries of medieval Europe. From the tenth to the twelfth centuries only the upper classes embraced Christianity. The process gained momentum over the next 300 years, which saw the expansion of the Church as an organisation: in 1500 there were about as many parishes as there are today over the same area. The Franciscan and Dominican orders were instrumental in consolidating a type of worship which gives prominence to the fundamentally humanitarian qualities of Christianity. In the Middle Ages were also laid the foundations of that intense devotion to the Virgin Mary which still remains the main feature of Polish Catholicism.

Throughout Poland's history the vigour and influence of Polish Catholicism have been closely linked with the fortunes of the Polish nation and people. The strong link between the Church and the state was manifested symbolically in the tradition which regarded the Polish primate as *Interrex*, who ruled between the death of one monarch and the coronation of the next. The Reformation in Poland had a relatively superficial influence, affecting mostly the upper classes, townspeople and people of non-Polish origin. Catholicism continued to be the national religion. In the late sixteenth century a relatively peaceful interdenominational contest ended with eventual victory for the vigorous Catholic Church. During the period of Poland's decline from the seventeenth century onwards, one which was exacerbated by ruinous wars, the consolidation of the Catholic faith continued. All the wars in which Poland was involved were against Islamic, Orthodox or Protestant powers, and this fact further underlined the centrality of Catholicism to Poles as a nation. The greatest threat to Polish Catholicism came at the end of the eighteenth century, with the partition of Poland among its three neighbours Austria, Russia and Prussia. It was during the subsequent 123 years, when Poland did not exist as a separate political entity, that patriotism and Catholicism became inextricably welded in the mind of the Polish people. Russification and Germanification went hand in hand with attempts to convert Poles forcibly to Orthodoxy or Lutheranism. In the Russian zone of partition, the Church was additionally persecuted for the support it gave to the two uprisings in 1830 and 1863.

Poland came into existence as an independent country again after the First World War, but was again occupied by Nazi

Germany and the Soviet Union in 1939. Over 2,500 bishops, nuns, monks, seminarians and priests perished in German concentration camps between 1939 and 1945. No data are available on the fate of the Church in the territories incorporated into the Soviet Union. When Poland was reconstituted in 1945 with altered boundaries, it became for the first time for centuries an almost homogeneous Catholic country: non-Catholics amounted to less than 3%. The majority of pre-war Poland's non-Catholics had lived in the lands annexed by the Soviet Union; German Protestants were expelled from Poland after 1945.

Four phases can be distinguished in the policy of the communist state towards the Roman Catholic Church since 1947.

The first phase, from 1947 to 1956, saw an attempt to nationalise the Roman Catholic Church in order to gain total control over it, despite a 19-point Accord signed by the Catholic hierarchy and the government on 14th April 1950. Catholic schools were declared illegal and all 'Higher Institutes of Religious Knowledge' closed down. Religious instruction was removed from the school curriculum and special atheist schools run by the 'Association of the Friends of Children' were set up. Catholic Action and other Church associations were also declared illegal and the government took over some 1,000 educational and charitable institutions run by 'Caritas'. The Church press was banned and the Church's property, with the exception of church buildings and their grounds, was confiscated. In 1953 the government announced that the state had the right to appoint and dismiss clergy; all priests and bishops were to take an oath of loyalty to the Polish People's Republic. When the Church refused to comply, Cardinal Wyszyński, the head of the Catholic Church, was arrested and confined to a convent. By the end of 1953, 8 other bishops, 900 priests and over 1,000 lay Catholic activists were in prison.

The second phase, from 1957 to 1970, saw an attempt to cripple the Church's activities using legal means accompanied by a vigorous ideological campaign portraying the Catholic Church as a 'bastion of primitive obscurantism and anachronism'. Severe restrictions were placed on permission for new church buildings.

In the third phase, from 1970 to 1980, the implacable ideological battle against religion was officially abandoned, but the government made efforts to stem the growth of Church membership and to cut the Church's links with the rapidly growing democratic opposition.

The fourth phase, from 1981, has seen a dual policy on the part of the government: an attempt to use the Church to uphold political stability while continuing to undermine its moral authority.

Only during times of acute crisis, when the political future of the state has been in jeopardy, and in the face of popular revolt (in 1956, 1970, 1976, 1980), has there been a notable easing of anti-religious policies and an effort by the state to seek a rapprochement with the Catholic Church.

The authority and personality of Cardinal Wyszyński dominated almost the entire period since 1945. His pastoral strategy was based on the strength of popular religiosity, reinforced by and expressed through festivals of faith dedicated mainly to the Virgin Mary, who is regarded by Polish Catholics as 'Queen of Poland'. In the 1960s Cardinal Wyszyński was subjected to criticism from some intellectual circles for the 'non-intellectual' nature of his pastoral work and also for obstructing Church reforms proposed by the Second Vatican Council. However, by the late 1970s all the Cardinal's critics agreed that it was his strategy which had placed the Church at the centre of Polish society and strengthened the people's sense of unity as Catholics against the oppressive tactics of the authorities, and that his slow and careful introduction of the reforms of the Second Vatican Council had spared Poland the division and confusion which had beset Catholic Churches in the West.

Throughout the post-war years, the Polish episcopate and clergy led by Cardinal Wyszyński were staunch promoters and defenders of human rights. In the 1970s they were joined by an increasing number of lay Catholics. These 'Catholic dissidents' undertook a number of initiatives in direct defiance of the authorities' aim of confining the Church to the strictly spiritual sphere of activity. Several Believers' Self Defence Committees were formed, as well as a Christian Association of Workers. Among the many unofficial publications which sprang up after

1977, two were produced by strictly Catholic dissident groups: *Spotkania* ('Encounters'), and *Krzyz Nowohucki* ('The Cross of Nowa Huta'). All the others contained special sections on the Church. The Church was also deeply involved in setting up the 'Flying University'—independent academic courses challenging the Party monopoly on education. In the diocese of Przemyśl some 100 churches were built without the government's permission. Most important was, however, the rapid development of the 'Light-Life' renewal movement, which in the late 1970s initiated a programme of renewal in the Polish church—educating baptised Christians to confirm their willingness to bear witness to Christ without compromise and to accept all the consequences of the faith. By the early 1980s over 350,000 Poles, mostly teenagers, had been involved in this technically illegal movement.

The Catholic community in Poland experienced heightened self-confidence after the election in October 1978 of Cardinal Karol Wojtyla as the first Slav Pope. Many nominal Catholics now joined actively in the life of the Church. The Solidarity period gave the opportunity for believers to engage in religious activities suppressed for years by government decrees. The government was forced to grant a number of important concessions, for example, allowing both the Roman Catholic Church and the Churches belonging to the Polish Ecumenical Council to broadcast religious services. Since the imposition of martial law many of these concessions have been cut back. Strict censorship of religious publications, lifted in 1980, has been reintroduced, and the amount of paper allocated for religious publications has been reduced; building permission for new churches, granted almost on demand during the Solidarity period, is again hard to obtain. Official abolition of state supervision of catechetical instruction in 1980 has been counter-balanced by the introduction of a pilot scheme of 'religious studies' as a compulsory subject in several Polish secondary schools. In order to get a good mark the children are expected to argue the scentific character of the Marxist world view and to denounce religion as a 'distortion of a person's natural needs'. Despite the Party's affirmation at the national conference of the PZPR in March 1986 that 'citizens of

Poland should not have to choose between loyalty to the state and their attachment to the church', a vigorous ideological campaign has been pursued since 1983, when the 13th Ideological Plenum of the PZPR called for confrontation with the Roman Catholic Church. Since 1985, ideological 'verification' of teachers has been carried out despite the Church's condemnation of this practice and doubts have been cast on the legitimacy of Party membership of religious believers.

The ideological offensive has not, however, deterred the religious revival which all denominations have been experiencing since the late 1970s. By the mid-1970s belief in the official ideology was in decline and few still thought that the Party could be reformed from within. Christianity, by contrast, was emerging as the main 'alternative ideology' which could unite people and give them a common purpose. In several schools children have actively protested against the removal of crucifixes from the walls of their classrooms, participation in services and religious pilgrimages is still at a high level, and Christian culture excluded from the state-controlled mass media has been flourishing in the churches. In 1983 the Party's atheist weekly *Argumenty* reported the findings of a series of opinion polls conducted among school pupils, which revealed that between 1977 and 1983 the percentage of those professing a religious world outlook has risen from 62 to 75, and of those believing that education should be based upon religious principles from 45 to 56. A similar census carried out among workers in 1985, by the Centre for the Study of Public Opinion, revealed that 75% of workers are practising believers, while a further 20% described themselves as believers who do not practise their faith.

Church structure

The territory of Poland is divided into twenty-seven bishoprics led by bishops ordinary, who are helped in their duties by a differing number of auxiliary bishops. In the case of three dioceses (Bialystok, Drohiczyn and Lúbaczów), which are parts of pre-war dioceses whose remaining territory is now within the Soviet Union, the bishops in charge act only as 'apostolic administrators'. According to historical tradition the ordinary bishop of Gniezno and Warsaw automatically becomes Primate of Poland and the head of the church. In 1986 there were 94 bishops in Poland and 3 cardinals. Four more bishops and two cardinals reside permanently in Rome.

The Plenary Conference of the Polish Episcopate, held several times a year in different places, is the highest authority within the Church. Historically, the Primate of Poland is also head of the Bishop's Conference. There is also a Main Council of the Polish Episcopate: all cardinals, all archbishops and a few elected bishops are its members. The secretary of the Polish Episcopate is in charge of communication with the political authorities.

All aspects of the Church's life are supervised by twenty-nine Episcopal Commissions, each consisting of a bishop and a certain number of priests, religious and lay experts. At the end of every Plenary Conference the Episcopate issues a communique in which current problems facing the Church and the country are discussed. The Episcopate also circulates pastoral letters. These communiques and pastoral letters are read out in all Catholic churches.

At diocesan level there are diocesan councils. Members include priests (both ex officio and elected) and, since the Second Vatican Council, lay experts. There are also two Conferences of Superiors of the Monastic Orders (for men and women).

Dioceses are divided into deaneries and these into parishes. In 1983 there were 7,299 parishes, of which 68 were created in 1981. After the war the Church acquired 3,297 church buildings, most of which had been Protestant, in the former Germany territory ceded to Poland. During the early post-war years the authorities allowed some churches destroyed during the war to be rebuilt, but from then until the rise of Solidarity necessary building permission for new churches was very difficult to obtain. By the end of 1983 there were 10,256 Catholic churches and 4,404 chapels.

Lay Catholic organisations There are four associations for lay Catholics, all of which aim to build bridges between the

Catholic Church and the communist authorities. In order of ideological proximity to the Polish Episcopate, they are: Znak, ODiSS, ChSS, and Pax.

Znak (the 'Sign' Movement) is a federation of associations and groups which collaborate on the basis of common principles. It focuses on the reforms of the Second Vatican Council, and sees its primary task as promoting the conciliar renewal of Polish Catholicism and assuring a Christian contribution to the social thought of the country, stressing the training of Polish Catholics as both church members and active citizens. It directly influences many Catholic intellectual circles and some of the clergy, who in turn influence a large number of the laity. During the Solidarity period, representatives of the Movement were among Solidarity's top advisers and also served on the Primate's Social Council, a body set up shortly before martial law was declared.

Prominent among the organisations associated with Znak are the Catholic Intellectuals' Clubs (KIKs), which were first formed after October 1956. Until the rise of Solidarity, 5 KIKs were allowed to function, in the cities of Kraków, Warsaw, Poznań, Wroclaw and Toruń, with a total of some 4,000 members. In 1980–1 the number of KIKs increased to 46, but after the introduction of martial law a few were closed down by the authorities on political grounds, and in 1983 the total was 33. The KIKs organise programmes of training and study on social, economic, moral and cultural subjects, with special emphasis on discussion groups. They also publish a certain amount of material on these themes. Each KIK is an autonomous association, but there is a co-ordinating secretariat in Warsaw.

The Social Institute of the Publication *Znak* in Kraków was founded in 1957. It produces the only national Catholic weekly *Tygodnik Powszechny* ('The Universal Weekly'), a highly prestigious socio-cultural publication, and the monthly *Znak*, dedicated to philosophy, theology and cultural questions. It also publishes about ten books a year.

The monthly *Więź* ('Bond'), concerned with social problems, which has been published in Warsaw since 1958, is also connected with the Znak Movement. The same publishing enterprise also produces a number of books every year. The editor of *Więź* was chosen to edit the Solidarity weekly, *Tygodnik Solidarność,* which appeared from 1980 to 1981.

In 1957 the Znak Movement, as seen earlier, was allowed to form a parliamentary grouping, also called 'Znak'. Between 1957 and 1961 it consisted of eleven members. As members tried to behave as if they were truly independent of the control of the Party, the group was punished by the loss of six members of Parliament in 1961. During the student revolt in 1968 members demanded an investigation into police brutality, and as a result all members were replaced by more subservient ones in 1969. In April 1976 the Znak Movement disassociated itself publicly from the new grouping, which later began to use the name 'Neo-Znak'. At the beginning of 1981, in response to the growing number of KIKs, Neo-Znak was instrumental in forming a new association called Polski Związek Katolicko-Spoleczny, or PZKS ('Polish Catholic Social Association'). PZKS does not enjoy the same support from the Polish hierarchy as the Znak Movement.

Ośrodek Dokumentacji i Studiów Spolecznych, or ODiSS ('Centre of Information and Social Studies'), was founded in Warsaw in 1967 as a split from the mainstream Znak Movement. It publishes *Chrześcijanin w świecie* ('The Christian in the World'), a bi-monthly with a French summary, and a few books every year. ODiSS is treated with some reservations by the Catholic hierarchy, who regard it as subservient to the government. In November 1981 Jerzy Ozdowski, a member of ODiSS, became one of the 7 deputy Prime Ministers of Poland, in charge of family and social policies. Later he became a vice-marshal in the Polish Parliament—a purely decorative post. Chrześcianskie Stowarzyszenie Spoleczne, or CHSS ('Christian Social Association'), was founded in Warsaw in 1957. It is a social and ecumenical group heavily involved in politics. It publishes a weekly newspaper *Za i Przeciw* ('For and Against') with a circulation of 50,000, a monthly journal *Novum*, a bulletin of information six times a year in English, French and German, and the occasional book. It manages its own enterprise, 'Ars Christiana', producing devotional articles which it sells in its own shops throughout the country. It has no official contact with the Catholic hierarchy and its social influence is limited.

The 'Pax' Association was founded in 1947 by Boleslaw Piasecki, whose aim was to collaborate with the new régime. The régime saw Pax as a vehicle with which to undermine or even destroy the reputation of the hierarchy, and to create a bloc of 'Catholic' opinion which was prepared to co-operate with the state on the Party's terms. During the Stalinist era in the early 1950s, the association was almost more Stalinist than the Communist Party, and in the 1960s it was in the forefront of a campaign against writers and students who were demanding a relaxation of censorship. Pax has never been recognised by the Catholic hierarchy, and priests are forbidden to join it. In 1964 Cardinal Wyszyński denounced Pax as a communist-front organisation. In the 1970s it had about 4,000 members, but it is now much smaller and it is mainly active in the field of religious publishing, producing between 80 and 100 books per year and the only 'Catholic' daily, *Slowo Powszechne* ('The Public Word'), with a circulation of 100,000. Pax also runs a centre for documentation and religious studies (Ośrodek Dokumentacji i Studiów Religijnych).

Church membership

Today the vast majority of the population belong to the Catholic Church, and are served by a large and growing priesthood. There is little difference in religious practice from one social class to another. The total percentage practising their faith, generally high in the rural areas and slightly lower in the cities, remains overall much higher than in Western Europe.

Over 90% of children are baptised into the Catholic Church. According to research findings at the Catholic University of Lublin in the 1970s, more than 86% of young people considered themselves religious and over 90% stated that they would be prepared to sacrifice their lives in the defence of the faith. 'Socialist ideals' emerged at the bottom of the list of values to be defended. In answers to another question concerning aspirations and aims, 'salvation' came second, ahead of 'education' or 'social advancement'.

Peasants still constitute some 40% of the population and form the basis of the Church's strength. Most of the clergy are of peasant origin—up to 90% in the rural dioceses and 60% in the industrial areas.

The industrial working class developed on a large scale only after the Second World War. By 1979 industrial workers constituted 22% of the population. Of recent rural origin, they brought with them their strong peasant religious traditions. According to research carried out by government sociologists between 1971 and 1974, over 93% of workers considered themselves to be believers and 57% regularly attended church services. The level of religious practice is not uniform, however, throughout the industrial areas of Poland; it is comparatively low in areas with a long tradition of socialism (such as Zagłębie Dąbrowskie, Łódź and Warsaw as well as several areas in the eastern part of the country, including the Lublin region); but other industrial centres have strong religious traditions, for example, Upper Silesia and the new industrial centres created after the Second World War, such as Nowa Huta.

The Polish intelligentsia has traditionally been non-religious, but this has been changing over the last twenty years. Nowadays, several attitudes can be distinguished among the intelligentsia. There is a declining group of older Catholics whose faith is based on Polish religious traditions: they are loyal to the Church, admire her cultural heritage, and respect her moral and disciplinary influence, while in doctrinal matters they are conservative, although their knowledge of the theological and social teachings of the Church is superficial. Another group of the intelligentsia is made up of former members of Catholic organisations banned by the Communist authorities, for example, Odrodzenie, Iuventus Christiana and Sodalicja Mariańska (Marian Sodality). Their relation with the Church is dynamic and they form a Catholic élite vitally interested in the life of the Church. The core membership of the Znak Movement is drawn from this group. A third group in the intelligentsia is the product of a new phenomenon: the growth of a sympathetic interest in religious questions, and especially Catholicism, among young people brought up in an indifferent or anti-religious spirit. In general, there has been an increasing rapprochement since the mid-1970s between the liberal intelligentsia and the Catholic Church.

The traditional strength of the church hierarchy in Poland has promoted a traditional passivity among the laity. Over the last few decades, clericalism in the Polish church has become still more firmly established because of the lack of religious organisations. Nevertheless, the role of the laity in the Polish Catholic Church has been growing in significance. Since the Second Vatican Council, lay movements which are not formally religious organisations have been developing on the initiative of the Church: The Movement of Catholic Families, Our Lady's Helpers, the Light-Life movement and others. Other lay organisations of various kinds have been springing up spontaneously. A specific role in the preparation of lay activists is played by the Catholic University of Lublin (KUL) and the Academy of Catholic Theology at Warsaw University. Lay activists are members of some commissions of the Polish Episcopate and of pastoral, diocesan and parochial councils. They take part in diocesan synods and have been playing an ever more important role in the life of the parishes and in formative work among laymen themselves.

According to *Annuario Pontificio 1985*, Poland has the largest number of vocations to the priesthood. The number of vocations had been rising steadily before 1978, and then in 1979, after the election of the Polish Pope, the number of first year seminarians doubled. It has continued to increase every year since then: in 1985 they numbered 1,854. Every third Catholic priest ordained in Europe in 1984 was a Pole and every tenth priest in the world is a Pole. In 1984 Poland had 22,381 priests altogether (both diocesan and monastic). Apart from Lúbaczów, every diocese has a seminary. There are also twenty monastic higher seminaries. The social prestige of priests is very high in Poland. They receive no financial help from the government, and rely on the generosity of the believers for their stipends. In order to remain totally independent of the government, the Church hierarchy has always rejected government offers to set up a pension fund for priests.

There are 45 monastic orders and congregations for men, and 104 for women. There are over 600 monastic establishments for men, housing 9,600 monks, 4,400 monastic priests and 1,400 friars. There are over 200 convents for women, housing some 27,500 nuns.

Current growth trends

As described in the 'History' section earlier (see p 115ff), the Catholic Church has been undergoing a revival since the 1970s, which involves not only an increase in the number of practising believers, but also, and more importantly, an enhancement of the quality and richness of their faith and witness.

The Eastern-rite Catholic Church

This Church was founded in 1595–6, when the Ukrainian and Belorussian Orthodox hierarchy joined the Catholic Church in the Union of Brest. The resultant Uniate Church expanded in the Polish-Lithuanian commonwealth and thrived under Austrian rule. Since the arrest of its bishops in 1945–6, it has had no hierarchy in Poland and it is not recognised as a separate denomination but as part of the Roman Catholic Church. Since 1956, however, Uniates have in fact been treated relatively tolerantly. The Uniates are subject to the Primate of Poland and are represented by two vicars-general, one for northern and one for southern Poland. Church membership is virtually all Ukrainian (including the Lemko ethnic group). The Church has between 300,000 and 500,000 lay members, 40 to 50 priests, about 23 Basilian monks and 140 nuns. There were six ordinations in 1984 and five in 1985; 24 candidates for the priesthood were reported in 1986.

The Polish Orthodox Church

This Church dates back to the fourteenth century, when Poland occupied the lands inhabited by Ruthenians professing Christianity of the Byzantine rite. In the fifteenth century there were ten well-organised Orthodox dioceses within the borders of the grand duchy of Lithuania, at that time united with Poland. They fell under the jurisdiction of the Patriarchate of Constantinople. After the Union of Brest only some dioceses remained faithful to Orthodoxy. In 1633 the existence of the Orthodox Church was officially recognised again. During the time of partition the Orthodox Church was used by the Russian tsars in their attempts to Russify the section of Poland under their control. In 1918, three million Orthodox, mostly Belorussians and Ukrainians, found themselves on the territory of the new Polish state. In 1924 the autocephaly (self-government) of the Polish Orthodox Church was approved by the Patriarchate of Constantinople. The Moscow Patriarchate recognised their autocephaly only in 1951. Since the war, the leaders of the Orthodox Church have enjoyed good relations with the authorities, but over the years church life has become gradually less active and membership has fallen. In the 1980s, however, an Orthodox movement among young people has been growing rapidly, giving the Church some hope for the future. It organises study groups which examine such topics as the renewal of the liturgy, ethical matters, theology, social work and liturgical music.

The Protestant Churches

Protestantism spread into Poland in the sixteenth century beginning with the Lutherans and later including Calvinists, Moravian Brethren, and anti-Trinitarian Polish Brethren and the Mennonites. Lutheranism found followers mainly among the townsfolk of German origin and Calvinism mostly among the aristocracy, the rich gentry and urban population. There was a brief period when Protestants had a majority in the Diet, which was composed exclusively of the gentry. Over the following centuries, however, the Protestant Churches declined in numbers: they failed to win wide support among the peasantry and were rent by factionalism on social and ethnic as well as theological lines.

In the second half of the nineteenth century free church

movements began to spread throughout the three territories of partitioned Poland. The Baptists, Evangelical Christians, Pentecostals, Seventh-day Adventists and the Church of Christ became especially vigorous after the First World War. Free churches found some followers among the Poles, but most of their members were Germans, Russians, Ukrainians, Belorussians and Jews. The Methodist Church developed out of a United States Methodist relief mission operating in 1921. Between the two World Wars, Protestants constituted 4% of the population. Only the Lutherans were recognised in law and were subject to legal restrictions; all other Protestant Churches operated freely.

At the end of the Second World War most Baptists and Pentecostals who lived in Eastern Poland found themselves in the Soviet Union, after the latter reincorporated Poland's pre-war eastern territories. Protestants of German origin in the western areas allocated to Poland at Potsdam in 1945 left through emigration, both forced and voluntary. As a result, the number of Protestants dropped dramatically: Baptists from 10,000 in 1939 to 1,800; Lutherans from 500,000 in 1939 to 200,000; Reformed from 30,000 in 1939 to a few thousand. Emigration has continued since then, encouraged by the signing of the Polish-German treaty in 1970 and the family reunification programmes undertaken since the Helsinki Agreement in 1975. By 1982 the Lutherans, the largest Protestant group, claimed just 80,000 members. Today Protestants are only a small minority of just over 100,000 Christians.

In the early 1950s some of the Protestant Churches suffered persecution. However, since 1956 the policy of the Polish authorities has been to protect the Protestant Churches, partly in order to offset the power of the Roman Catholic Church and partly to gain the image in the West of being tolerant towards religion. All Protestant Churches were granted legal status after the war. Most are members of the Polish Ecumenical Council, which was created in 1945 and has links with the World Council of Churches.

The Protestant Churches have shared in the country's general religious revival in the 1980s. Church membership has increased and some converts have been won from Catholicism.

Baptists and Pentecostals (who constitute a part of the United Evangelical Church—a Federation of five evangelical Churches) seem to be the most vital and fast growing. The Baptist Church, for which Billy Graham's visit to Poland in 1978 was a welcome boost, received some 200 new members in 1985.

Quasi-Christian groups

The two largest groups are the Jehovah's Witnesses and the Church of Jesus Christ of the Latter-day Saints (Mormons).

Jehovah's Witnesses were banned until 1956. Since the end of the 1970s, they have received a degree of official backing; at the same time the Roman Catholic Church has expressed concern over the increasing activities of Jehovah's Witnesses among the Catholic population. In January 1980 the head of the Office for Religious Affairs stated that Jehovah's Witnesses would not be imprisoned for refusing military service. Though not officially registered as a religious association, they have been allowed to hold 41 public meetings attended by some 9,000 people. Passports were issued to 5,000 Jehovah's Witnesses, to travel to Austria for a congress, and over 40,000 Jehovah's Witnesses, including some from the West, took part in a three-day rally in the south of Poland in August 1985.

Before the Second World War, Mormons had one congregation, but it disappeared as a result of emigration after 1945. 1977 saw the resumption of Mormon activity: a Mormon community was set up in Szczecin. By a decision of the Office for Religious Affairs on 30th May 1977, it was included in the Register of Associations and Religious Unions. It remains in union on dogmatic and ideological matters with the Central Church of Jesus Christ of the Latter-day Saints, based in Salt Lake City (USA). In 1979 it claimed 24 believers.

CHRISTIAN ACTIVITIES

Evangelism and Mission

The Catholic Church became involved in missionary activity on a large scale only after Poland regained independence in 1918, though even before that date there were a number of outstanding Polish missionaries. Among them, the most famous are Mother Maria Teresa Ledóchowska (1863–1922), founder of the Congregation of St Peter Claver's Missionary Sisters, working in Africa; and Jan Beyzym (1850–1912), a Jesuit who from 1899 worked among the lepers in Madagascar, where he built a lazar house from Polish offerings and directed it until his death.

In 1974 the Polish Episcopate decided, in response to an appeal by the Second Vatican Council, to send 1% of its clergy abroad on missionary activity. In 1979 Polish missionary personnel numbered 1,064: 607 regular priests, 283 sisters, 44 lay brothers, 122 diocesan priests and 8 laymen (these figures do not include the personnel ministering to émigré Poles throughout the world). There are seventeen male orders and eleven female orders involved in missionary activities.

The missionary target countries have included New Guinea, Japan, Zaïre, Togo, Ghana, Cameroon, Polynesia, Iraq, Madagascar, Algeria, Zambia, Libya, Burundi, Rwanda, Congo (Brazzaville), Tanzania, Brazil, Argentina, Paraguay, Peru, Australia, Bolivia, Guatemala and Chile. In Bolivia and Paraguay, Polish missionaries have been involved in establishing the basis for a Light-Life movement. One feature of Polish missionary activity worth noting is that missionary personnel from communist Poland are granted permission to work in certain countries (especially African) which call themselves 'socialist' and which have expelled missionaries from 'imperialist' countries.

Broadcasting

Since 1965, the Polish Evangelical Church has produced a daily radio programme with government approval. Programmes entitled *The Voice of the Gospel* have been produced in Poland and shipped to Monte Carlo for broadcasting. Since 1972, Sunday programmes for children have also been produced in the same way.

After the signing of an agreement in August 1980, between Solidarity and representatives of the government, the Churches gained direct access to the Polish mass media. Catholic masses are now broadcast every Sunday, as well as services for sailors. Since 24th January 1982, Churches associated with the Polish Ecumenical Council have been able to transmit services on the first and third Sundays of each month and on Christian festivals. The future of these services is uncertain as, according to Party plans intercepted by Solidarity, they should be discontinued at the first opportune moment.

Literature

In January 1985, thirty-one periodicals published in Poland were recognised as Catholic by the Roman Catholic Church. Only three of them are published by lay groups: *Tygodnik Powszechny* ('The Universal Weekly'), and two monthlies, the academic *Znak* ('The Sign', published since 1957) and the more popular *Więź* ('The Bond', published since 1958). The remainder are published by dioceses and religious orders. Six began publication only after 1980 in a wave of concessions to the Church. The most important by far is the bi-monthly *Communio,* a theological review which was first published in the West after the Second Vatican Council. It aims to promote modern Catholic thought. Cardinal Wojtyla, now Pope John Paul II, was one of the founders and editors of the original journal, as well as the originator of the idea for a Polish edition. After his election as Pope, he also secured a Polish monthly edition of *L'Osservatore Romano*, published at the Vatican and distributed inside Poland by the Church since April 1980.

Despite years of petitions by the Church, the authorities still refuse to allow a Catholic daily. There is a daily *Slowo Powszechne* ('The Universal Word'), but as it is published by the government-sponsored Pax organisation, it belongs to that category of publications described by the Church as 'papers for Catholics' rather than 'Catholic papers'. Into the former category come all the periodicals published by Pax, ChSS, PZKS and Caritas. They are favoured by the government as they all reflect government policies. Pax and ChSS produce a number of periodicals in many foreign languages, which are widely promoted in the West as giving the full picture of religious life in Poland. It should be noted, however, that Pax published many valuable religious books in the post-war years—though many experts argue that these were part of an attempt to make Pax more attractive to the hierarchy of the Church.

There are several Catholic publishing houses throughout Poland producing religious books, and some books published in the West are allowed to be imported to Poland, notably those published by the Paris-based *Edition du Dialogue*.

All other recognised denominations have a regular periodical and are allowed to publish a few books a year.

All Catholic papers are subject to strict censorship. Since the introduction of martial law in 1981, they have been allowed to indicate to their readers the places where the censors have intervened. Even *L'Osservatore Romano* is censored, in violation of the special understanding between the Polish authorities and the Vatican. Between 1980 and 1984, three issues of *L'Osservatore Romano* were even prevented from entering Poland. Since 1986, the authorities have tried to limit the influence of the Catholic press by cutting the paper allocated for printing by 20%.

Religious themes are present in all Polish *samizdat*. Among the religious *samizdat* periodicals, the most prestigious by far is *Spotkania* ('*Encounters*') which began to circulate in October

1977. It was published by a group of young Catholic intellectuals from Lublin. By 1978 it had grown into a movement which strives to develop a consciously Catholic attitude towards the world and to foster understanding and co-operation with all democratic opposition groups in Poland, as well as to disseminate knowledge about the situation of the churches throughout Eastern Europe. *Spotkania* is one of the very few *samizdat* periodicals which has continued to appear since the imposition of martial law. The 'Spotkania' group has also published several books in *samizdat*.

Bible Translation and Distribution

For over 300 years, until 1975, there were two commonly used Polish Bible translations: the Catholic Wujek Bible, first published in 1599, and the Protestant Gdańsk Bible of 1632. The British and Foreign Bible Society opened an agency in Warsaw in 1816 and published both Bibles, meeting the needs of both the Catholic and Protestant communities.

The Bible Society was closed during the Second World War by the German occupation forces (and the building burnt down), but it was reopened in new premises in 1946, still as a branch of the BFBS. It is now a full Bible Society and a member of the United Bible Societies, as well as of the Polish Ecumenical Council.

In 1966 a modern Polish New Testament was published, followed by the full Bible in 1975. It is known as the Millennium Bible as the New Testament appeared during the celebrations of Poland's 1000th anniversary. A 'Good News' style translation is currently being made.

The Bible Society now distributes largely to the non-Catholic churches through church bookstalls, but also by mail-order and to personal customers at its shop in central Warsaw. Since 1969, when large-scale distribution became possible, the Bible Society has printed or imported well over one million Bibles and New Testaments, as well as hundreds of thousands of Gospels and Scripture portions. One of the most popular books is the New Testament with colour illustrations, of which over a quarter of a million have been produced. The main problem has concerned paper supply, for which state sponsored publications get priority. The United Bible Societies regularly provide paper and sometimes other printing supplies, thus subsidising the Polish work. An arrangement has now been worked out whereby Scriptures destined for other parts of the world are printed in Poland out of the profits made from sales in Poland.

Production of Bibles for Catholic parishes is largely decentralised, with many dioceses arranging their own printing and distribution. For some dioceses the quantities have been substantial, but total figures are unknown.

Although Bible distribution is aimed primarily at churchgoers (about 80% of the population) there is a general interest in reading the Bible, especially among young people, with whom the illustrated New Testament is particularly popular. Despite the relatively high production, supply does not altogether meet demand, and people are prepared to pay more than the official selling price to obtain a copy. The Baptist and United Evangelical Churches record daily evangelistic broadcasts which are transmitted by Trans World Radio in Monte Carlo. Listeners are invited to write in for New Testaments, and thousands of copies have been distributed as a result.

Bible distribution in all Churches is now well established and sales are likely to continue at a high level for the foreseeable future. There is a strong demand for children's Bibles and for the illustrated New Testament, and the 'Good News' Bible can be expected to stir considerable interest.

Education

Schools

Before the Second World War there were a number of primary and secondary schools run by the Catholic Church. Religious instruction was obligatory for all denominations recognised in law. The Reformed Church, although it did not have legal status, was still allowed to give religious instruction to Calvinist children in schools and to run Bible study groups and parish Sunday schools. The Methodists, also not legally recognised, were allowed to run a Bible school which trained future Methodist pastors, Sunday schools and a primary school in Klarysów.

Today, apart from a few centres for mentally handicapped children run by Catholic nuns, all primary school education is in the hands of the state. At the secondary level, the Catholic Church has one school for boys and a few for girls.

Higher Education

Poland boasts the only independent Christian university in Eastern Europe: the Catholic University of Lublin (KUL). It is financed solely by the Church and the generosity of the faithful in Poland and abroad. KUL was established after the First World War. When the communists came to power, it was reduced to four faculties: theology, canon law, Christian philosophy and the arts. In 1981, during the Solidarity period, KUL was allowed to reopen its department of social sciences abolished in 1952. It consists of three sections: sociology, psychology and pedagogics. 60% of all students at KUL are laypeople.

The Academy of Catholic Theology at Warsaw (ATK) was created in 1954, after the forced merger of the theological departments of Kraków and Warsaw Universities. It is financed by the state and is still not recognised as a Catholic academic institution by the Vatican. Each degree has to be verified on an individual basis by the Catholic Church. ATK has three faculties: theology, canon law and Christian philosophy. More than half the students are laypeople.

In addition to these two institutions, there are also four pontifical theological faculties: at Kraków, Warsaw, Wroclaw and Poznań. There is also the Institute of Theology in Warsaw and the Institute of Philosophy in Kraków, both run by the Jesuits. The theological faculties have over 4,000 students. They are 'acknowledged' by the state, but are regarded as part of their respective diocesan seminaries and not as academic institutions. Any academic degrees conferred by the Institutes are not, therefore, recognised by the state, although they are recognised in the West. The Catholic Church has struggled for years for full recognition of pontifical Institutes and during the Solidarity period (1980–1), when the Church was given a number of concessions, it almost succeeded in achieving it. After martial law was declared on 13th December 1981, the whole issue was dropped by the authorities and negotiations resumed from the beginning.

The Christian Theological Academy was set up in 1954 to replace the Department of Evangelical Theology of Warsaw University. It contains an evangelical section and an Old Catholic section. A third section was added in 1957 for the Orthodox Church.

Catechesis

Catechesis (Catholic doctrine) classes have been allowed in schools between 1945 and 1952–3 and again between 1957 and 1960, but the state authorities finally banned them in 1961, and at the same time brought pressure to bear on both priests and lay catechists in the parishes to accept payment from the state. The Church, however, did not give in.

At the national level, catechesis is organised by an episcopal conference, through its catechetical commission. Each diocesan chancellery has a section in charge of catechesis. At parish level catechetical instruction is under the authority of the parish priest or another priest or nun delegated by him. In recent years the church has encouraged a growth in the number of parish catechetical councils. All expenses, including the salary for catechists, fall on the parish.

Instruction is given on parish premises or in private homes. In 1979, there were 21,229 places where catechism was taught. Catechesis is received before schooling (up to the age of 6) by 15% of children, during primary schooling (from 7 to 15) by 80–90% of children, and from 16 to 19 by between 30% and 70%. Some categories of children are however difficult to reach systematically—for instance, those in orphanages and boarders. In 1978 over 17,000 priests, religious and laypeople were involved in catechesis. Of these, only 2,000 were laypeople, whom it is difficult to employ in this work, since present legislation provides no pension or social security for catechists.

There is good training for catechists, and they are helped by the bi-monthly *Katecheta* ('The Catechist').

Pastoral Activities at University Level

There are over 300 centres, each run by a priest, which specialise in this kind of work. Their aim is to foster Christian communities, and in the absence of specifically Catholic youth movements, these centres play a varied role and attract a significant proportion of Polish students. University chaplains are given an excellent theological and pastoral training. Pastoral work among students is seen as very important by the Catholic Church: it is the means of forming a Catholic intelligentsia and of deepening religious faith. University centres have played an important part in liturgical revival over the last fifteen years.

Since 1981, the number of independent 'universities' has rapidly increased. In 1983 in Warsaw alone there were some 200 active academic groups. The most popular are courses organised in the Church's so-called Christian Workers' Universities. The scope of these courses in usually wide, with lectures on history, sociology, family life and biblical studies and liturgy.

Social Concerns

The Roman Catholic Church has a long tradition of involvement in social issues. Before the Second World War it set up Christian Workers' Universities, and a Christian Trade Union. The Primate's Social Council was also very active.

Since 1945 the Church's involvement in many social issues has often led to a direct conflict with the state. The church has spoken on social problems through memoranda sent to the government, through communiques of the Polish Episcopate and through pastoral letters written by the entire Episcopate or by individual bishops. Social issues are also raised by parish priests in their Sunday sermons. The Church has spoken out against the forceful collectivisation of peasants and against exploitation of workers by the state, and has demanded that the right of intellectuals to unhindered academic enquiry be respected.

Over the years the Church has also attempted to combat national social problems such as alcoholism. In the late 1950s it initiated a very successful anti-alcohol 'crusade', which, however, came to an end when its founder, Fr Blachnicki, was arrested. It was resumed again on a national scale in 1980 within the Light-Life renewal movement, as part of a Crusade for the Liberation of Man. The Church has also been very quick to respond to the drug problem, which has been escalating since the late 1970s, and has set up a special unit to carry out pastoral work among drug addicts. Since 1955, when abortion was legalised in Poland, the Church has tried, unsuccessfully, to change the law. Several 'pro-life' groups are active throughout Poland and many church centres for single mothers have been set up. During the Solidarity period over a million people signed a petition to Parliament to make abortion illegal again.

In recent years the most spectacular, albeit unsuccessful, venture by the Church has been an attempt to create an 'Agricultural Fund' to revive Polish agriculture. Some two thousand million American dollars were to be raised by Western churches and governments, and channelled through the Church to private farmers. By the end of 1986 it became clear that the Polish government had decided to kill the Fund for ideological reasons. A more limited scheme was, however, set up in 1987 under the Church Agricultural Committee. The Catholic Church continues to distribute general relief aid from the West. The Polish Ecumenical Council and individual non-Catholic churches have also been active in distributing aid received from abroad. The Ecumenical Council has been the main channel for aid received from the World Council of Churches and Western ecumenical relief agencies.

CHAPTER 3

Hungary

HUNGARY: OVERVIEW

The country; the people; brief history

The Hungarian People's Republic today occupies an area of
36,000 square miles. Before dismemberment at the end of the
First World War, the former kingdom of Hungary included
Slovakia, Transylvania and parts of Yugoslavia and Austria.
Much of present-day Hungary is flat land, especially the eastern part of the country. There are, however, extensive upland
regions in the west, and the foothills of the Carpathian Mountains line the border with Czechoslovakia. The country is dis-
sected by two major rivers, the Danube and its tributary the
Tisza. The climate is noted for its hot summers and bitterly
cold winters.

The Hungarians, known as the Magyars in their own language, occupied the Carpathian basin at the end of the ninth
century. They came from the region between the Volga and
the Urals, and they belong to the Finno-Ugrian linguistic
group. The Magyar invaders assimilated most of the indigenous tribes, though large Slavic and Wallachian minorities
remained in the peripheral regions of the Carpathian basin.
Subsequent Cuman, Pecheney, Jazygian, German and Jewish
settlers have further enriched the Hungarian nation. The present population of Hungary is 10,700,000. Another 4,000,000
Hungarians live outside the country's borders. Over 98% of
the present population speak Hungarian as their mother-
tongue; there are small German, Romanian, Serbo-Croat and
Slovak enclaves.

Hungary became a kingdom in 1001 when the Magyars' first
Christian ruler, István (Stephen), received the 'holy crown'
from Pope Sylvester II. Hungarian kings of the fourteenth and
fifteenth centuries rivalled German and Bohemian monarchs
for hegemony in Central Europe. This was achieved during the

143

reign of Matthias Corvinus, who in 1485 established his court
in Vienna. But the Hungarian nation was unable to consolidate
this favourable position. Weakened by internal division, the
Hungarians were defeated by the Turks at Mohács in 1526. For
nearly two centuries the Turks occupied much of the country
and exercised suzerainty over Transylvania. Meanwhile, the
holy crown passed to the Habsburgs, who controlled the north
and west of the country. By the end of the seventeenth century
the Turks had been expelled from most of the country.

Tensions between the Habsburgs' centralising tendencies
and Hungarian aspirations for self-government resulted in the
rebellions of Bocskay (1604–6), Thököly (1678–85) and
Rákóczi (1703–11), and the national uprising of 1848–9. The
Compromise of 1867, which created the Austro-Hungarian
Empire, gave extensive autonomy to Hungary. The Austro-
Hungarian defeat in the First World War led to the loss of two-
thirds of the Hungarian crown lands to Czechoslovakia,
Romania and Yugoslavia, and the establishment of a republic
in 1918. In March 1919 the Communists and left-wing Social
Democrats assumed power and proclaimed a Soviet Republic.
Five months later this was overthrown and the constitution of
the old kingdom was restored, with Admiral Horthy as regent.
Under Horthy's rule Hungary came increasingly under German domination, culminating in the occupation of the country
in 1944 and the establishment of a Nazi government later that
year. By the spring of 1945 the Soviet army had defeated the
German and Hungarian forces. The occupying Soviet military
prepared the way for the Communist takeover of the late
1940s.

In 1956 the nation revolted against the imposition of Soviet-
style communism. This uprising was crushed by the Soviet
Army, which restored to power the Communist Party with
János Kádár at its head.

The economy: social conditions; political life

The Hungarian economy is dominated by the state, with over

95% of the country's wealth produced by state-owned and co-operative enterprises. The country is a member of COMECON, and the Soviet Union is its major trading partner. Hungary remained primarily an agricultural country until after the Second World War. Now industry accounts for about half of the national income. The state gives direction to economic development by issuing five-year plans. Since the introduction of the New Economic Mechanism in 1968, however, the tendency has been away from a Soviet-style central planning system. Decentralisation, incentives and market forces are key concepts among Hungary's ascendant economic planners. The economy is heavily dependent upon Western loans.

Since the end of the Second World War, the Hungarian social structure has undergone radical change. The classes of large-scale landowners and capitalists were liquidated and titles were abolished. Most of the working population became employees of the state or of co-operatives. In 1949, 53% worked as manual agricultural workers, while in the 1980s about the same proportion was employed as non-agricultural manual workers. The class of professional workers has steadily increased to its present figure of 27% of the population. Acute social problems have accompanied the socialist transformation of Hungary. The country has among the highest rates of suicide and alcoholism in the world, and while economic reforms have allowed a small wealthy class to re-emerge, increasing numbers of pensioners and unskilled workers have incomes near or below the official subsistence level. One in three Hungarian marriages ends in divorce.

The Hungarian People's Republic is a one-party communist state in which the Hungarian Socialist Workers' Party plays the 'leading role'. According to the Constitution, the nation's Parliament is the highest state organ, but supreme de facto power resides with the Party's Central Committee, under the leadership of First Secretary Károly Grósz. In 1985 the Party had over 870,000 members. Party statutes exclude believers from membership, but the Communist régime seeks to enlist the supportive participation of non-party members in the political process by means of its 'policy of alliances'. Non-party members, including believers, therefore, have a high profile in the Parliament, and in such semi-official political organisations as the Patriotic People's Front and the National Peace Council—though all key leadership positions go to communists. In the 1980s the government introduced reforms that require the nomination of at least two approved candidates for all constituency parliamentary seats, and permit greater public discussion of public affairs than is found in most other Soviet-bloc countries.

Hungary has a small, fragmented 'democratic opposition' movement. It is to a large extent tolerated by the authorities, but activists are subjected to periodic police action and threats of loss of employment or educational opportunities. In the spring of 1988 there were 154 conscientious objectors to military service in Hungarian gaols. With few exceptions, they have taken their stand on religious grounds. Apart from the conscientious objectors, there are no known political prisoners.

THE STATUS OF CHRISTIANITY

The religious complexion of the country

The Magyar tribes had limited contact with Byzantine Christianity before they reached the Carpathian basin. According to legend, Magyar warriors encountered both St Cyril and St Methodius during their westward migration. When the Magyars entered the basin in 896 they found a largely Christian population there. Christianity had been first carried to the region by the Romans in the third century. Szombathely and Pécs became diocesan centres. It became the dominant religion shortly before the Magyar occupation, as a result of the missionary activities of the Frankish church and of Orthodox priests from the Bulgarian Empire. During the first decades of Magyar rule, Christianity was tolerated but paganism again became ascendant. Sensing their vulnerability in the midst of

Christian Europe, however, tenth-century Magyar princes began to encourage mission activity. They first turned to Constantinople, where several distinguished Magyars were baptised, but after suffering defeat by the Germans at Augsburg in 955, the Magyars leaned towards Rome. In 972 the German Emperor sent the missionary Bishop Bruno of Sankt Gallen to Hungary at the request of Prince Géza, who was baptised together with his family. Within a few years Bishop Bruno and his co-workers baptised several thousand of the Magyar élite. Bishop Adalbert of Prague built upon the work of Bruno in the 990s. Two of Adalbert's followers, the monks Sebastian and Anasztaz, were instrumental in the intensive Christianisation of the Magyars during the reign of Géza's son, St Stephen.

Christianity has been the dominant religious force in Hungary since the conversion of King Stephen. Despite the long Turkish occupation, Islam did not make great inroads among the native population. Today there is a small Islamic community in Hungary. Jews constitute the country's largest non-Christian religious group, numbering around 80,000 (before the Holocaust the Jewish population was over 800,000). The state recognises the National Representation of Hungarian Israelites, which encompasses both liberal and orthodox congregations. The Jewish seminary in Budapest is the only one remaining in Eastern Europe. Hungary also has an officially recognised Buddhist Mission with roughly 100 adherents. About 15% of the population are thought to have no religious convictions.

Since the Second World War, Christianity has lost its ascendant position within Hungarian society. The state proclaimed the separation of church and state, nationalised most church schools, abolished compulsory religious education, dissolved most religious orders and established the hegemony of Marxist-Leninist ideology in public life. In 1947 the government decreed the equality of all Christian denominations and of the Jewish community before the law. However, differences in status between Churches continue to exist. The Catholic, Reformed, Lutheran and Unitarian Churches are recognised as legal entities and they receive regular state subsidies, while the Orthodox and smaller Protestant groups associated with the Free Church Council are recognised but are not regularly subsidised. Some small Churches and religious groups have not received state recognition, and only members of recognised Churches and groups enjoy the constitutional right of free religious practice.

During the inter-war years over 95% of the population identified themselves as Christians. Since then, the Christian proportion of the population has fallen steadily and substantially. This decline may be attributed to a combination of various factors: restrictions placed by the state on religious activity; the Party's ideological struggle against religious belief; the breakdown of tradition accompanying rapid industrialisation and urbanisation; and the growing strength of materialism and consumerism. Sociological surveys conducted in the mid-1980s suggest that roughly half of the population hold some kind of religious belief and that about 10% are regular church-goers. Among the religious believers, 80% declare themselves to be religious 'after my own fashion' as opposed to 'in accordance with the teachings of the church'. Religious faith is strongest among the elderly and in the countryside. In recent years Christianity has recovered some lost ground among the better-educated young people of the towns. Disillusionment with Marxism-Leninism and the search for a caring community are often cited as reasons for the revival of faith among the young.

The State's attitude to religion

The Hungarian state promotes the classical Marxist-Leninist view of religion: it is seen as a by-product of social evolution which will disappear when socialist societies are transformed into communist utopias. Communist statesmen of the late 1940s and the 1950s tended to anticipate the rapid demise of religion, but the enduring strength of religious belief, especially among the younger generation, has led the country's present leadership to conclude that Christianity will long remain an important factor in national life. Meanwhile, the Communist Party's 'policy of alliances' governs the state's attitude to Christianity. According to this policy, the state makes a political distinction between Christian groups which allegedly have the potential for making a positive contribution to the building of socialism and those which do not. The former are tolerated and, in some cases, supported by the state, while the latter generally find state power ranged against them.

After the Communist take-over the authorities were convinced that the major Churches—the Catholic, Reformed and Lutheran—were dominated by elements which obstructed the development of Marxist-Leninist socialism. The state, therefore, formed alliances with small groups within the Churches which were prepared to support its policies. It guaranteed their ascendancy over the so-called 'clerical reaction' led by those who sought to defend their Church's independence, such as Cardinal Mindszenty, the Reformed Bishop László Ravasz and the Lutheran Bishop Lajos Ordass. The authorities imprisoned Mindszenty and Ordass on false charges in order to limit their influence. Meanwhile, the 'progressive' successors of the 'clerical reaction' were assigned the role of enlisting the support of believers in Hungary and churchmen abroad for key aspects of the Party's political programme. Protestant bishops and leaders of the Catholic 'Peace Priests' were given seats in Parliament and a high profile in political organisations, such as the Patriotic People's Front and the National Peace Council.

Since the 1956 uprising, the Kádár régime has gradually come to accept that it should to some extent back the Churches' efforts to promote traditional Christian ethical values in order to combat the socially destablilising effects of growing cynicism and 'nihilism' among the population. It has, therefore, given the Churches greater scope for evangelism, Christian education and social work. However, some unrecognised Churches and groups are still seen as incompatible with socialist construction, and suffer harassment from the authorities. Imprisonment is rarely used today against those with unacceptable Christian views, except in the case of conscientious objectors to armed military service.

In March 1988 the Catholic bishops called for greater freedom for the Churches. They urged the government to allow the re-establishment of religious orders, the formation of associations, greater access to the media, and alternative, unarmed service for conscientious objectors. The Prime Minister, Károly Grósz, called the requests reasonable, and said they would be studied carefully by the government. Shortly before the bishops publicly made their requests, the Justice Minister announced in the Parliament that new legislation on church-state relations would be forthcoming shortly.

THE VARIOUS CHURCHES

The Roman Catholic Church

History

The Catholic Church has worked continuously in the Carpathian basin for twelve centuries. After the defeat of the Avar Empire at the end of the eighth century, Charlemagne sent Latin-rite missionaries to what is now western Hungary. Their converts laid the basis for the conversion of most of Hungary to Latin-rite Christianity during the reigns of the Magyar ruler Prince Géza and his son St Stephen. Géza and Stephen chose to promote the activities of missionaries under the jurisdiction of Rome rather than of Constantinople because the Western connection offered Hungary greater security for its independence. In 1001 Stephen received the holy crown from Pope Sylvester II, and Hungary officially became a Catholic state. The Hungarian Church was organised into ten dioceses with the help of the Benedictine followers of Bishop Adalbert of Prague. The Benedictines were followed in the twelfth century by the Cistercians, the Knights Hospitaller, the Norbertines and the Knights Templar, and in the thirteenth century by the Dominicans and Franciscans. The establishment of the Catholic Church was not achieved without bloodshed. Recurrent pagan uprisings were suppressed by armed might as late as the mid-eleventh century. According to the law of Stephen, every ten villages had to build a church and all Hungarians—fire-minders excepted—had to attend church on Sunday.

Although the Hussite movement gained ground in Hungary, Catholicism was not seriously challenged until the early sixteenth century when Reformation influences began to filter into Hungary from Germany and the Hungarians were defeated by the Muslim Turks at Mohács (1526). By the end of the century an estimated 90% of the population had become Protestant, the Catholic Church had lost most of its lands and many bishoprics remained unfilled for decades. The Catholic Church succeeded in recovering its lost ascendancy during the Counter-Reformation under the guidance of the Jesuit Archbishop of Esztergom, Péter Pázmány (1570–1637), a persuasive scholar and orator. The re-Catholicisation of Hungary was given momentum by the advance of Habsburg power in the seventeenth century, and the influx of foreign Catholic settlers after the expulsion of the Turks. However, large Protestant minorities remained. The influence of the Catholic Church was somewhat diminished as a result of the policies of the Emperor Joseph II (1741–1790), whose reforms resulted in the dissolution of all non-pastoral and teaching orders and the restriction of papal power in the Habsburg dominions. The Josephine reforms also included the extension of state supervision of the Church. Legislation passed after the Austro-Hungarian Compromise of 1867 brought about the equality of all 'received' Churches—the Catholic, Reformed, Lutheran, Unitarian and Orthodox Churches—and deprived the Catholic Church of virtually all its previous legal privileges.

The Hungarian Catholic Church first experienced communism at the time of the Hungarian Soviet Republic of 1919. Most Church property and all Church schools were sequestrated. Practising believers were subjected to state-sponsored anti-religious propaganda. Opposition to the communist dictatorship grew strong within Catholic circles. After the Soviet Republic was toppled, Church property was restored and the work of the 'received' Churches was encouraged by the Horthy régime. Bishop Ottokár Prohászka and the Jesuit Fr Béla Bangha gave impetus to a spiritual revival during the inter-war years, a revival which led to the establishment of many Catholic social and political institutions. In 1944 the German army occupied Hungary and the Hungarian government ordered the arrest of clergymen who opposed the persecution of the Jews, and the country's role in the war. Among the arrested were two future primates, Jósef Mindszenty (1892–1975) then Bishop of Veszprém, and his secretary László Lékai (1910–86).

After the war the communist-dominated government set in motion a process of secularisation which by 1950 resulted in the loss of Church lands, the nationalisation of all but eight Catholic schools, the end of compulsory religious instruction and the dissolution of nearly all the monasteries and convents. The means used to achieve secularisation were often brutal, and included the arrest of thousands of priests and religious—Cardinal Mindszenty among them—a violent press campaign against the 'clerical reaction', the harassment of zealous believers, and state sponsorship of the pro-communist 'peace priest' organisation. As a result of this kind of pressure, the hierarchy signed an agreement with the state on 30th August 1950 in which the state promised to subsidise the Church financially while the bishops undertook to support state policies and to discipline politically dissenting priests. The agreement also narrowly defined the Church's sphere of legal activity. During the 1956 uprising Cardinal Mindszenty was set free and acted as head of the Church for five days before seeking refuge from the invading Soviet army in the American Embassy, where he remained until 1971. In 1964 the Vatican and the Hungarian state signed a 'partial agreement', which established principles for the appointment of bishops and stipulated that Church leaders must swear to uphold the laws of the Hungarian People's Republic. The 'partial agreement' paved the way for the completion of the hierarchy, with the appointment of László Lékai to succeed Cardinal Mindszenty as Archbishop of Esztergom in 1976. Cardinal Lékai's policy of firm conformity to the state's political directives has coincided with an easing of tight restrictions on Church activities. Archbishop László Paskai (born 1927) succeeded Lékai as Primate in April 1987. Under Paskai's leadership the bishops have continued Lékai's policy of political conformity, but have trodden fresh ground by publicly asking the government for greater freedom for the Church.

Church structure and membership, current growth trends
The Hungarian Catholic Church is divided into eleven dioceses, including the Eastern-rite diocese of Hajdúdorog. National Church policy is established by the Conference of Bishops. The chairman and leading member of the Conference is the Archbishop of Esztergom, who has traditionally been recognised as Primate of Hungary. The Primate is the main link with the state. Parish councils assist with administration at the local level.

Since 1950, only four teaching orders remain active. In the mid-1980s the state approved the establishment of a new order of sisters to undertake social work. The Church runs eight grammar schools—six for boys and two for girls—with a total of over 2,000 students. Six seminaries exist for the teaching of priests. These are located at Budapest, Esztergom, Eger, Szeged, Győr and Nyíregyháza (Greek Catholic). In 1986 there were 32 graduates. Since 1978, the Budapest seminary has run a correspondence course for the laity. In the 1984–5 academic year 567 students were enrolled. Seminarists and priests may also study at the Hungarian Papal Institute in Rome, which is under the direct jurisdiction of the Vatican, but receives financial support from the Hungarian state.

Before the Second World War, *Actio Catholica* was the umbrella organisation for the country's numerous associations. Since the dissolution of most Catholic associations in 1946, it has been responsible for organising national religious festivals, supervising the St Francis of Assisi Hospital in Budapest and organising trips abroad for Hungarian churchmen; it also publishes the weekly newspaper *Új Ember* ('New Man') and the monthly literary and theological journal *Vigilia*. The Catholic Peace Committee of the National Peace Council was founded with state backing in 1950, with the aim of applying pressure on the hierarchy to submit to state supervision and commit the Church to help in the building of Marxist-Leninist socialism. In 1957 the hierarchy agreed to the establishment of *Opus Pacis*, with a bishop at its head to work in conjunction with the Peace Committee. The Roman Catholic Charity Service operates old folks' homes, mostly for aged priests and nuns.

There are approximately 5,000 small local groups of Catholic believers, or 'basis' communities, with an estimated total membership of 70,000–100,000. Because of the strict state supervision of the Church, these groups have taken on an unofficial character and seek to retain as much autonomy as possible. The largest organised network of basis communities is *Regnum Marianum;* the next largest is *A Bokor* (*'The Bush'*), which is led by the pacifist priest Fr György Bulányi. There are also Charismatic, Focolare and Taizé groups.

Among Hungary's Churches, the Catholic Church contains the widest cross-section of the population. Approximately 62% of Hungarians have been baptised as Catholics, though not many more than half regard themselves as 'religious'. Among the 'religious' Catholics, only 20% describe themselves as 'religious in accordance with the teachings of the Church'. Between 10% and 15% of the country's Catholics regularly worship in church. In 1950 there were over 6,000 parish priests and monks. By the mid-1980s the number had diminished to 2,500 of whom over half were older than 50. A further drop of between 25% and 30% by 1990 is forecast.

There is a continuing decline in the total number of Catholics in Hungary, and the elderly and rural percentage of Church membership steadily increases, indicating that it is among the young city-dwellers that the decline has been steepest. Nevertheless, there are at the same time signs of renewal, especially in the basis community movement. These unofficial communities are succeeding in instilling a high level of commitment, among the better educated youth.

The Eastern-rite Catholic Church

Eastern-rite (or Uniate) Catholicism was established in Hungary in 1646 when 400 Orthodox priests in Ungvár (Uzhgorod)—now in the Soviet Union—united with the Roman Catholic Church. The Uniate variety of Catholicism has traditionally been strong among Slavic and Romanian peoples in the eastern territories of the old Hungarian kingdom, which are now divided amongst Hungary, Czecho-slovakia, Romania, Yugoslavia and the USSR.

In 1873 a district vicariate for Hungarian-speaking Uniates was founded, which in 1912 became the Greek Catholic dio-cese of Hajdúdorog, under the Bishop of Hajdúdorog. His jurisdiction was extended in 1920 to include the apostolic exar-chate of Miskolc, encompassing parishes formerly belonging to dioceses which after the First World War had mostly been transferred to the successor states of the Austro-Hungarian Empire. In 1968 the pastoral care of the whole Eastern-rite Catholic diaspora throughout Hungary was entrusted to him. Outside the diocese of Hajdúdorog there are seven diaspora centres in Budapest, Szeged and Makó. The Uniates have a seminary in Nyíregyháza with fifty theology students.

Although most of the country's Uniates are of Slavic or Romanian descent, most of them speak Hungarian as their native language. In 1980 there were about 250,000 Uniates and 146 priests. No Uniate parish is without a priest.

The Reformed Church

History

The Swiss Reformation began to leave its mark on Hungary in the middle of the sixteenth century. Among the most impor-tant Hungarian disciples of the Swiss reformers were István Szegedi Kiss, Péter Melius and Márton Kálmáncsehi. At the Debrecen Synod of 1567, the Reformed Church became organisationally and theologically distinct from the Lutheran Church. Reformed doctrine found favour primarily among the Hungarian-speaking population of eastern Hungary and Trans-ylvania. Reformed Christianity became known as the 'Magyar faith', on account of its close association with the cultural and political aspirations of this element of the population. By the end of the sixteenth century, Reformed Christians out-numbered Catholics and Lutherans in the Hungarian crown lands. During the Counter-Reformation, the Reformed Church, along with the Lutheran, suffered great losses to the

Catholic Church, but Joseph II's Toleration Patent of 1781 lifted many of the restrictions which had been imposed on the Reformed Church at that time. Further rights were won during the 1848 uprising, but these were short-lived. Only after the Austro-Hungarian Compromise of 1867 did the Reformed Church achieve a legal standing almost equal to that of the Catholic Church. The transfer of Transylvania from Hungary to Romania at the end of the First World War meant the severance of over 600,000 Reformed members of an important Reformed cultural centre from the rest of the Hungarian Reformed Church.

After the Second World War, the Church experienced sharp conflict between those wishing to see the Church serve the state in the building of a society based on Marxist-Leninist principles and those seeking to preserve its traditional social role and autonomy within the state. The former group prevailed when Albert Bereczky replaced László Ravasz as bishop in 1948, but its ascendancy was strongly challenged in 1956 by the 'Confessing Church' movement, which succeeded in bringing Ravasz back as Church leader. After the defeat of the 1956 uprising Ravasz was again replaced by Bereczky, whose main policy lines are followed by the present Reformed leadership. The present head of the Church is Bishop Károly Tóth, who succeeded Tibor Bartha as presiding bishop in 1987.

Church structure and membership; current growth trends
The Hungarian Reformed Church and its sister church in Transylvania are the only Churches within the worldwide Reformed fellowship which have bishops. The General Synod is the highest authority within the Hungarian Reformed Church, according to its constitution of 1967. The General Synod is presided over jointly by a bishop and a lay leader, though real power lies in the hands of the bishop. This pattern of joint lay-episcopal leadership applies also to the six districts, 29 deaneries and about 1,500 congregations. The Church's constitution recognises the supervisory powers of the state. There are Reformed theological seminaries in Debrecen and Budapest, and a grammar school in Debrecen. The Church publishes a weekly newspaper *(Reformátusok Lapja)*, a

monthly magazine for pastors *(Református Egyház)*, and a theological journal *(Confessió)*. Nine homes for the elderly and seven centres for the handicapped are operated by the Church. The Church belongs to the Hungarian Ecumenical Council, the World Reformed Alliance and the World Council of Churches.

The Reformed Church has 1,900,000 baptised members, 363,334 of whom are on congregational electoral rolls. About 10% of baptised Calvinists are thought to attend church regularly. Reformed congregations may be found throughout the country, but the Calvinist stronghold remains the area east of the Tisza. There are over 1,200 clergymen engaged in pastoral work. In the 1984-5 academic year 170 students were enrolled in the seminaries, and another 143 participated in a correspondence course for the laity.

The Lutheran Church

History

The teachings of Martin Luther first filtered into Hungary soon after the proclamation of the 95 Theses. To counteract this influence the Archbishop of Esztergom in 1521 ordered the condemnation of Lutheran doctrines from all pulpits, and Hungarian Diets approved anti-Lutheran laws in 1523 and 1525. The acceptance of Luther's teachings gained momentum after the Turkish victory at Mohács in 1526. Among those in the forefront of the Lutheran movement were Mátyás Dévai (known as the Hungarian Luther), Mihály Sztárai and Péter Bornemisza. By 1570 an estimated 60% of the population was Lutheran. The great majority of them were soon lost to the Calvinists, especially in the more homogeneous Magyar territories occupied by the Turks. The Lutherans suffered further losses during the Counter-Reformation when they were faced with a combination of legal restrictions and a revitalised Catholic Church. The Toleration Patent of 1781 increased the opportunity for Lutheran worship, but apart from a brief interlude in 1848–9 the Lutheran Church did not achieve rights broadly equal with those enjoyed by the Catholic Church until after the Austro-Hungarian Compromise of 1867. The loss of Slovakia, Transylvania, the Banat and Burgenland after the First World War deprived the Hungarian Lutheran Church of 706 out of 1,110 congregations.

The Lutheran leadership offered strong resistance to the assault on the Church's social role and autonomy by the Communist-dominated government in the late 1940s, but its resistance crumbled after the arrest and imprisonment on false charges of Bishop Lajos Ordass in 1948. In that year the non-imprisoned Church leaders signed an agreement with the state which marked the beginning of a new era of strict state supervision and restricted activity. In 1956 Bishop Ordass was rehabilitated by the state and resumed his episcopal office. Two years later the state again withdrew recognition of Ordass, who was replaced by Zoltán Káldy. Under Bishop Káldy the church has preached and practised the so-called 'Diakonia Theology', which explicitly commits its adherents to positive support for the policies of the state. Káldy who was elected President of the Lutheran World Federation in 1984 died in 1987 and was succeeded as Presiding Bishop by Gyula Nagy and as Bishop of the Southern District by Béla Harmati.

Church structure and membership; current growth trends
Since 1952, the Lutheran Church has been divided into two districts, each headed by a bishop. Each district comprises eight deaneries. Altogether there are 324 parishes and 270 active pastors. At the head of the national Church stands the Presiding Bishop, who is elected by a General Synod with the prior approval of the state. Pastors are trained at a Lutheran theological seminary in Budapest. The seminary also sponsors a theological correspondence course for lay leaders. The Church owns a retreat centre at Gyenesdiás on Lake Balaton and operates sixteen institutions, providing care for the elderly and handicapped. The Church's press department publishes a weekly newspaper (*Evangélikus Élet*), a monthly pastoral aid (*Lelkipásztor*) and a twice-yearly theological journal (*Diakonia*). The Church belongs to the Hungarian Ecumenical Council, the Lutheran World Federation and the World Council of Churches.

Lutherans tend to be concentrated away from the geographical centre of the country. Though Hungarian is today the native tongue of the great majority of Lutherans, 3,000 services are conducted annually in Slovak and German. The Lutheran Church has a diaspora character, with one out of four Lutherans living some distance from a congregational centre.

Official figures from 1949 indicated that there were 430,000 Lutherans in Hungary, but estimates suggest that today there are about 350,000 (3.3% of the population). About 10% of baptised Lutherans attend church regularly. The annual number of baptisms has fallen by half since 1956 and in 1984 there were 2,974 baptisms compared with 4,834 funerals.

The Baptist Church

History

Baptists first came to Hungary in 1846. In that year János Rottmeyer (1818–1901) and several co-workers returned to their native Hungary from Hamburg, where they had been associated with the German Baptist missionary J G Oncken. In Budapest the tiny Baptist congregation co-operated with Reformed and Lutheran evangelicals in distributing Bibles and tracts. They were forced underground by the Habsburg authorities after the Hungarian War of Independence was lost in 1849, and were able to re-surface only in the 1860s. Though still sometimes harassed by the authorities, Baptist evangelists such as Heinrick Meyer and Mihály Kornya succeeded in establishing congregations throughout the country by the end of the century. In 1905, one section of the divided Baptist community received state recognition, while the other, which opposed recognition, continued to be regarded as an unrecognised sect. The two groups reunited in 1920 to form the legally recognised Federation of Hungarian Baptist Congregations. In 1947 the Baptists and all other recognised Free Churches achieved legal equality with the Catholic, Reformed and Lutheran Churches. In 1955 the Federation was transformed into the Hungarian Baptist Church. A new Constitution and

Confession were approved by the state in 1967.

Church structure and membership; current growth trends
The highest decision-making body of the Hungarian Baptist Church is its General Assembly, which represents the congregations, seminary teachers and Church leaders. The highest executive organ is the national Presidium. The Church is divided into four districts, each with its own Presidium and Assembly. The Church has 430 congregations and about 100 ordained pastors. They are trained at the Baptist seminary in Budapest. *Békehírnök* ('Herald of Peace') is the Baptists' weekly newspaper. The Hungarian Baptist Church is a member of the Ecumenical Council, the Free Church Council and the Inter-Church Peace Committee.

The Baptist faith made its first inroads among Hungary's German-speaking population, but by the end of the First World War the character of the Church was largely Hungarian. Baptist beliefs first found acceptance mostly among rural people and skilled workers. The social composition of the Church still reflects these roots. The Church has 22,000 members. Some estimates which take regularly-worshipping non-members into account (children and adults who have not experienced believer's baptism) put the number of Baptists as high as 50,000. In the 1980s the Church has recorded its first increase in membership in many years.

The Orthodox Church

History
Eastern-rite Christianity was practised in the Carpathian basin before the Magyar occupation. It enjoyed parity with Latin-rite Christianity until St Stephen accepted the 'holy crown' from the Pope in 1001. Thereafter the Eastern rite suffered a gradual decline. In the mid-seventeenth century there was a large-scale transfer of allegiance to Greek Catholicism in response to anti-Orthodox pressure from the state. The Toleration Patent of 1781 lifted many restrictions imposed upon the

Orthodox. In 1895, two Orthodox dioceses were founded.

Church structure and membership; current growth trends
The Orthodox community in Hungary is divided by nationality.
Szentendre is the ecclesiastical centre of the Serbian Orthodox
vicariate, which is divided into eighteen parishes. There are
about 7,000 baptised Serbian Orthodox in Hungary, who are
served by 12 priests. Their episcopal vicar is subordinate to the
Patriarch of Serbia. The seat of the episcopal vicar of the
Romanian Orthodox is at Gyula. The Romanian vicariate
numbers 18 parishes, 10 priests and 16,000 baptised members.
The episcopal vicar is under the jurisdiction of the Patriarch of
Romania. Budapest is the centre of the Hungarian Orthodox
vicariate, which consists of 8 parishes and 5,000 baptised members. The vicariate is subject to the Patriarch of Moscow, and
includes both Russian and Hungarian parishes. The Bulgarian
Orthodox number 500 and are organised into one parish, which
falls under the jurisdiction of the Patriarch of Bulgaria.

Other Protestant Denominations

The Adventist Church
Adventist missionary work started in Hungary with the visits of
the American Bible seller L R Conradi in the 1890s. The first
converts were among Baptists in Kolozsvár (Cluj) in Transylvania, but the faith soon spread to Hungary proper. Today the
Adventist Church has 5,500 members, 131 congregations and
35 pastors. The Church is however, divided, with between
1,000 and 2,000 Adventists belonging to unrecognised congregations: they have been periodically harassed by the
authorities. The recognised Adventists, like several of the
smaller Protestant denominations in Hungary, are members of
the Free Church Council.

Christian Brethren
The 2,200 strong Congregation of Christian Brethren traces its
spiritual heritage to the Plymouth Brethren of Britain. The first

Hungarian converts were won in the 1920s. Today the Church has thirty local congregations and belongs to the Free Church Council.

The Pentecostal Church and other Charismatic denominations

The Pentecostal faith reached Hungary at the end of the First World War, when a small group of prisoners of war returned from Russia, where they had been converted, and the movement gained momentum a few years later when Hungarian émigrés to the United States returned to their native land. The largest of the Pentecostal groups is the Fellowship of Evangelical Pentecostals, which has nearly 4,000 baptised members and 5,300 regular worshippers. The Fellowship has 35 ordained pastors, 18 of which are in full-time ministry, and 155 congregations. Other recognised charismatic denominations belonging to the Free Church Council are the Free Christian Congregation (600 members), the Congregation of the Living God (600 members) and the Ancient Christian Apostolic Church (2,200 members). One of the largest groupings of unrecognised charismatic congregations is the Congregation of God, which reportedly has 3,000 adherents and 23 pastors.

Another is the Faith Christian Fellowship. This is a charismatic denomination which grew out of a small prayer group in 1978. It has approximately 600 regular worshippers. The largest of its several congregations is in Budapest. The Fellowship is not legally recognised and encounters periodic harassment from the authorities.

The Methodist Church

The first Methodist minister in Hungary was Otto Melle, who was sent from Dresden in 1900 to the village of Szenttamás (now in Yugoslavia). Five years later he started Methodist work in Budapest. The Methodist Church split in the 1970s, and was left with 1,800 members. The new church to emerge from the division, the Community of Evangelical Brethren, has 900 members. The Evangelical Brethren were recognised in 1981, but their relationship with the Free Church Council has not yet been settled.

The Congregation of Nazarenes Believing in Christ
The oldest of the 'free churches' in Hungary is the Congregation of Nazarenes Believing in Christ, which was established in Hungary by followers of the Swiss Nazarene S H Fröhlich in the 1830s. The Nazarenes are strongest in central and southeastern Hungary. They are noted for their pacifism, and this has traditionally brought them into conflict with the secular authorities. The Nazarenes were recognised by the state in 1977, and although they do not belong to the Free Church Council, this body handles its relations with the state. The Nazarenes claim 7,000 members and 112 congregations.

Some estimates put the number of small unrecognised evangelical churches at over thirty-five.

Quasi-Christian groups

The Jehovah's Witnesses began their work in Hungary in 1913. They are not recognised by the state, and are subject to harassment by the authorities. In April 1988, 146 Jehovah's Witnesses were in prison for refusing to perform military service. They are believed to number about 5,000 and have 140 congregations. They evangelise zealously and membership is on the increase.

The Unitarian Church

The Unitarian movement in Hungary began in the midsixteenth century when anti-trinitarian ideas were introduced in Transylvania. They found favour at the court of Prince János Zsigmond (d1571), where they were promoted by Ferenc Dávid (c1520–1579). The teachings of Dávid made their biggest impact on the Magyars. Kolozsvár (Cluj) became one of the leading European centres of Unitarian spiritual and intellectual life. The Counter-Reformation took a heavy toll on the Unitarians, especially in Hungary proper, where Unitarianism was virtually eliminated. Unitarian services started in Buda-Pest (sic) in 1869 for the benefit of government officials who had come to the work in the Hungarian capital from Transylvania after the Austro-Hungarian Compromise of 1867. By 1938 there were 6,920 Unitarians in Hungary. Most of them had roots in Transylvania or had transferred their denominational allegiance from the Reformed Church. Until 1971, Unitarians in Hungary proper and Transylvania (in Romania) were united in one Church. Since then, those in Hungary have had a separate Church organisation which is headed by a bishop and a lay superintendent. Today there are approximately 5,000 Unitarians in Hungary, most of whom live in Budapest. The Church has eight parishes and eleven pastors.

CHRISTIAN ACTIVITIES

Evangelism and Mission

Public evangelisation and mission were severely restricted during the anti-religious persecution of the early 1950s. Most Catholic associations were dissolved as early as 1946. All but a handful of church schools were nationalised in 1948, and obstacles were put in the way of children attending optional religious instruction. In the same year Protestant evangelical organisations belonging to the Union for Inner Mission were disbanded. Catholic orders were dissolved in 1950. Over the past decade, however, the state has come to accept that limited public evangelism can contribute to social stability by satisfying the missionary impulses of the churches and by imparting positive ethical values to the country's large and rapidly growing 'nihilistic' element. Accordingly, the churches have been allowed to expand their evangelistic and missionary activity. Some Catholic parishes have developed dynamic religious instruction programmes aimed at evangelism. In the early 1980s a Catholic retreat centre at Leányfalu was opened. In recent years the Protestant Churches belonging to the Ecumenical

Council have participated in an Alcoholics Mission and a Mission to Wayward Youth. The more evangelical Protestant Churches have hosted visits by Billy Graham, Nicky Cruz and lesser known Western evangelists.

Though the churches now enjoy greater opportunities for public witness, their evangelistic activities still remain limited by comparison with the pre-war period. Much of the evangelism that takes place in Hungary is carried on without official approval, by foreign Protestant mission organisations and by indigenous Catholic basis communities and evangelical Protestant fellowships.

Broadcasting

Religious broadcasting is limited to one half-hour programme at 7 am each Sunday. The Catholic Church is allotted fifteen to twenty slots per year, with the rest divided up between the country's other recognised Churches, according to size and historic significance. Most of the broadcasts take the form of abridged worship services. It is estimated that about 140,000 people, or 2% of the adult population, listen to *The Religious Half Hour of the Catholic Church*.

In recent years Hungarian television and radio have broadcast educational programmes on religio-cultural subjects, and these have included contributions from Christian scholars.

Trans World Radio (an evangelical braoadcasting station based in Monaco) broadcasts a wide variety of evangelical programmes in the Hungarian language.

Literature

Christian publishing in Hungary experienced a sharp decline after the Second World War, when most Christian publishing houses were nationalised and censorship of the religious press was introduced.

In 1946 there were approximately 20 Catholic publishing houses. Today there are two: Ecclesia and the St Stephen Society. Since the 1970s, the two have published between 15 and 30 books per annum. These include not only ecclesiastical works but also poetry, novels and historical writings. In 1946 Catholic newspapers and magazines represented over 11% of all those published in Hungary; now the figure is less than 1%. Today the Church publishes five periodicals: the weekly newspaper *Új ember* (circulation 100,000); the fortnightly 'peace priest' paper *Katholikus szó* (17,000); the monthly literary-theological journal *Vigilia* (11,500); the quarterly scholarly theological journal *Teologia* (4,000); and the news service in Hungarian, French and German *Magyar kurir*.

Protestant publishing has suffered a similar decline with the demise of the dozens of Protestant publishing houses which flourised before the Second World War. Each major Protestant Church, the Ecumenical Council and the Free Church Council have been able to retain their own publishing houses. They produce relatively few publications, but manage to cover a wide range of subjects and genres. The Reformed Church publishes a weekly newspaper, *Reformátusok lapja,* with a circulation of 32,000, a monthly pastoral magazine, *Református Egyház*, and a scholarly quarterly, *Confessió*. The weekly *Evangélikus élet,* with a circulation of 12,000, is the official newspaper of the Lutheran Church. The Lutherans also publish the monthly pastoral aid *Lelkipásztor* and a twice-yearly theological journal *Diakonia*. The Ecumenical Council publishes the bimonthly theological review *Theologiai szemle*. For foreigners, the Ecumenical Council offers the monthly newsletter *Hungarian Church Press* in English and German.

The Hungarian religious press operates under the constraints of self-censorship, so as to ensure that all publications are compatible with the joint interests of the state and of the state-approved church leaders. The State Office for Church Affairs sets fixed limits on the print-run of church books and periodicals. Religious *samizdat* is rare in Hungary but such writings are produced and circulated by the small unofficial groups. Articles on religious affairs appear in political *samizdat* periodicals such as *Beszélő* and *Hírmondó*. Much religious literature is sent to Hungary, both officially and unofficially, by Western agencies to meet unfulfilled needs.

Secular publishers in Hungary produce some reference books, and scholarly and popular works on religious subjects— for example, lexicons on religious history or the Bible and books on the Marxist attitude to religion. A wide variety of religious music—for example, Gregorian chants, Protestant psalms and so on—is also available.

Bible translation and distribution

The first complete translation of the Bible into Hungarian was completed by the Reformed clergyman Gáspár Károli in 1590. The Károli translation was widely distributed and soon became the 'authorised version' of Hungarian Protestants. A translation for Catholics was prepared by the Jesuit György Káldi in 1626. Both the Károli and Káldi versions were extensively revised early in the present century. A completely new translation was published by the Catholic St Stephen Society in 1973. A new Protestant translation in modern Hungarian was published by the Hungarian Bible Council, an affiliate of the United Bible Societies, in 1975. The St Stephen Society and the Hungarian Bible Council are the official agencies responsible for Bible distribution. Bibles may be bought at non-prohibitive prices at several religious bookshops in Budapest and Debrecen, and directly from local churches. Some state bookshops now sell Bibles too. Since its foundation in 1948, the Bible Council alone has distributed over half a million Bibles. Bibles are also sent to Hungary by some Western mission organisations. There are more than enough Bibles available to meet the needs of believers. There is a substantial flow of Bibles sent unofficially from Hungary to the Hungarian minorities in Transylvania (Romania) and Slovakia. In 1980 the first Hungarian Bible in Braille was published.

Education

Before the Second World War the Catholic, Reformed and Lutheran Churches dominated the Hungarian educational system. The Catholic Church operated over 3,000 schools, including primary schools, secondary schools, colleges of higher education and law schools. The Reformed and Lutheran Churches had nearly 2,000 schools and colleges between them. Altogether church schools represented almost two-thirds of all Hungarian educational institutions.

After the nationalisation in 1948 the Churches were left with fewer than a dozen schools. The Catholic Church now has six grammar schools for boys at Pannonhalma, Győr, Esztergom, Szentendre, Budapest and Kecskemét; and two for girls at Budapest and Debrecen. Over 2,000 students attend the Catholic grammar schools. The Reformed Church has one grammar school at Debrecen with about 400 students. The two Lutheran grammar schools remaining after nationalisation were turned over to the state in 1952. The Baptists lost their only school in 1948. The State has given approval for the re-establishment of two grammar schools—one Reformed and the other Lutheran.

The Catholic Church trains candidates for the priesthood at six seminaries located at Budapest, Esztergom, Eger, Szeged, Győr and Nyíregyháza (Eastern-rite Catholic). Two hundred and thirty-four seminarists were enrolled in 1984. The two Reformed theological academies are at Budapest and Debrecen from which 25 students received diplomas in 1986. The Lutherans and Baptists have one seminary each at Budapest. The Free Church Council sponsors an extension course for the training of pastors in co-operation with the seminaries of the other Protestant Churches.

Religious education in state schools ceased to be obligatory in 1949. Optional religious education classes are, however, available in state schools, but the law stipulates that they must take place before or after school hours, that teachers of

religion must be authorised by the state, that students may not
be graded and that no disciplinary action may be taken against
students. In 1949, about 90% of students participated in religious instruction. Today very few still take part. This sharp drop
may be attributed to the combined effect of the decline of
religious faith and of administrative measures which discourage
registration.

In the Catholic Church religious instruction in the churches
was limited to short-term first-communion and confirmation
classes. The Church-State Agreement of 1950 permitted
further instruction in churches for those not receiving it in
school. According to norms set by the state, instruction in
churches was to take the form of a monologue and children
were not to ask questions. Such restrictions were not strictly
enforced in all parishes. In 1976 there was an agreement
between the bishops and the state which allowed parishes to
offer instruction for two hours per week to each age group.
About 8% of school children participate in parish-based religious instruction. Each parish may have no more than 160
children enrolled in religious instruction. Since the early 1970s,
new books have been published for Catholic religious instruction to replace those written during the inter-war period.

Confirmation classes form the back-bone of the religious
instruction programmes of the Reformed and Lutheran
Churches. These classes run from December to April, and
must be preceded by a twelve month Bible study course. Like
the Catholic Church, the Protestant Churches may offer two
hours of instruction per week to each age group. One hour
must be offered on Sunday. In 1987 and 1988 the Reformed
Church and the Lutheran Church respectively signed agree-
ments with the state to regulate parish-based religious instruction beyond the traditional confirmation classes.

Notwithstanding limited resources and state-imposed restrictions, some imaginative and energetic clergymen have succeeded in offering dynamic programmes of religious instruction.

The teaching of the Bible as literature in state schools has
been allowed since 1980. The aim is to expose students to a
great literary work and to help them become familiar with the

biblical imagery to be found in secular works. Teachers have been instructed by the state not to use these 'Bible-as-literature' classes as an opportunity for religious or anti-religious education.

Over the past decade theological correspondence courses for laypeople have been set up by the seminaries of the various Churches. They are intended to train laypeople for pastoral work. Successful graduates may conduct religious instruction classes.

Social Concerns

The churches in Hungary have traditionally played a role in the provision of social services—indeed, before the Second World War they did more in this field than the state itself. The Catholic and Protestant Churches alike ran many associations sponsoring work among young people, orphans, the elderly, the handicapped and the sick. Most social work organised by the Lutheran and Reformed Churches was carried on by trained deaconesses; monks and nuns played the main role in the social work of the Catholic Church.

By the early 1950s, however, the state had brought most church social work to an end. In 1946 most Catholic associations were dissolved and in 1950 virtually all monasteries and convents suffered the same fate. In 1948 the Protestant associations belonging to the Union of Inner Missions were dissolved. Church hospitals were nationalised. The state restricted the social work of the churches to limited care of their own elderly and handicapped people. The Church Charity Service was founded in 1950 to direct Catholic social work. Its main task is to look after the monks and nuns who were left homeless and unemployed after the dissolution of the religious orders. The Charity Service operates 17 old people's homes serving over 800 people, and 7 rest homes for priests. A new Catholic home for handicapped children was opened in 1986. In 1953 the Charity Service founded *Solidaritas*, a co-operative employing several hundred religious in small workshops or in cottage industries. The Reformed Church was left with eight old folks' homes, six residential centres for the mentally handicapped, one nursing home and one hospice. The Lutheran Church has about as many homes for the elderly and mentally handicapped as the Reformed Church, which altogether care for 600 people. Among the smaller Churches, the Baptists have two old people's homes, while the Adventists, Unitarians and Methodists have one each.

In the 1980s the Protestant Churches have begun missions for alcoholics and wayward young people; these seek to meet spiritual, physical and psychological needs. In the more tolerant climate of the 1970s and 1980s some parishes and congregations have been able to increase their local social work. The Protestant Churches have recently sponsored collections for mission and relief work in Africa. With the Catholic Church, help is given to the work of Mother Teresa of Calcutta. In 1988 the churches have been allowed to respond to the flood of refugees from Romania by establishing centres for the provision of material assistance and counselling.

CHAPTER 4:

Czechoslovakia

CZECHOSLOVAKIA: OVERVIEW

The country; the people; brief history

Czechoslovakia, in the very heart of Central Europe, came into existence as recently as 1918, when the Austro-Hungarian Empire dissolved at the end of the First World War. It is a country consisting of two nations, the Czechs in Bohemia and Moravia and the Slovaks in Slovakia; they speak Czech and Slovak respectively. The first Republic, under T G Masaryk, lasted from 1918 to 1938, when, to appease German demands, the British, French and Italians made a pact with Hitler in Munich whereby the German-speaking border area, the Sudetenland, was ceded to Germany, while other parts of Czechoslovakia were transferred to Hungary and Poland. The remainder of Czechoslovakia was invaded and occupied by Germany in 1939.

After the Second World War, all of Czechoslovakia's pre-war territory was restored to her, with the exception of Car-patho-Ukraine, which was claimed by the Soviet Union in 1945. Virtually all the German speaking inhabitants of Czechoslovakia were expelled from the country in the same year, and the Sudetenland was resettled by Czech speakers.

In 1946 elections were held, and the Communist Party under Klement Gottwald emerged as the largest party, gaining 38% of the votes cast. A coalition government was formed with Gottwald as Prime Minister, and after the resignations of other ministers there was a Communist take-over in 1948. A hardline Stalinist régime then remained in power until 1963, when a new cabinet was formed with Jozef Lenárt as Prime Minister. A period of liberalisation followed, climaxing in 1968, with Alexander Dubček as Party Secretary, Ludvík Svoboda as President, and Oldřich Černík as Prime Minister. The liberal

175

reforms of this government were seen by the other Eastern bloc countries as a threat to their unity and in August 1968 Warsaw Pact armies occupied Prague and other major cities. Dubček was ousted and replaced by Gustáv Husák, a hardliner: a purge of the Communist Party ensued and most of Dubček's supporters were removed from government posts.

The economy; social conditions; political life

Czechoslovakia is a member of the Council of Mutual Economic Assistance (COMECON) and over 70% of its trade turn-over is accounted for by fellow member countries, principally the Soviet Union, on which Czechoslovakia depends for many raw materials. The economy is based on heavy industry and agriculture, but, although once prosperous, the country is in serious economic trouble. While eager to trade with the West, the Czechoslovak authorities are not prepared to go to the necessary lengths to achieve this. Czechoslovakia's technology is obsolete and many of its products are second-rate, offering no competition for those of its Western rivals. Furthermore, the economy is centrally planned and has been severely constrained by the government's unwillingness to embark on economic reform. However, under the leadership of Miloš Jakeš (elected December 1987) the Party has committed itself to a measure of economic restructuring, including the introduction of some private enterprise.

Despite the serious state of the economy, the people of Czechoslovakia enjoy one of the highest standards of living in Eastern Europe. Shops are relatively well stocked and people can afford to buy what they sell. A considerable number of families have second homes in the country to which they retreat at week-ends and holidays. A large number of people own private cars: these are principally Czech-made Škodas, but cars imported from the West are a common sight. Despite their wealth, it is very difficult for people to travel to the West, for two reasons: it is prohibitively expensive (it is cheaper to go to Cuba on holiday than to Great Britain) and it is hard to get permission to travel. However, new legislation introduced in 1988 should simplify the procedure and allow Czechoslovak citizens to travel to non-socialist countries every three years.

Those who enjoy the most material comfort are those who conform to the requirements of one of the most rigid political systems in Eastern Europe. People are encouraged to join the Communist Party, but apart from a very few committed communists, most of the members do so for purely careerist motives, as membership of the Party opens many doors. Nevertheless, those who do so are looked down on by the majority of citizens who do not join the Party at all.

Political indoctrination begins at an early age. As in other communist countries, when children enter their teens they are expected to join the 'Pioneer' movement. This movement resembles the Boy Scouts or Girl Guides, but in addition to excursions and summer camps, it also provides a structured political teaching programme. At university students have to pass exams in Marxism-Leninism, and at work people are expected to attend political lectures regularly. Political dissent is not tolerated and is treated in much the same way as religious dissent.

THE STATUS OF CHRISTIANITY

The religious complexion of the country

Despite some Christian missionary activity from Rome in the eighth century, Christianity made its real impact on what is now Czechoslovakia as a result of the work of the missionary brothers, Sts Cyril and Methodius. They came to Greater Moravia in the ninth century, having been sent there from Constantinople. By the end of the Middle Ages, Bohemia was at the heart of the Reformation: in the early years of the fifteenth century, Jan Hus led a rebellion against what he saw as the social and religious corruption of the Catholic Church, and was burnt at the stake in 1415 by the ecclesiastical authorities. Throughout the centuries since then, Bohemia and Moravia have retained a strong Protestant tradition, while Slovakia, despite the strong influence of Lutheranism in the sixteenth century, has remained essentially Roman Catholic.

It is very difficult to establish reliable figures for the number of Christians in Czechoslovakia, as statistics are hard to come by. In 1985 a government official quoted some apparently quite credible figures. He reported that 1.3 million non-Catholics paid membership fees to their churches. It is generally accepted that Catholics outnumber non-Catholics by a ratio of seven to three, and this would indicate that there are just over three million practising Catholics, although other observers of the Czechoslovak religious scene put this figure at over four million. There would, therefore, be a total of between four and a half, and five and a half million active Christians in Czechoslovakia out of a total of fifteen million inhabitants. This figure represents a considerable drop since the census of 1950, which was the last occasion on which the number of believers was recorded. According to that census, 94.6% of the population declared themselves to be believers, so it would appear that under Communist rule the various Churches have lost up to two thirds of their membership.

As well as a Protestant tradition, Bohemia also has a splendid Jewish history. The Alt-Neue Synagogue in Prague is the oldest remaining synagogue in Central Europe and the city was one of the great centres of European Jewry. In the 1930s there were approximately 350,000 Jews in Czechoslovakia, of whom 250,000 were killed by the Nazis. At the time of the Communist take-over, there were 48,000, more than half of whom emigrated to the newly-founded state of Israel. By the 'Prague Spring' of 1968, the number was down to somewhere between 12,000 and 15,000 and it now stands at approximately 5,000.

The state's attitude to religion

Christianity in Czechoslovakia is currently enjoying a considerable revival in the face of hostility from the state. In the 1950s all religious orders were outlawed. Countless numbers of priests and members of the religious orders were imprisoned. During the more liberal years following 1963, many of them were released and rehabilitated. In March 1968 the new Party leader, Alexander Dubček, abolished censorship and all the Churches enjoyed a freedom which they had never previously nor have since enjoyed under Communist rule. Since the invasion of the Warsaw Pact countries the following August, the Churches, and especially the Catholic Church, have been fighting a non-stop battle for their survival. The approach of the various denominations has differed, and this in turn has resulted in their receiving different treatment from the state. By and large, the various Protestant denominations have been prepared to accept the limitations imposed upon them and they now manage to function to some extent. This has, however, meant paying a degree of lip-service to various government policies, so that, for example, any prominent religious assembly dealing with any subject will invariably issue some statement reflecting the state's position on the arms race.

The position of the Catholic Church is far more complicated. The aim of the state would appear to be to destroy the Catholic Church from within. In the 1950s, the plan was first to persuade the Church to break away from Rome and form a National Catholic Church, led by pro-government clergy. This attempt failed, but the authorities did succeed in setting up an organisation of priests who actively supported the régime. Its contemporary equivalent is a group called 'Pacem in Terris' (which will be described in more detail later). Suffice it to say for the moment that this organisation has succeeded in causing disruption within the Church. It has left ordinary believers bewildered, not knowing whether to choose the slightly easier option of supporting these priests at the risk of compromising their faith, or to follow their consciences and voice their dissent where necessary.

Whilst the state is ultimately set on the elimination of religion in Czechoslovakia, this does not prevent it from exploiting the Churches for its own ends. Thus the Christian Peace Conference, founded in Czechoslovakia in 1958, has over the years become the forum for the expression of an exclusively Soviet perspective on the struggle for peace. The state cannot ignore great religious figures in Czechoslovakia's history, as it is impossible to deny the part they played in cultural and political affairs. Whenever they are mentioned, however, they are described as great political or social reformers rather than as religious figures; so, for example, Jan Hus is praised for taking a bold stand against the foreign influence of Rome in his capacity as a great Czech nationalist. In 1985 Czech Christians commemorated the 1100th anniversary of the death of St Methodius. The Minister of Culture attended a huge rally of Christians at Velehrad, where St Methodius is thought to be buried, and delivered an address in which he presented the mission of Cyril and Methodius to Great Moravia simply as an event of cultural importance, linking it to the constructing of socialism.

THE VARIOUS CHURCHES

The Roman Catholic Church

History
The Catholic Church in Czechoslovakia has a long and troubled history. The eighth-century Teutonic missionaries from Rome were largely unsuccessful in their attempts to convert the inhabitants of Greater Moravia because they were seen as imposing a foreign culture on the indigenous population. However, when Cyril and Methodius arrived from Constantinople, they were well versed in Slavonic and they brought to the Moravians a vernacular liturgy which they had not been offered before. In the tenth and eleventh centuries, after the schism of 1054 between Rome and Constantinople, the Christians of Moravia and Bohemia (the Czech Lands) remained loyal to Rome. The Catholic Church flourished there until the late fourteenth century, when Jan Hus, who was heavily influenced by the teachings of the Englishman, John Wyclif, led the

Bohemian Reformation. He combined strong nationalist sentiment with protest against what he regarded as the external
authority imposed by Rome. Despite Hus' execution in 1415,
the Reformation continued and reached its peak in the late sixteenth century. In 1621, the Catholic Habsburg Empire took
control of the Czech Lands, and suppressed Protestantism; in
later centuries, however, edicts of toleration were introduced
to protect Protestant believers. With the end of the First World
War, came the founding of the state of Czechoslovakia. The
First Republic (1918–1938) was marked by tolerance of religious diversity and it was during this period that the latest schis-
matic group broke away from Rome. In 1921, a group of clergy
demanded the use of the vernacular in the liturgy and permission for priests to marry. Rome refused to give in to this group,
and so it broke away to form the Czechoslovak Church, which
was renamed the Czechoslovak Hussite Church in 1972.

Until 1918, Slovakia developed quite separately from the
Czech Lands. While they were at the heart of the Reformation,
Slovakia remained Catholic and culturally remains essentially
Catholic today. While the Czech Lands were under the Aust-
rian part of the Hapsburg Empire, Slovakia came under Hun-
garian rule. Although Slovakia was united with the Czech
Lands in 1918, the two nations were separated again by the
Nazis. While the Czech Lands were invaded and occupied,
Slovakia became a Nazi puppet state under the leadership of a
Catholic priest, Fr Josef Tiso, and Slovak Catholics are still
vulnerable to accusations of having collaborated with the
Nazis.

Since the Communist take-over of Czechoslovakia, the
Roman Catholic Church has always been one of the chief
targets for elimination as part of the state's ideological struggle. In 1948, two laws were passed aimed at undermining the
Church's influence and power. The first resulted in the confiscation of all Church property, thereby depriving her of a vast
proportion of her income. The second led to the closing down
of all Catholic schools and the abolition of religious instruction.
In the course of one year, the Church was, thus, seriously
crippled in two important areas of its activity.

The 1950s saw an uninterrupted struggle between the state

and the Catholic Church under the remarkably strong leadership of Cardinal Beran, who spent most of his career before leaving the country in 1965 under virtual house arrest. The state made inroads into every aspect of church life, putting pro-régime clergy in charge of the Catholic media and in other places of influence. A Catholic priest, Fr Josef Plojhar, joined the government and despite Cardinal Beran's order that he resign, he refused to step down and was eventually excommunicated.

Throughout the 1950s, the state imprisoned many priests and religious, and employed a wide range of methods in its attempt to destroy the Church. After the comparatively liberal 1960s, a harsh régime was reintroduced under Gustáv Husák, and throughout the 1970s and into the 1980s the régime has been continuing in its struggle against the Church, albeit in a somewhat less crude fashion than in the 1950s.

Church structure and membership; current growth trends
One of the most effective ways in which the state is succeeding in limiting the influence and growth of the Catholic Church is by controlling the Church hierarchy. The state is able to exercise control at all levels, from the seminarian to the bishop. To enter a seminary, a candidate has to be accepted not only by his bishop, but also by the secular authorities, and thus only politically 'reliable' candidates are accepted for the priesthood. Once in the seminary, seminarians are required to study courses in Marxism-Leninism and atheism, subjects which are taught by staff members approved by the secular authorities. Furthermore, the number of men admitted to the two seminaries in Czechoslovakia is severely restricted by the authorities, so that often fewer than half the applicants are accepted and the shortage of priests gets worse all the time as older priests die. Once he is ordained, a priest is permitted to exercise his vocation only if he is given a state licence to do so. He risks losing his licence if he does any more than the bare minimum required of him—which is, to say the Mass. Furthermore, priests are encouraged to join the government-sponsored organisation *Pacem in Terris*, whose main function is to endorse government peace propaganda. In March 1982 the

Pope banned priests from belonging to any political organisation, and this was taken to include *Pacem in Terris*. Before the ban, approximately half of Czechoslovakia's priests belonged to *Pacem in Terris*, but its membership declined drastically afterwards. Now, although just 9% of Catholic clergy belong to the association it is still members of *Pacem in Terris* who control the Catholic media and teach in the seminaries.

The appointment of the bishops of Czechoslovakia is subject to state approval. On the whole the current Vatican policy is to allow bishoprics to remain vacant, rather than fill them with unreliable bishops. The result is that of the thirteen Catholic dioceses (including the Byzantine-rite diocese of Prešov), only three have bishops, of whom one is a member of *Pacem in Terris*. In addition, there are four bishops who have been barred by the authorities from holding office. Since December 1987, the Czechoslovak government has been locked in negotiations with the Vatican over possible new episcopal appointments. In May 1988 it was announced that three new appointments would be made.

The head of the Catholic Church in Czechoslovakia is Cardinal František Tomášek, now in his late eighties. In 1965, he became Apostolic Administrator of Prague, and was secretly made a cardinal in 1976, a fact which became known in the following year. He was installed as Archbishop of Prague in 1978. He is seen by Catholics in Czechoslovakia as a great figurehead who is not afraid to speak his mind. However, there is considerable concern that he will not be replaced when he dies.

The Catholic Church remains far stronger in Slovakia than it does in the Czech Lands. Throughout Slovakia, the majority of people marry in church, baptise their children and have religious funerals; the only exception to this is Bratislava, the capital of Slovakia, where just over a quarter of the inhabitants are married in church. These statistics may give a slightly exaggerated picture of religiosity in Slovakia, as baptising a child or holding a religious funeral is often done for traditional and cultural reasons.

The Catholic Church in Slovakia is strongest in rural areas and weakest in the cities, especially in Bratislava. The reverse is true of the Czech Lands, traditionally more secular than

Slovakia, and hostile to Catholicism. Here the Catholic faith is now finding itself strongest in the two largest cities, Prague and Brno, where it is gaining an increasing following among the dissident intelligentsia. Catholicism remains strong in some Moravian villages, but this is not the case in Bohemia, where outside Prague the only real stronghold of Catholicism is in the far south of the region.

The Catholic Church is unable to function properly because of the artificially low number of priests available. Because of government restrictions, there are just 3,500 priests to serve the country's 4,600 or so parishes. Priests are terribly overworked, and there is no real opportunity for them to structure a proper parish life; hence the sense of a parish community is usually absent.

The situation for the religious orders is even worse. In 1950 they were forbidden to receive novices, all their hospitals and schools were closed down, and members of the orders who were not gaoled were forced into special homes. The orders are still prevented from accepting new members, and so they have been forced to operate underground. They have managed to form tiny communities of maybe four or five members who live in the same flat. Recently, however, the orders have become a little bolder. At pilgrimages in 1985, some members appeared in their habits. The Franciscans seem to be especially courageous and are causing the greatest concern to the authorities, since they are proving to be very popular and influential among young people. In recent years, many members of the order have been arrested and detained by the authorities.

Despite the numerous factors designed to discourage active religious witness in Czechoslovakia, it seems that a considerable revival of Catholicism has begun over the last few years. Statistics have been fairly constant for the last five years or so and indicate a very slight decrease in religiosity overall. However, these statistics would appear to be misleading in the light of many reports emerging from Czechoslovakia. These speak of an increasing interest in religion among young people living in the cities. This interest would appear to be, in part at least, a reaction to the emptiness of the official ideology, and is especially noticeable among students. In addition, the religious orders have attracted more and more young people, despite the difficulties that this inevitably entails and the abnormal conditions under which the orders are forced to function.

A very important indication of the growth in religious activity is attendance at pilgrimages. The pilgrimage at Velehrad in July 1985 attracted up to 250,000 participants, a number which clearly took the authorities by surprise. Furthermore, the mood of the pilgrimage was one of defiance, with the government speakers being derided and vociferous demands for religious freedom being made. A fair conclusion to draw, therefore, is that an increasing number of Christians who had been prepared to practise their faith quietly and discreetly in the past are now coming out into the open to proclaim their faith to the world. By and large, all denominations (other than the Roman Catholic) have managed to establish a working relationship with the state, and there are comparatively few cases of individuals coming into open conflict with the authorities.

The Eastern-rite Catholic Church

The Eastern-rite Catholics of Czechoslovakia, also known as Uniates, Greek Catholics or Byzantine-rite Catholics, are principally of Ukrainian and Slovak nationality, although there is also a small number of Hungarians; and the vast majority of them live in Eastern Slovakia, although some Uniate churches are to be found in Prague, Brno and Bratislava. Until the Second World War, there were approximately 550,000 Uniates in Czechoslovakia, but at the end of the war, with the annexation by the Soviet Union of Carpatho-Ukraine, the number went down to between 250,000 and 300,000. In 1950, the Uniate Church was forcibly merged with the Orthodox Church by the government, which then attempted to force priests to join the Orthodox clergy. The majority refused to do so and were imprisoned. Among them were Bishop Pavel Gojdič, who died in prison in 1960, and his auxiliary, Vasil Hopko, who was held in a psychiatric hospital until 1963, when he was moved to an old people's home. All Church property was handed over to the Orthodox.

The brief freedom of 1968 saw the complete rehabilitation of the Uniate Church. Individual parishes held elections to decide whether to remain Orthodox or to revert to Catholicism and, with few exceptions, they chose the latter course. In 1969 a Slovak, Ján Hirka, was appointed Ordinary in charge of the eparchy (diocese) of Prešov, which incorporates all the Uniates of Czechoslovakia. This caused considerable bitterness within the Church as the more likely candidate, to the Ukrainians at least, would have been Bishop Hopko. However, he remained an auxiliary bishop under Hirka until his death in 1976.

Compared with other denominations, and in view of its exceptionally difficult history, the Uniate Church is surviving very well. According to the Vatican yearbook in 1985, the eparchy of Prešov had 355,320 faithful (representing an increase of up to 100,000 since the Second World War), served by 207 diocesan priests and 16 religious priests. The Uniate Church does not regularly come under attack in the way that the Latin-rite Roman Catholics do and the main danger to it appears to be internal divisions between its Slovak and Ukrainian elements.

The Czechoslovak Hussite Church

The latest figures (for 1977) indicate that this Church has a membership of about 650,000 in 350 parishes. There are not enough priests for all the parishes. About eighty of the priests are women. There are six bishops, headed by a Bishop Patriarch who is *primus inter pares*. Priests train at the Hus Czechoslovak Faculty in Prague.

The Evangelical Church of the Czech Brethren

This Church came into existence in 1918 as the result of the union of Christians of the Lutheran and Reformed traditions, together with some former Roman Catholics. It has about 200,000 members and 521 places of worship in 270 parishes. Just over one quarter of these are unoccupied. There are about 250 ministers, of whom about 30 are women. The Church has a presbyterian form of government and is administered on a synodical basis. Local congregations are grouped in seniorates, each averaging twenty churches, and the supreme body of government is the general assembly, known as the Synod, which meets every two years. Ministers and laity share responsibility at every level of church life, and the lay members are usually well trained and vigorous in their witness. About 3,000 of them serve on Church committees. The ministers train at the Comenius Evangelical Faculty in Prague. Of all the non-Catholic denominations, this one has encountered the greatest difficulties with the authorities. A number of clergymen and laymen have been imprisoned, mainly for their involvement in Charter 77, a human-rights movement founded in 1977. However, those who have been tried and imprisoned have had very little support from any official Church body. The one exception to this occurred in 1985, when the Synod expressed its support for Jan Keller, a minister who was on trial after he had organised prayer and Bible meetings for young people. Around twenty-five ministers are thought to be currently without a state licence to exercise their ministry.

The Lutheran Church

This Church is split into two groups, the Slovak Lutheran Church and the Silesian Lutheran Church. The former has 369,000 members, 384 places of worship and about 350 ministers, while the latter has about 46,000 members, 41 places of worship and 21 ministers. Ministers train at the Slovak Evangelical Faculty in Bratislava. The Lutheran Church rarely encounters trouble with the authorities, although in recent years a minister has been placed on trial for his evangelical activities among young people and a number of youths have been arrested for distributing Bibles. This Church seems to be growing in popularity in Slovakia.

The Reformed Church

This church is Calvinist and of Hungarian origin. It has 130,000 members, 95% of whom are Hungarian speakers and the others Slovak speakers. It has about 300 places of worship and about 150 pastors. In 1987 23 new pastors were ordained. These were the first ordinations in ten years.

The Czechoslovak Orthodox Church

Originally this Church came under the jurisdiction of the Serbian Orthodox Church, but after the Second World War the Russian Orthodox Church took it over and eventually granted the Czechoslovak Orthodox Church autocephaly in 1951. There are about 150,000 Orthodox believers in Czechoslovakia today, most of whom are to be found in eastern Slovakia; there are about 190 churches altogether, although there are only 38 parishes in the Czech Lands. Priests are trained at the Orthodox Faculty in Prešov, in Slovakia.

Other Denominations

Brethren
The Church of Brethren has 8,000 members, 29 churches and 30 pastors and the Unity of Brethren (or Moravian Brethren) also has 8,000 members, but only 18 churches and 20 pastors.

The Baptist Church
The Baptist Church has just under 4,000 members on its roll, but probably twice as many regularly attend worship. They are

fairly evenly distributed throughout the country and there are twenty-eight churches besides many other informal places of worship. The largest congregations are in Prague, Brno and Bratislava, and there are twenty-one full time ministers as well as some lay pastors. Ministers train at the Comenius Evangelical Faculty in Prague or the Slovak Evangelical Faculty in Bratislava. A noteworthy feature of the life of the Baptist Church is its vigorous youth department, which organises study conferences and camps, and has a mobile work group, consisting of young people who give up their week-ends and holidays in order to assist with the building of new churches.

The Methodist Church
This Church has just over 1,500 members and a total community of nearly 5,000. They worship in forty-two places and are served by eighteen ministers and six retired ministers. Ministers are trained at the Hus and Comenius Faculties in Prague and the Slovak Evangelical Faculty in Bratislava.

The Old Catholic Church
The Old Catholic Church seems to have a following of 3,000. Until the end of the Second World War it had a large following in Czechoslovakia among the *Sudetendeutsch,* and its numbers were drastically reduced when they were expelled after the war. They have just one diocese, Varnsdorf, which is served by five priests.

Others
The Unitarian Church has 2,000 members in four congregations, the New Apostolic Church has 500 members, the Darbyites have 5,000 in 140 congregations, and Seventh-day Adventists have up to 7,000 followers. There are two Christian denominations which have no legal status: the (Pentecostal) Church of the Apostolic Faith with 1,000 believers, which, however, has legal status in Slovakia, and the Exclusive Brethren, who have 400 followers in 10 congregations.

Quasi-Christian groups

The only quasi-Christian group active in Czechoslovakia is the Jehovah's Witnesses. They are an illegal sect and are, therefore, forced to operate underground. However, they are exceptionally well organised, managing to avoid detection, while at the same time being very effective in distributing religious literature. They usually come to the authorities' notice when, as pacifists, they refuse to perform military service. Estimates of their numbers vary from 5,000 to 8,000.

CHRISTIAN ACTIVITIES

Evangelism and Mission

There is no scope on an official level for evangelical and missionary activity, but nevertheless such activity does take place. People who are engaged in evangelical and missionary work run the permanent risk of being prosecuted for 'obstructing state supervision of the church', which carries a maximum sentence of two years' imprisonment and, in the case of the clergy, the possibility of losing their licences to perform their pastoral duties. However, it would seem that this is not a sufficient deterrent to prevent fairly widespread evangelical work, particularly by the Franciscans. A number of Czech Brethren ministers have also run into difficulties with the authorities because of their zealous evangelism.

Broadcasting

There is no broadcasting of a directly religious nature within Czechoslovakia. The activities of the Christian Peace Conference may occasionally be reported and, quite exceptionally, a report of the Velehrad pilgrimage of 7th July 1985 was shown on Czech television. However, this was broadcast at the same time as Austrian television, which can be picked up in many parts of Czechoslovakia, reported the pilgrimage, and it omitted scenes of the crowd interrupting the government official who addressed them. In the absence of a domestic religious broadcasting service, Christians in Czechoslovakia rely on Vatican Radio and Trans World Radio for religious information, as well as the BBC and the Voice of America, which also regularly broadcast religious news.

Literature

There are three broad categories of religious literature in Czechoslovakia: literature published inside the country with official permission; *samizdat*, which is produced secretly and which is, of course, completely uncensored; and literature brought in secretly from abroad.

The Roman Catholic Church is the most severely restricted in what it may publish. It has few regular publications: a slender yearbook; *Duchovní pastýř* ('The Spiritual Pastor'), a journal for priests; and *Katolické noviny* ('Catholic News'), a paper for the laity. In addition, there is a monthly publication for the Uniates, *Slovo* ('The Word'). All these publications, with the exception of *Slovo*, are under the editorship of *Pacem in Terris* priests. Consequently, Cardinal Tomášek has in recent years withdrawn his imprimatur from them on the grounds that they serve as the mouthpiece of an organisation forbidden by the Vatican, and have no business describing themselves as 'Catholic'. In addition to these publications, the Czech Catholic publishing house *Charita* occasionally produces hymn booklets as well as the odd book dealing with uncontentious issues in church history.

The other Churches between them enjoy much wider scope for publishing. Each denomination has its own regular news publication and books of high academic quality regularly appear, dealing principally with biblical scholarship and exegesis ('safe' topics for study). Prayer-books and hymn books, some even designed specifically for children, are published in reasonable quantities.

Far more important than the officially approved religious publications, however, are the many clandestinely produced *samizdat* books and journals. The various *samizdat* publications cover a very wide range of subjects: literature, art, philosophy, politics, music and religion, to name but a few. As far as the religious publications are concerned, the Roman Catholic Church seems to have the best-structured *samizdat* network. Catholic *samizdat* began to have a significant impact in the mid-1970s and since then, has continued to grow in quality and quantity, despite the trial and imprisonment of six apparent ringleaders in 1979 and trials in 1985–6 of people allegedly involved in the printing and distribution of religious *samizdat*.

There are now at least nine Catholic *samizdat* journals circulating in Czechoslovakia, covering various aspects of the Catholic faith. One is a journal of catechetics, aimed specifically at children, which explains the various tenets of Roman Catholicism as well as serving as a family magazine. There are also several theological journals which attain a very high standard of scholarship. The most important Roman Catholic *samizdat* journal is, however, the monthly *Informace o Církvi* ('Church Information') first published in 1980, and which covers currrent news about the Catholic Church. It is principally through this journal that Catholics learn of arrests and imprisonments of their fellow-believers, and it is this periodical, rather than *Katolické noviny,* which supplies a conscientious record of the activities of Cardinal Tomášek. It also provides details of the teachings of the Pope, other theological writings, and features on moral issues; and each issue finishes with a survey of the church in various countries throughout the world.

Another important *samizdat* journal is the secular publication put out by the Czech human-rights movement Charter 77, *Informace o Chartě 77.* This is essentially a news bulletin about arrests and imprisonments, and since it first appeared in 1978 has come out up to 16 times a year. Because of very strong Christian participation in the movement, principally by Roman

Catholics and members of the Evangelical Church of the Czech Brethren, this journal inevitably carries news of their activities, insofar as these have led to conflict with the authorities. Furthermore, it records all Charter 77 documents; these deal principally with issues concerning human rights and so, naturally, persecution of religious believers is a recurrent theme.

Apart from the regular and occasional journals which appear, a large number of *samizdat* books by Christian authors are also published. These are concerned with many of the subjects covered by *samizdat* journals, but, of course, treat them at greater length. It is impossible to exaggerate the importance of *samizdat* to believers and to banned writers, both religious and secular. The writings which appear in *samizdat* provide the basis for something approaching normal, healthy academic debate between intellectuals whose views the authorities would prefer to supress.

The second source of uncensored religious literature is the material which is brought in secretly from abroad. Many émigré Czechs and Slovaks feel a strong obligation to help their co-nationals still living in Czechoslovakia, and succeed in finding funds to finance such operations on a fairly large scale. There are several Czech and Slovak publishing houses in the West, representing all shades of religious and political opinion, and a considerable number of their books find their way into Czechoslovakia. Some of them are by writers in Czechoslovakia who have succeeded in having manuscripts taken secretly out of the country; others are by Czech and Slovak émigrés or by other authors translated into Czech or Slovak.

It is dangerous to make firm predictions about future trends in the unofficial production and import of religious literature. The most helpful indication for the future is that even when people are arrested and imprisoned for such offences, the production and circulation of unofficial religious material does not seem to be significantly hampered. It seems that previously inactive Christians are prepared to step into the shoes of arrested religious activists, and this fact indicates the likelihood that such activity is not likely to decrease in the future.

Bible translation and distribution

The first translation of the Bible into the vernacular which appeared in what is now Czechoslovakia was completed by Sts Cyril and Methodius in the ninth century, and in the following centuries various partial and complete translations were published. The most important translation into Czech was the Kralice Bible, produced by the Unity of Brethren between 1579 and 1593. Revised editions of the Kralice Bible came out in 1596 and 1613, but the onset of the Counter-Reformation and the persecution of Protestants which ensued made it impossible for work to continue on revising the translation. The first major Protestant translation of the Bible into Czech since the Kralice Bible was the ecumenical Bible brought out in 1979 to mark the 400th anniversary of the Kralice edition. Since the Kralice Bible came out, there have also been various translations into Czech which have met with the approval of the Roman Catholic authorities. Translations have appeared both within Czechoslovakia and abroad. The Bible has also been translated into Slovak, again both at home and abroad. The Lutheran Church has been responsible for domestic translations and the Christian Academy in Rome has produced a Catholic translation.

Apart from these full translations, there is an illustrated Catholic children's edition of the Bible published and printed in Yugoslavia.

Despite the existence of good translations, it is, however, very hard to get hold of a Bible in Czechoslovakia. This is because of severe restrictions imposed by the authorities on the number of Bibles which may be printed or imported. The Protestants generally succeed in securing more copies than the Catholic Church, but everywhere demand invariably exceeds supply. The number of Bibles legally in circulation is supplemented by Bibles brought into the country secretly, either by individuals acting on their own initiative or by those working for Bible agencies.

Education

Religious education for the children of Catholics is legally available in schools in Czechoslovakia, but is not an easy option. The Protestant Churches are permitted to run their own Sunday schools. If parents decide to register their children for religious education classes, those children will have great difficulty in getting into university or finding jobs suited to their abilities. This fact goes some way towards explaining the apparently catastrophic decline in attendance at religious education classes over the last 18 years: at the height of the period of religious freedom in 1968, as many as two-thirds of the country's children enrolled for classes throughout Czechoslovakia, whereas by 1984 the number had dropped to as low as 0.9% in some of the most heavily secularised areas.

The authorities go to great lengths to prevent children from enrolling in religious education classes. In order to enrol a child must present a form signed by both his parents, stating their desire that their child attend them. At the beginning of every academic year, reports reach the West of the problems caused by this procedure. If priests remind their parishioners to enrol their children, they are accused of 'interfering with family life'. On other occasions, pupils have not been allowed to enrol because their parents have been Party members who nevertheless wish their children to receive religious instruction. An incentive to teachers to lower the number of pupils receiving religious instruction is a bonus of 200 crowns per pupil persuaded not to attend those classes (teachers receive approximately 3000 crowns salary per month).

With all these constraints on legal religious education in school, it is inevitable that many children receive their religious education illegally elsewhere. Much religious instruction is given directly by parents, and priests will often give classes in private. To help with religious education there is the children's *samizdat* publication *Vzkříšení* ('Resurrection').

The situation is far from satisfactory then; but it would

appear that despite difficulties and powerful disincentives, parents do succeed to a remarkable degree in passing on their faith to their children.

Social concerns

The religious orders in Czechoslovakia have a long history of involvement in social concerns. The thirteenth-century princess Blessed Agnes of Bohemia, for example, was the foundress of a religious nursing order. Despite a virtual ban on the religious orders in 1950, nuns have continued to work in social care institutions. Many such institutions are only kept going by the tireless work of nuns. However, without novices to assist them, it seems unlikely that the few remaining nuns will be able to continue this service.

On a less formal level, conscientious priests have on many occasions involved themselves in helping the disadvantaged and needy—for example, gypsies (who are treated as second-class citizens in Czechoslovakia), alcoholics and drug addicts. The state authorities, however, discourage this kind of activity, often by depriving such priests of their licences.

In 1958 the Christian Peace Conference was founded in Czechoslovakia by the Protestant theologian Josef Hromadká to promote discussions on peace between Christians from East and West. For a decade it was indeed genuinely a forum for creative encounter, and much of value was achieved; but after 1968 it has served principally as the mouthpiece for a pro-Soviet political line. Nowadays, priests in Czechoslovakia are encouraged to join the priests' association *Pacem in Terris* and to come out actively in support of Soviet peace propaganda. Thus, as in the Soviet Union, 'peace' work is the only field of social activity in which clergy receive any encouragement from the government to become involved.

Ecumenical activity

There is a great deal of ecumenical activity in Czechoslovakia, involving all the main Churches with the exception of the Roman Catholic Church. Ecumenism has a comparatively long history in what is now Czechoslovakia: in 1905, the 'Union of Constance' was established as a forum for co-operation between the Protestant Churches. In 1969, this organisation changed its name to 'Christian Unity'. All the main Churches apart from the Roman Catholic Church also belong to the 'Ecumenical Council of Churches in Czechoslovakia', which is responsible for organising the annual week of prayer for Christian unity and various ecumenical conferences.

CHAPTER 5

The German Democratic Republic

THE GERMAN DEMOCRATIC REPUBLIC: OVERVIEW

The country; the people; brief history

Of all the countries of Europe, the German Democratic Republic is the most difficult to categorise. There are no German natural frontiers. A single unified German nation did not come into being until 1871, and was relatively short-lived: not a few German citizens who experienced the dismemberment of their country in 1945 were old enough to remember the proclamation of Union 74 years before. The present frontier between the Germanies was agreed by the Allies early in 1945 as the provisional boundary between the Soviet and the British and American forces' zones of occupation. The eastern frontier of the GDR, adjoining Poland, was determined when the shape of post-war Poland was under discussion. The northern and southern boundaries of the GDR, following the Baltic coast on the one hand and the watershed in the south, are not at all controversial.

The GDR came into being in 1949, when the occupying Soviet forces handed over their powers to the newly proclaimed Republic. The GDR's official attitude to frontiers and to nationhood has developed over the years, and will no doubt develop further. At first, there was a tendency to think of the GDR as part of the larger German nation, in that the reunion of the two halves of Germany was not unthinkable; but since the building of the Berlin Wall in 1961, prospects of reunion have faded and the existence and frontiers of the GDR have come to be regarded as fixed and irreversible. Presentation of German history by the spokesmen of the GDR varies according to the socio-economic needs of the moment. In the mid-1980s it became normal to present the GDR as the incorporation of all that is noble and forward-looking in the German tradition. Various historical characters—for example, Luther,

Frederick the Great, Stein, Clausewitz, Bismarck and Wagner —have been re-evaluated and shown to be at least partially progressive. At the same time the Federal Republic is often depicted as reactionary, the haven of war criminals and unrepentant Nazis, a showcase of developed capitalism moving inexorably to its doom.

The population of the GDR is almost exclusively German. The only noteworthy exception is the Sorbish (Wendish) people living in the south-east part of the state around Bautzen. Much stress is laid on the fact that they are allowed to use their own language and practise their national customs.

The economy; social conditions; political life

The economy is, all things considered, a strong one—by far the most advanced of the East European economies. Advanced technology is used to a considerable extent. The average standard of living is comparable with that of several West European countries. The average wage-earner is helped by the state's policy of charging low rents and subsidising the price of fares and basic food-stuffs; on the other hand, he faces constant problems in securing all kinds of everyday requirements, such as household articles, spare parts for cars, materials for home decoration and repairs and so on.

The economic strength of the GDR is to some extent artificial, however, relying to a significant extent on imports from the West. The Federal Republic has recently provided credits on a very generous scale; tourism and gifts (for example, via the churches) help; but trade with the West remained in deficit for a number of years. No doubt the régime would like to scale down the present level of defence expenditure, but at present such an idea is out of the question.

The official description of the situation in the GDR is that of 'real, existing Socialism'. The vast majority of the industrial workforce is employed in 'nationally owned enterprises' (*Volkseigene Betriebe*); nearly all farms are collectively owned and operated. Over 80% of the younger working age group is skilled. Officially, at least, unemployment does not exist.

Formally, the government of the GDR is an 'anti-fascist' political alliance known as the Democratic Bloc. The leading party is the Socialist Unity Party (SED), a fusion of the Communist and the Social Democratic Parties achieved in the then Soviet Zone of Occupation in April 1946. In practice, the government is entirely in the hands of the Central Committee of the SED.

Citizens of the GDR are generally well-informed. They are the only citizens of an Eastern European socialist state who have regular access to Western television in their own language; such viewing is not punished, cannot be prevented, and is almost universally practised, even by Party members. Freedom of thought and speech exist to a certain degree, within certain tacitly agreed limits. The security service exists to keep a watch on citizens, to dissuade them from going beyond those limits, and to punish those who do. Citizens practise certain standard ways of displaying 'commitment to Socialism': sending their children to the *Jugendweihe* or secular youth dedication ceremony, serving as combatants in the armed forces, taking occasional part in demonstrations, voting (preferably for the official list of candidates), using official phraseology in school, university, and professional and public circles.

All organisations other than the churches, officially speaking, owe some measure of allegiance to the Marxist-Leninist régime.

STATUS OF CHRISTIANITY

The religious complexion of the country

The German lands that later became the GDR were never part of the Roman Empire and did not come under the influence of Christianity in Roman times (unlike the territories south of the Rhine-Danube, including western and southern Germany).

For some time heretical traditions of Christianity, such as Arianism, held sway side by side with paganism. By the eleventh century, Germany east of the Elbe may be said to have been Christianised. After several centuries of Roman Catholicism the area which now comprises the GDR became the heartland of the Reformation under Luther.

The GDR contains very few members of non-Christian religions. The Jewish community is extremely small, and declining in numbers—fewer than 500 in 1986. There was no resident rabbi in the country until 1987. All the main cities are provided with synagogues, mostly rebuilt since 1949. These buildings are seen by the government as symbols of the country's claim to have eradicated anti-Semitism root-and-branch. Though Jewish religious life remains at a very low ebb, there are signs of change in official policies, which might lead to an increased number of synagogue services.

The majority of Christian believers are of the Protestant faith—mostly Lutherans belonging to the eight major provincial churches. The figure of 7.7 million Lutherans was quoted in a semi-official publication for foreign consumption in 1983; but the Secretary of State for Religious Affairs, Klaus Gysi, speaking in Poland recently, suggested that the real figure is about 3 or 4 million. There are, in fact, no reliable figures, and even GDR Protestant Church leaders stress the futility of trying to arrive at accurate statistics. The number of practising believers has certainly declined steeply during the life of the GDR, and is possibly continuing to decline. Even the figure quoted by Gysi is almost certainly too high.

The strength of the Roman Catholic Church is easier to quantify. The figure quoted officially early in the life of the GDR was 1.3 million; in 1987 Roman Catholic sources gave a revised estimate of just over a million. Though there are Roman Catholic communities spread throughout the country, their main strength is in the south, near Erfurt and Dresden.

Some half a million citizens belong to the various Free Churches and other independent Christian communities: prominent among these are the Methodists and the New Apostolic Church, the Baptists, and there are also Seventh-day Adventists, Mormons and members of the Orthodox Church.

The only formally proscribed community are the Jehovah's Witnesses; but it is only fair to say that little police action is taken against the activities of this group at the moment, unless they refuse military service.

Several factors militate against the spread of religious faith. Firstly, there is the general thrust of education which, although rarely attacking Christian doctrines or belief in God head-on, presents religious believers as fish out of water as far as a modern scientific society is concerned. More specifically, the religious believer is almost certainly debarred from the major professions (the civil service, the law, the police, commissioned ranks of the armed services, and positions of responsibility in the teaching profession). A third factor is one which affects the West as well as the more industrialised Eastern European countries—the anonymity, rootlessness and materialism associated with life in big cities which make all kinds of mission effort difficult.

Over and against these considerations are factors which tend to encourage the growth of interest in religion. Firstly, there is widespread disillusionment with Marxism-Leninism as a living philosophy. Secondly, the major Churches have considerable spiritual strength. The Protestant Church maintains its spiritual integrity. Refusing to deny what it sees as its God-given responsibility for the people as a whole, believers and non-believers alike, it insists on proclaiming the truth of the gospel in response to social and political developments. Meanwhile, the Roman Catholic Church has traditionally remained apart from any involvement with the state apparatus and stresses its spiritual independence. The law gives the Churches the chance to preach to the unconverted, which they often make use of.

The state's attitude to religion

It may fairly be assumed that the basic aims of Party and government in the GDR are fundamentally the same as those of most Marxist régimes elsewhere: while recognising that religion will in fact continue to exist in the foreseeable future, they try to limit as far as possible the churches' practical influence, and to confine their activities within the 'spiritual' sphere; but at the same time, where feasible, to harness the churches' energies in 'useful' causes, thus blurring the distinction between the church and the world, and enlisting institutional religion as an agent of socialism.

Both aims have been pursued since the war. Legislation in 1945 established a rigorous distinction between church and state, and took education out of the hands of the former. At the same time, the government exploited the left-wing 're-volutionary' potential it discerned in the churches, cultivating the Christian Democratic Union (CDU), especially after 1949, as a means of rallying the social and political forces within the churches behind the SED. The CDU continues to operate as a political party for Christians, but it enjoys very little support or popularity among believers.

The division between church and state is no mere empty theory: the churches have always refused to be dominated by the state. There have been important meetings in 1978, 1985 and 1988 between leaders of the Protestant Church and the state, with the aim of setting up a framework for a co-operative relationship. At the same time, it is a constant aim of the government's propaganda to present church-state relations as much warmer than they in fact are. Statements by church leaders reported in the official press are almost invariably abbreviated to show the speaker as being in agreement with state policies.

THE VARIOUS CHURCHES

The Federation of Protestant Churches

History
From the sixteenth century the states of eastern Germany had what may be described as an 'established church'. Protestan-

tism was part of the structure of the state; 'Throne and Altar' was the watchword. From the end of the eighteenth century, when universal compulsory education was introduced, confirmation tended to become a *Volkssitte*, a national custom, which was, as a rule, carried out at the end of the period of compulsory schooling. A specifically religious tax, quite separate from the other elements of taxation, was deducted by the state and handed over to the Church authorities. A grandiose cathedral was built close to the Imperial Palace, symbolising the complementary nature of church and state.

The new constitution of the Weimar Republic (1918–33) ended the long-standing alliance between the state and the Protestant Church. New laws decreed the separation of the state from religion. After the advent of Nazism the policies of Hitler caused dissension within the Churches. In 1934 the Nazi régime entered into an agreement or 'Concordat' with the Roman Catholic Church, supposedly guaranteeing the integrity of the Church in return for its undertaking not to interfere in political life. Hitler attempted to subvert and dominate the Protestant Church; his principal agent in this attempt was the new 'National Bishop' Müller, a man who saw the Nazi movement as the guardian and purifier of the Lutheran Church, and who tried to rally Christian believers in the service of the Führer. Some believers saw, or professed to see, the new movement as the salvation of their country; many millions more tried to keep religion out of politics. There was also a sizeable minority which tried to hold fast to the gospel in the face of modern idolatry: they were known as members of the 'Confessing Church' ('*Bekennende Kirche*' or 'BK'). It should be stressed that the BK was a movement, not a new denomination. Their number fluctuated, but thousands remained true to the BK's ideals, and held the membership card right until 1945. Thousands were imprisoned, and there were many martyrs. As it became clear that the Concordat with the Vatican was not working, the Protestant resisters were joined by Roman Catholic confessors and martyrs. Thus it came about that believers of both denominations found themselves side by side with communists in prisons and concentration camps.

When the war ended, the leading German Christians were

dismissed from their high offices—some, indeed, found themselves under arrest. Members of the BK, many of them emerging from obscure country parishes or military service or indeed from imprisonment, found themselves in the vacant positions. It was a situation which well suited the occupying Soviet authorities, whose avowed policy was to 'denazify' their zone. They dismissed all Nazi Party members and sympathisers from the major professions, notably the law, the civil service, local government and teaching, and appointed bourgeois non-communists to those posts with a high formal position, while appointing communists to positions of less prestige but more power. As early as 26th June 1945, the CDU began life in the Soviet Zone of Occupation in response to permission for the founding of 'anti-fascist' parties; the CDU's manifesto appeared only a few days after those of the Communist and Social Democratic Parties.

In the circumstances, it is not surprising that the Soviet authorities and their German colleagues looked on the Christians as potential allies, with a reservoir of anti-fascist energies which might be harnessed in the struggle to gain willing support for the Socialist cause. When on 30th–31st October 1945 orders were issued for the confiscation of vast amounts of property belonging to industries and other large enterprises, the Churches were exempted, as they were when far-reaching land reforms were introduced later in the year. The Churches were, therefore, left as large-scale property owners, owning and running hospitals, orphanages, welfare homes, children's homes, hospices and the like. The subventions made regularly to the Churches before 1945 were considerably reduced, but not abolished. When the new GDR constitution came into force in 1949, redefining the separation of church and state, the Churches had the very considerable asset of a legal and economic power base. Moreover, from the beginning the GDR state authorities refrained from interfering to any noteworthy extent in the internal affairs of the Church. It is impossible to establish how far this non-interference reflected a definite decision by the authorities; but it is easy to see why they might have reached such a decision. Thousands of examples of resistance by believers to Nazism would have made the new rulers wary of antagonising the Churches. It would also have been clear that there were some Church members with left-wing political views who would be likely to support a humanitarian socialist system. Another factor to be borne in mind would have been the close institutional and personal links between the Churches in the eastern and western German zones, and the probable adverse reaction of the latter to overt anti-church measures.

The Church members had a wide range of attitudes to the new régime. There were those who had no great love for it, but thought it an improvement on the Third Reich; there were enthusiastic left-wingers who worked energetically through the CDU (like Gerald Götting, who later rose to be President of the People's Chamber); there were not a few who thought that the only significant difference between the old and the new rulers was that the former wore brown shirts and the latter red. And then there were, of course, the pragmatists who believed that, whatever their personal feelings, some kind of modus vivendi between the church and the government must be worked out.

As time went on, it became necessary for the Protestant leaders to define the Church's attitude to the new régime. The attitude of the BK towards the secular authorities had been appropriate for the Nazi period (1933–45), when the most basic features of the ruling ideology were seen to be incompatible with Christianity. In 1945 the church in Eastern Germany came under the sway of Marxist-Leninists, whose theorists had always declared that religion must die. To such a régime the Christian church could not give its blessing. In practice, however, the Soviet occupation forces were surprisingly tolerant towards religion. And Soviet power had, of course, destroyed the old tyranny.

What of the practical aims of the new society? Much was said about brotherhood, justice, equality, peace and so on. If these were in fact true descriptions of the practical policies of the régime, then the Church could indeed give its blessing to any measures or laws which were calculated to advance such aims. But constant vigilance was called for. The Church was not a political party or pressure group, and could not become an integral part of a society which set out to eliminate religion. The Church decided that it must represent the interests of believers in an atheist society, must be at all times ready to make its voice heard in defence of the gospel, and to criticise the temporal power if its actions or policies conflicted with some vital aspect of the teaching of Christ.

The Church's progress towards this policy was neither quick nor easy. In the 1950s and 1960s there were various conflicts among Church leaders who stood for widely differing attitudes vis-à-vis the state. Only during the 1970s, under the leadership of Bishop Schönherr, did there emerge anything like a consensus, summarised by the terms 'the Church in Socialism' and 'critical solidarity'. The tactics employed by both state and Church in this uneasy relationship have, of course, changed over the years. Leaders of both sides have become a good deal more adroit and sophisticated in their handling of problems. The state has responded to the situation by being a good deal less crass in its propounding of atheism, and the official view is that there is an excellent working relationship despite occasional problems. State newspapers and radio programmes carry only very carefully doctored versions of Church views, principally sentences (sometimes taken out of context) which profess to give full support to government policies. Criticisms made by synods and on other Church occasions meet with little publicity. Specific criticisms, or requests for discussions on controversial matters, are often met with silence, or at best with the offer of a meeting with an official from the Secretariat of State for Church Affairs. It is thus possible for the official media to maintain the fiction that the Church is almost invariably in favour of the government's policies.

It would nonetheless be untrue to suggest that the Protestant Church has abandoned its prophetic stance in exchange for privileges and a quiet life. Two aspects of the Protestant Church's understanding of itself as the 'Church in Socialism' have brought it a great deal of publicity. Firstly, there is its claim to speak fearlessly for the gospel as and when that gospel impinges directly on the life of the nation; and secondly, its claim to bear God-given responsibility not merely for believers, but for the nation as a whole.

Questions concerning peace and war have constantly led to controversy between Church and state. For the Marxist-Leninist, the challenge is clear: 'Socialist' countries, merely by being what they are, are striving for peace against the forces of 'imperialism', whose very nature drives them to plan aggresive war. Thus the 'Socialist' camp must always be fully armed and fully alert. Such an attitude, though based on Marxist-Leninist ideology, is held by the GDR authorities to be self-evident, and therefore to be supported by all citizens of goodwill— including religious believers. On the other hand, the Christian cannot possibly recognise the doctrines of an atheist creed as the proper basis for analysing the nature of peace and the causes of war; here the gospel is paramount.

The Protestant Church has never followed a fully pacifist stand-point, but has always interceded for those whose consciences have not allowed them to respond to the Republic's call to arms. Thus, in 1962, the Church spoke in defence of those young men who, on conscientious grounds, refused to obey the new law on conscription. It was no doubt mainly due to the influence of the Church that a new regulation came into force two years later, setting up unarmed units ('construction battalions') for conscientious objectors. Since then, the Church has interceded for those who object even to unarmed military service, and, since the 1970s, has repeatedly called for 'peace service' (a special clause allowing conscientious objectors to opt for a period of social service in place of service in the army). During the last ten years there have been organised schemes of peace education in parishes, and every November programmes called 'ten days for peace' have been held by congregations throughout the GDR. The Church's witness for peace has always remained strikingly independent of the Party line. Moreover, there is no doubt that the Church has in this way given expression to the views of younger people who do not claim to be Church members, or even believers. Since 1983, the Church's witness for peace has been modified somewhat. The feeling then grew that the stationing of medium-range rockets on German soil had brought the international situation to a new stage, and induced a new sense of powerlessness and fatalism. In 1987, however, the withdrawal of such weapons

convinced many Protestants that their stand had been vindi-
cated. Nowadays, there is much emphasis on the defence of the
environment as being an immediate task, about which the ordinary churchman and citizen can do something practical. Other
problems often raised by Protestants concern aspects of personal freedom, such as restrictions on the freedom to travel
abroad and on the freedom to criticise, as well as the continued
denial of equal rights to Christian citizens, despite what is
stated by official spokesmen.

The relationship between the state and the Protestant
Church rarely develops steadily or smoothly. A period of
détente is often followed by one of storm and stress. The
period of 12 months from the spring of 1987 to the spring of
1988 gave a very clear example of this change of atmosphere.
The final preparations for the Berlin Protestant Kirchentag and
for the Dresden Catholic assembly, both held during the summer of 1987, signalled an unusual degree of harmony in
relationships with the state. These events took place in a
remarkable atmosphere of freedom. In September, Church-
based peace groups took part in the 'Olof Palme' peace
marches, carrying their own banners—something unpre-
cedented in GDR history. In November, however, Church premises in East Berlin were raided and searched by security personnel; no such direct action had been taken against the
Church since the 1950s. Later many arrests took place of members of Church-based independent groups, some of whom were
sentenced and packed off to the West. There was an atmosphere of tension and suspicion when Bishop Leich, the Chairman of the Federation of Protestant Churches, met Erich Honecker in March 1988—10 years after the Schönherr-Honecker
meeting on 6th March 1978. All that can be reliably predicted
is that the future course of Church-state relationships is
unlikely to be smooth.

Church structure and membership
To describe the Protestant population of the GDR as essentially Lutheran is a commonplace, but is only partly true. That
part of the established church of the German Empire which is
now in the GDR is made up of eight provincial *Landeskirchen*,

of which only three could be described as Lutheran. The other five Churches are on the territory of the 'Prussian Union' and although predominantly Lutheran, were considerably influenced by the Reformed Church.

Broadly speaking, the Church boundaries follow pre-war lines. In 1945 the Churches, of course, found themselves deprived of their eastern territories; in the West, more than one of the *Landeskirchen* found some of their adherents assigned to the British or American zones. For nearly twenty-five years the eight provincial Churches maintained their membership of the *Evangelische Kirche in Deutschland,* thus giving outward expression to the notion of an all-German Protestant Church. There were, of course, constant difficulties in administration. In 1969 the decision was taken to make the East German Protestant Church administratively independent of that of the Federal Republic, and a union of the East German Churches, the 'Federation of Evangelical Churches in the GDR' was formed. It was and remains, however, a Federation, as later efforts to achieve a closer union have come to nothing.

Any attempt to quote total figures for the membership of the eight regional Churches, as has already been pointed out, is foredoomed to failure. It is true that the total number of those attending churches and taking an active part in parish life is only a small fraction of the nominal membership, but a degree of 'residual faith', though it cannot be measured, does exist. There is more than a grain of truth in the comment often made by Party leaders in their more candid moments that the Party and the Churches command between them less than 10% of the population, and that these two rivals are actively competing for the allegiance of the great majority.

There are some 7,200 parishes, the majority of which have incumbents. Candidates for the ministry are trained both in theological faculties at state universities and in Church training institutions. Those at present under training should be numerous enough to fill most of the parish vacancies; nor is there any shortage of candidates at the moment: in 1984, for example, one Church seminary had to turn away over 40% of those who applied, after an exhaustive selection process. An increasing number of young men (and women) come forward who have already had some years of experience in other jobs and professions. For some time the ministry has been open to women, and there are many parishes with female ministers. There are a number of specialist ministries: chaplains with special responsibility for work among young people; those in charge of church music; those charged with legal or financial tasks; hospital chaplains; and even a small number of prison chaplains (there are legal provisions for spiritual care in penal institutions).

Current growth trends

Such figures as are available make it clear that the total number of baptisms and confirmations, which declined steeply during the first two decades of the GDR, still continue to decline—though nothing like as sharply as in the 1950s. In the regional (Evangelical-Lutheran) Church of Mecklenburg, for example, the total number of baptisms in 1950 was 20,264 and of confirmations 11,583; in 1970, 4,656 and 6,401 respectively; in 1982 2,393 and 2,327. These figures, however, take no account of the quality of the new members of the Church. One may quote, for example, the experience of a fourteen-year-old boy in one of the northern towns of the GDR. He not only became a candidate for confirmation (the only one in his class at school), but invited the whole class to the ceremony. Moreover, two-thirds of them actually came. It is impossible to measure the impact of this Christian witness on a group of young people who knew almost nothing of Christian doctrine. Every year there are a few hundred adult baptisms—not a large number, but a significant one. Great efforts are made to see that religious education is attractive and effective, and it is well-known that half the members of many classes are unbaptised children, with little in the way of church background. It may well be that among the young—those under twenty-one—the influence of the Christian faith is slowly but steadily increasing.

The Roman Catholic Church

History

The events of the Reformation meant that Germany east of the Elbe was largely lost to Rome. By the time of Hitler, Catholics were vastly outnumbered by Protestants in this area. The movements of refugees in 1945 meant that large numbers of Germans from the eastern territories (which became part of Poland) came to settle west of the river Oder, and in this way the Catholic population of the Soviet Zone of Occupation came to exceed 1 million. The Sorbs (living around the district of Bautzen and Cottbus) remain predominantly Catholic.

A noteworthy feature of Roman Catholicism in the GDR is the Church's feeling of being beleaguered, a church of the 'diaspora'. Catholics constitute a diaspora in two senses of the word: as Christians in an atheist society, but also as a small island of Catholic Christians in a lake of Protestantism. A defensive mentality is thus common. The Church has devoted a considerable proportion of its energy to maintaining its own identity, rather than to increasing its effective witness within society. The Church leaders, for their part have tended to be wary of what they consider the dangers of professing to be a 'Church in Socialism'. They have done their best to maintain a sharp distinction between the church and the world, and to insist that the Catholic faith is totally foreign to Marxism. On the other hand, they are often applauded by the state authorities for not involving themselves in state affairs. At the same time, processions, acts of witness in the open air and family loyalties have all served to 'preach the gospel' in a very telling way.

Another factor which for many years caused dissension between the state and the Roman Catholic Church is the fact that ecclesiastical boundaries do not coincide with the political frontier: the civil authorities have not, therefore, been able to deal with the 'Roman Catholic Church in the GDR'. The Church's decision to set up 'episcopal districts' has gone some way towards meeting the state's demand for an alteration in this situation.

The vigour of the Catholic Church in defending aspects of the Christian faith in the face of state laws or policies cannot be denied. The so-called 'Döpfner Decree', issued by the Bishop of Berlin on 20th November 1957, insisted that all authoritative pronouncements about current problems affecting the country could come only from the whole body of bishops. The local bishop, of course, might pronounce on matters affecting his own diocese, but individual clergy were forbidden to make statements on their own responsibility which might be taken to represent the view of the Catholic Church. Within the context of this decree there have been several declarations and pastoral letters which have represented firm attitudes on controversial affairs. Examples are: the strong stand taken by the Catholic Church on the legalising of abortion (3rd January 1972); the pastoral letter read on 17th November 1974, challenging the monopoly of education which requires the teaching of 'socialist' and 'scientific' values in all schools; the declarations made in 1954 and subsequently which have made it clear that the *'Jungendweihe'* cannot be undertaken by Catholic believers; and more recently, the pastoral letter of January 1983 which clarified the Church's attitude to militarism and peace. It is clear, then, that although the aim of the Catholic Church has traditionally been to insulate itself from the contamination of Marxism, it has also to some degree, at least, tried to influence the legislation of the society in which it exists. The principles of 'the Church in Socialism' do indeed have some application to the Catholic Church in the GDR.

Church structure and membership; current growth trends
There are two mainly Catholic areas in the GDR: in the neighbourhood of Erfurt, and in the south-eastern corner of the country, around Cottbus and Bautzen in Lausitz (Lusatia).

In accordance with Catholic Church policy of avoiding concessions to the state, while insisting on the integrity of the Church, diocesan boundaries have not been redrawn to coincide with the frontiers of the GDR.

The governing body of the Church is the Berlin Bishops'

Conference, presided over by Cardinal Meisner. The only seats of bishops in the GDR are Berlin and Dresden-Meissen. The latter has lost a few parishes to Poland, and the former a sizeable area. The Apostolic Administration of Görlitz covers a small area of the Breslau diocese. In the western part of the GDR three Episcopal Districts (Mecklenburg, Magdeburg and Erfurt-Meiningen) cover parts of dioceses whose bishops have their seats in the Federal Republic. The diocese of Berlin includes the whole of West Berlin. There are monastic communities in some 300 priories and other institutions. A number of different orders are represented. There· are over 1,000 parishes or pastoral communities, served by about 1,300 priests.

The estimate of about one million Roman Catholics is a fairly realistic one. Although the Church has been slowly declining in numbers, considerable efforts are made at parish and family level to ensure that religious belief remains alive and that young people do not fall away from the faith. Though there are no very clear signs of growth, the fact that some Protestant leaders are worried about proselytising activity argues that some converts are being made.

Other mainstream Christian groups

Besides the eight evangelical provincial Churches and the Roman Catholic Church, there are a number of smaller religious communities. Notably enough, the third largest religious body is the New Apostolic Church, with at least 100,000 adherents. This community, although avoiding publicity as far as possible, is strongly entrenched in the GDR and continues to grow in numbers, if slowly. It is well led and organised; relations with the state are generally good. Evangelical Lutherans ('Old Lutherans', who claim that the main provincial bodies have strayed from the basic principles of the reformer) have about 11,000 members; the Old Catholic Church (not in communion with Rome) numbers over 1,000 members. In the southern part of the country the Evangelical Methodist Church

has some 20,000 members. There are a small number of Orthodox believers, Baptists, Seventh-day Adventists, Free Evangelical and Evangelical Reformed congregations, Moravians and
Mennonites.

Quasi-Christian groups

It is claimed by the East German authorities that small religious communities defined as 'sects' are not discriminated
against. There is some substance in this assertion. The Mormons (Church of Jesus Christ of Latter-day Saints) have various congregations and a purpose-built temple.

The Jehovah's Witnesses are the only group of this kind
which is technically illegal. In 1933 there were about 25,000 of
them in the whole of Germany; of these nearly 2,000 were executed or died in camps or prisons by 1945. After May 1945 they
were fêted as 'anti-fascists': the Soviet authorities put nothing
in the way of their preaching activities. In August 1950, however, by which time over 21,000 Witnesses were active in the
GDR, the movement was proscribed on grounds of espionage,
unconstitutional activities, stirring up hatred against socialism,
sabotage and so on. In five years there were about 2,800
arrests, and 468 Witnesses were still in solitary confinement in
1960; 33 had died under arrest. Underground activity continued. Since that time, although the Witnesses are still technically illegal, active persecution has all but ceased. Door-to-
door work goes on; the names of only the most openly zealous
are noted by the police. If there are arrests, they take place
because of refusal to do military service. A significant development since 1950 has been the emergence of a group called
'Christian Responsibility' (*Studiengruppe Christliche Ver-
antwortung*) with a journal of the same name. It was formed
about 1959 by ex-Witnesses. The avowed aim of the group is to
give instruction about the true nature of the Watch Tower Society to disillusioned Witnesses or support to those who wish to
leave the movement. 'CR' has the tacit approval of the state,
and gains legal supplies of paper for its journal.

CHRISTIAN ACTIVITIES

Evangelism and mission

Evangelism—the winning of the uncommitted to Christ—has a number of different aspects in East Germany. Not surprisingly, the main target of almost all evangelical efforts is the younger generation. Members of the older generations, the grandparents and indeed the great-grandparents, were born before the Second World War—some indeed before the First World War. Most of them are at least formal members of the Churches; at the same time the great majority of them have learned to accommodate themselves to the new régime. The younger generation, those born since the mid-1960s, have experienced only a régime which has gained immense experience in shepherding the vast majority along the paths of conformity and isolating the minority of nonconformists. There are, of course, members of this age group who have made a conscious decision to become church members, but most of them know nothing of church life, prayer or Bible reading. At the same time, a widespread desire among the younger generation is to escape from compulsory conformity and to avoid the formal 'statements of belief' which are inevitably associated with schools, universities and professional life. Special events organised by the Churches attract young people by dint of their atmosphere of freedom; but these same young people are on the whole extremely reluctant to become members of the Churches, as such a step would mean being tied down to a range of credal statements which might turn out to be almost as demanding as the compulsory beliefs required by the Party. A current joke runs: 'Can you be a Communist *and* a Christian?' 'In principle, of course—but why make life twice as difficult?'

In these circumstances, the evangelist has to work extremely hard to find fertile ground. Some extremely effective forms of evangelical witness make no headlines in the church press. Young conscripts who opt for the unarmed construction units on grounds of conscience sometimes run informal prayer groups and Bible study sessions in their spare time, drawing in some of the disillusioned and uncommitted. Protestant clergy often complain about the vast size of the church buildings which they have to maintain, sometimes in quite small towns; however, even these places can evangelise. Large numbers of visitors come during the summer who know nothing of religion; these people can sometimes be successfully confronted with the claims of the gospel.

One distinctive method of bringing the message of the gospel to the notice of those outside the church as well as within it is the *Kirchentag* (an untranslatable word, inadequately rendered as 'church congress' or 'church conference'). A number have been held in the GDR since the war. The largest gathering of this kind was held at Leipzig in 1954, when (some time before the building of the Berlin Wall) about half a million people took part. During 1983, the year of the Luther Quincentenary, no less than seven separate *Kirchentage* were held in different parts of the GDR. A *Kirchentag* has no set programme. A typical pattern includes a number of elements. There are normally open-air as well as formal services, discussions in small groups, Bible study sessions, meditations, musical events, counselling, and special events for children. Even though in 1983 only small numbers could come from the West, at least two of the seven attracted over 100,000 visitors. *Kirchentage* continue to be held, and to influence the uncommitted— especially the younger generation.

The most difficult areas for evangelism are undoubtedly the suburban housing estates in the large cities like Berlin, Leipzig, Erfurt and Karl-Marx-Stadt. Lack of church buildings is a handicap, though a number of new churches and parish centres have been opened by the Catholics as well as the Protestants. The main method of spreading the Word remains the activity of small groups in individual flats, where the Bible can be read, hymns can be sung and prayers offered, and where the impact of the faith on life's many problems can be discussed. Nevertheless, the percentage of believers in the newer part of the cities remains very low—between 1% and 2% in some cases.

Evangelical rallies and assemblies certainly have their place in the GDR. Billy Graham made a much-publicised tour in 1982, with considerable impact. After a thirteen-year gap, visits from West German evangelists were resumed in 1979; Gerhard Bergmann and Wilfried Reuter conducted meetings in Görlitz. Several events have been held by GDR evangelical leaders. An outstanding evangelistic event is the annual Convention of the GDR Evangelical Alliance, held every year since the foundation of the GDR at Bad Blankenburg in Thuringia. As many as 5,000 people may come—most of them aged under 25. There is drama and brass band music, but the main fare is solid Bible teaching of a conservative kind. In 1985 there were nearly 6,000 present, most of them young people sleeping at a nearby camping site. Six hundred were there for the first time. The decade of the 1980s was designated as the GDR Missionary Decade by representatives of missionary societies and established Free Churches under the motto 'Life For All: Jesus'. It was felt that not enough efforts were being made to exploit available oportunities, and there is evidence that this call has been followed up.

The singer Gerhard Schöne is an evangelist of a very different kind. His attractive style of singing is enormously popular, and he is often welcomed at Protestant Church events. Young people flock in their thousands to Protestant churches to hear his recitals. He does not shout loudly for conversions; he says quite simply that he is a believer; his songs speak only obliquely of the Lord, but the message—if not always crystal clear—is at the same time disquieting and thought-provoking.

The Roman Catholic Church, as has already been said, is conscious of being a minority Church. It is, therefore, not surprising that it directs its efforts towards the strengthening of the faith of those already within the fold, rather than at the evangelisation of outsiders.

In the areas where the Roman Church is strong, however (in the Eichsfeld district in the far west, in the city of Erfurt, and in Lusatia among the Sorbs), processions and pilgrimages represent a powerful witness to the gospel and no doubt make an impression on the unbelieving public. Neuzelle and Rosenthal are two of the best-known places of pilgrimage in Lusatia.

Broadcasting

Religious broadcasting existed before the establishment of the GDR. As early as 1946 the Soviet Military Administration gave permission for religious programmes. Every Sunday between 7.30 and 8.20 am the Churches now have the opportunity to broadcast: the Roman Catholic Church once a week, the Free Churches once every three months, and otherwise the provincial Protestant Churches are responsible for the programmes. Ultimate responsibility has, however, always lain with the state broadcasting authority. There is no formal censorship of preaching, but the authorities have the chance to object to a particular preacher or a particular text.

It has always been difficult for the Churches to assess the needs and wishes of listeners. Nevertheless, the Churches are able to make a good use of their opportunities. They have built up a considerable body of listeners over the years, and letters are received after nearly all programmes, asking for transcripts of the sermons or for pastoral guidance in some particular problem. Broadcasting can, therefore, be said to have a pastoral function.

Naturally, there are fears on the part of the Churches that religious transmissions may be used to further the political aims of the state. Side by side with the regular religious programmes, there is a regular commentary on church-state affairs; this is wholly under the control of the state broadcasting authority.

Television coverage of religious topics has been regular since the 1978 meeting between Erich Honecker and Bishop Schönherr. (It should be pointed out that the Roman Catholic Church has not shown any interest in this opportunity.) At that time the Protestant Churches had no one experienced in this medium, but since 1979 they have gained quite a good understanding of the audience they are aiming to reach and the kind

of material which is appropriate to television. Regular programmes go out at Christmas, Epiphany, Easter, Pentecost, on
Reformation Day (31st October), and on the last Sunday in
August, when attention is focused on the Churches' social
ministry. On this August Sunday the problems of the blind, the
deaf and those with other handicaps are highlighted. Otherwise
there is a strong stress on informative programmes, meditations and portrayals of the church's life and work. There are, of
course, the inevitable difficulties. As no prior approval can be
given, live transmissions are the exception rather than the rule.
On occasions programmes have had to be cancelled at the last
moment, or last-minute changes made to satisfy the
authorities. On the whole, however, the Protestant Churches
regard this access to television as a positive gain.

Literature

Apart from the Bible Societies (mentioned in the next section)
there are three major religious publishing houses: the
Evangelischer Verlagsanstalt (Protestant) working in Berlin and
Leipzig; the *St Benno Verlag* (Roman Catholic) working in
Leipzig; and the *Union Verlag* in Berlin, belonging to the
Christian Democratic Union. The latter is not under the control of either of the Churches, but produces a number of religious titles. The fact that of the 6,109 titles issued in the GDR
during 1980, rather more than 5% could be classified as 'religious' is somewhat misleading; it should be made clear that of
the 1.5 thousand million copies of books produced that year,
only 5 million were 'religious', which is a third of 1%. There
are various factors limiting the output of the religious publishing houses. They do not have printers or bookbinders of their
own. However, the responsibility for the acceptance of manuscripts, the granting of licences, and the apportioning of paper
supplies falls in every case to officials of the Ministry of Culture. Such supervision is reflected in the range of titles: works
dealing with, for example, the philosophy or sociology of religion never appear, and teaching aids and children's books are

few in number. Nevertheless, a fair number of attractive and thoughtful books do appear, and have a ready sale. They are not normally obtainable in the state bookshops. Every major city has its pair of church bookshops—Catholic and Protestant—where the available range of religious books, provided that they have not already been sold out, is on view. The level of production of religious literature is without parallel in Eastern Europe, apart from Poland.

The Protestant Church also produces its own weekly news service, the *ENA* (*Evangelischer Nachrichtendienst*). Only some 600 (duplicated) copies of this service are produced; its distribution is not generally interfered with by the state authorities, though there has been at least one recent occasion when foreign subscribers have been prevented (presumably by GDR government decree) from receiving their copies. It is not available to the general public in the GDR. The Catholic Church does not operate a similar news service.

There are over thirty church magazines and journals of which the best known are *Die Kirche* (Protestant) and *St Hedwigsblatt* (Catholic). The Methodists, the Union of Evangelical Free Church congregations and the Seventh-day Adventists all have their own publications. The Sorbs have two church publications in their own language—one Catholic (*Katolski Posol*) and one Protestant (*Pomhaj Boh*). Church journals are only obtainable by post from the distributors; the sale of individual copies at kiosks is not permitted, though they are sometimes sold in church buildings. (The exceptions to this rule are the two periodicals published by the Christian Democratic Union [the political party which claims to represent the interests of Christians]: they write almost entirely in favour of government policies.) The Post Office, through whose agency periodicals are ordered, therefore controls the list of readers.

There is no pre-censorship of periodicals, but a necessary condition of publication reads as follows: 'This licence is granted on the condition that the nature of the material published is in accordance with the legal requirements of the GDR'. It thus falls to the lot of the editor of the periodical in question to use his judgement in order that the law—whatever it may be—shall be observed. Whereas in the 1950s and 1960s there were quite frequent examples of issues failing to win state approval and having to be pulped, such occasions have been rare in the 1980s. Possibly editors have become more circumspect; but even when the mark has been overstepped, government officials have proved unwilling to act as heavy-handed censors. Even with these various restrictions, church periodicals in the GDR contain a fair amount of readable material; some of it, indeed, is lively and stimulating. The *Mecklenburgische Kirchenzeitung* has gained a not undeserved reputation for bold and independent thinking. Even the Christian Democratic Union publications are sometimes worth reading.

The churches may legally produce duplicated or photocopied material without the need for censorship of any kind. It is assumed that such writings are intended for internal church use; hence the designation '*Nur für Dienstgebrauch*' ('For Official Use Only'). In this way, for example, the discussions of synods and other church governing bodies are publicised, including some plain speaking on some very sensitive subjects. Such comment is, generally speaking, prevented from reaching the general public.

There are some writings which cannot be legally circulated in any form. Conspicuous among these are appeals or open letters addressed by church people to government leaders, if such documents fail to gain the support of a recognised church authority, and call in question the Constitution of basic 'socialist' principles. An example of this type of document was a letter sent in January 1986 to the government of the GDR. It was signed by a number of people who had no formal links with the church, but also by the Protestant pastor Rainer Eppelmann and a few other Christians, and it called for an end to travel restrictions, an end to prosecutions under certain articles of the Criminal Code, the legalising of conscientious objection, an extension of the democratic process, and a more genuine freedom of speech and association. Protestant leaders may well have thought (rightly or wrongly) that these demands represented an unjustified church intrusion into the political arena. The state authorities no doubt believed that the demands went far beyond practical politics, and (knowing that if they were publicised, they would find a large degree of popular support) preferred to acknowledge the letter neither publicly nor privately. The fate of the letter shows that there is no legal possibility for churchmen to publicise an unwelcome message within the country.

Bible translation and distribution

The total number of Bible Societies working in the GDR is usually given as twelve. The chief organisations are: the *Evangelische Hauptbibelgesellschaft* in Berlin, the Altenburg Bible Society, the Saxony Bible Society and the Christian Service to the Blind. The remainder are smaller bodies, with no full-time personnel. The General Secretary of the GDR Bible Societies co-operates with the United Bible Society.

In recent years some 50,000 Bibles and New Testaments have been distributed annually in the GDR; the total over the first 30 years of the Republic is reckoned as about 3 million. The evidence is, then, of a regular supply of Bibles which goes a fair way towards meeting the demand.

The great majority of the Bibles have been reprints of the traditional Luther translation. Naturally, there have been demands for revisions and modern language versions. A careful revision of the Luther New Testament, undertaken jointly by the Protestant Church of the GDR, the Federal Republic and Austria was completed in 1984 after two years' work. An edition of the New Testament in the 'Good News' version was made available in 1975, and the 140,000 copies printed were soon sold. There continues to be a demand for this version. Various works have been produced by the church in the GDR in an effort to stress the Bible's relevance—for example, a selection of Bible passages published by the main Bible Society in 1959.

Bible congresses and other gatherings have played a considerable role in the church life of the GDR. There have been two congresses: one at Karl-Marx-Stadt in 1982 and another at Görlitz, on the Polish frontier, two years later. The 1982 congress entitled 'Time for the Bible', lasted four days. Two thousand people attended. The Görlitz congress was also well attended. The theme was 'Living with the Bible'. Besides Lutherans and members of the Reformed and Free Churches, Adventists and Roman Catholics were in attendance. Themes covered were 'The Bible in the Worship and Preaching of the Churches', 'Bible—Lifestyle—Peace', 'Translation of the Bible into our Present-day Setting', and 'The Bible and Man's Image'. It was stated that 52,000 copies of the revised Luther translation (New Testament) were to be had.

A regular Bible conference has been held for many years by the Evangelical Alliance at Bad Blankenburg in the Harz mountains.

Education

There is no teaching of religion in the schools of the GDR. Such teaching was abolished immediately after the war, in accordance with the principle that church and state should be totally separate. There was only muted opposition among church people to this new measure, as 'Christian' teaching had been so misapplied during the Nazi régime. The Churches were, however, allowed to organise their own religious education, and the earliest (1949) Constitution of the GDR, in fact, guaranteed their right to do this on school premises. During the 1950s, however, difficulties multiplied for the Churches. Catechists were denied access to school rolls; religious teaching might only take place long after school hours; head teachers began to claim that attendance at religious education classes was a sign of social unreliability.

Nowadays, it is unthinkable for religious teaching to take place on school premises. The only pupils to whom the church has ready access are children from the families of believers; otherwise catechists must search out likely candidates and make visits to issue invitations. These efforts at mission are by no means unsuccessful, as unbaptised children involved in Protestant religious education often make up a third—sometimes as much as half—of the total number in a class. The instruction usually begins at the age of seven, and carries on up to the age of twelve. Confirmation instruction begins normally at thirteen and takes two years. The favourite age for confirmation in the Protestant Church is fifteen. Confirmation instruction is not generally of a formal kind; it is almost always a gradual initiation into the life of the local Christian community. Part of the aim of the instruction is to equip the young person to live a Christian life in secular society. Christians of all ages in the GDR tend to regard themselves as pupils, constantly learning more about the problems of acting as followers of Christ in a Marxist environment. The result is seen in the common watchword for the Protestant Church: *Kirche als Lerngemeinschaft*— the church as a learning community. The learning programmes of all the Protestant Churches take for granted the twin foes of the gospel: on the one hand, the pervasive secularism, which seems to be the inevitable hallmark of a technically-minded consumer society, and on the other, the educational programmes of the Marxist régime, which either mute the message of the gospel or present all religions as harmful and obsolete superstitions. The churches have constant difficulty in commending the Christian faith systematically to interested outsiders; yet it is calculated (May 1986) that the youth work of the Protestant Churches reaches 4% of the country's young people—in the circumstances, no mean achievement.

Young members in the Protestant Churches are grouped together under the title '*Junge Gemeinde*' (literally, 'Young Congregation'). In the early years of the GDR the Protestant Church participated in helping to set up the 'Free German Youth', a country-wide organisation under the umbrella of the SED, but friction inevitably developed. In March 1951 the existence of specifically religious youth movements was made illegal, on the grounds that they were organisations in the service of imperialism. The title *Junge Gemeinde* is, therefore, preferred today, as it is—in theory at least—neither a society nor an organisation. Statistics and membership lists are not to be found.

Careful attention is paid by the Roman Catholic Church to the education of its younger members. Of particular significance are the 'Religious Children's Weeks' and the 'Happy

Hours given to the Lord God'. The latter are run jointly by pastoral assistants, catechists and mothers of families, and take place weekly. They are for children of pre-school age. The aim of these lessons is officially defined as follows: 'In play, in daily life, in artistic creation and in what he sees and hears the child shall absorb new things and make them his own; in this way he learns to see life's experiences through the eyes of faith'. The aim, therefore, is not to instil a body of knowledge, but to make a first step in Christian education. The 'Children's Weeks' are for those of school age. A working group associated with the Bishop's Office at Magdeburg puts forward proposals for activities: special children's afternoon programmes (ie after school), handicraft activities, children's services, catechetical work and so forth. Both the 'Children's Weeks' and the 'Happy Hours' have been specially commended at Rome. In the work with older children and students there is a special effort to make them feel part of the church as a community of people. Week-end meetings, spiritual exercises and pilgrimages play an important part in this educational work. Like the Protestants, the Catholics find that young people want to ask basic questions about the meaning of life. Many of the young people concerned are fully committed, but a proportion have by no means identified themselves with the church's teaching and discipline.

No account of the subject of education would be complete without some reference to the Youth Dedication ritual, the so-called '*Jugendweihe*'. This ceremony dates back to the nineteenth century, when many workers' children studied socialism and swore a solemn oath to be true to the cause of the workers. There was a reluctance to revive this custom during the earliest years of the GDR, as many Party leaders feared that it would prove divisive. It was brought in, however, in 1954, for the eighth class (14-year-olds) as part of the prevailing offensive against the Churches. The programme of instruction contained elements of atheism. Both the major Churches opposed the new move bitterly, declaring that the 'Youth Dedication' was incompatible with Christianity. The Catholic Church was in a much better position to resist, firstly because (lacking an 'established' tradition) it had far fewer merely nominal members than the Protestant Churches, and secondly because Catholic young people, unlike Protestants, were brought to confirmation ('*Firmung*') well before the age for Youth Dedication. By the early 1960s the vast majority of the 14-year-olds of the GDR were taking part in the Youth Dedication ceremony, and today the proportion stands at over 97%. The Catholic teaching on the incompatibility of confirmation and Youth Dedication remains unmodified. Most of the Protestant Churches try to avoid a merely negative stand; they acknowledge that most nominally Protestant young people will go through the ritual, but make it clear that this does not mean that they cannot continue to be Church members.

At present the policy of the state is to try to prevent the Youth Dedication (which remains voluntary) becoming a source of division. The atheist element has almost disappeared; true, the young people swear to be true socialists, to be friends of the Soviet Union, and to devote themselves to peace and progress, but there is no oath to deny God. It is alleged that the young people themselves help to shape the syllabus; the Youth Dedication is presented as a gigantic national effort involving parents, sponsors, old Party fighters, teachers— indeed more or less the whole nation in action. Those who refuse to take part in it, therefore, automatically appear to be wilfully rejecting society.

Social concerns

The massive involvement of the GDR Churches in social service, running hospitals, old people's homes and the like, is not paralleled in any other East European country. The reasons for this involvement need careful examination. What is to be said applies to both the Protestant and the Catholic Churches, so it will not on the whole be necessary to distinguish between the work of the two major denominations.

Social service (now known as '*Diakonie*' in the Protestant Church and '*Caritas*' in the Roman Catholic) has a long history in Germany. Although attempts were made by the Nazi authorities to commandeer Church institutions in this field, such efforts were not generally successful and in 1945 a whole range of such places remained in the possession of the Churches. Such was the need among refugees, orphans, bombed-out families and the rest that the compassionate labours of the Churches seemed to be almost indispensable. The Protestants' emergency measures became known as 'Hilfswerk der EKD'. As has been indicated in an earlier section, the Churches were seen by the Soviet occupying forces as generally 'progressive' and 'anti-fascist', and it was the policy of the latter to restore confiscated properties to the Churches. The work of Christians such as Pastor Braune, who as director of the Hoffnungstal Institute at Lobetal had resisted the Nazi programme of euthanasia with great courage, was by no means forgotten. The contribution of the Churches thus became accepted in the late 1940s as a normal feature of 'Socialist society'.

In 1949 the newly constituted Democratic Republic, though carrying on the policy inherited from the occupying forces, questioned its rightness. The SED, or some elements within it, aimed to bring all aspects of national life under the direct control of the Party; they saw in the social work of the church a stronghold of the ideological foe, a 'bridgehead of imperialism' which might in the long run undermine and menace the established régime. Accordingly efforts were made in certain cases to question the competence of the church authorities in the running of hospitals, and certain institutions were taken over by the state. There are clear indications that the political leaders of the GDR were conscious of a dilemma: if the Churches continued to have a considerable presence in social affairs, an area would exist in which the Churches were almost totally free to propagate an alien ideology; yet the propaganda value of having a 'subservient' church serving the people would be considerable, not forgetting the financial value of allowing the Churches to carry out social projects at their own expense. Certain church ventures were terminated: thus the Church's Railway Missions were made more or less impracticable by state regulations, and so many difficulties were put in the way of the Inland Waterway Mission that the church abandoned it.

But discussions between church and state leaders in 1958 led to a working arrangement, according to which the Churches' right to social work was in principle recognised.

It is scarcely necessary to give full details of the Churches' work, but some statistics may be of interest. Taken together, the Catholic and Protestant Churches maintain over 12,000 beds in 82 church-owned hospitals; in other words, some 7% of the whole hospital capacity of the GDR. No fewer than thirty-four of these hospitals are Roman Catholic ones. The Protestants are very much to the fore in the care of the mentally and physically disabled—they run eighty-nine such homes. Both denominations run large networks of local nursing stations. There are considerable numbers of both children's homes and children's day care centres. Between them, the major Churches provide places for nearly 15,000 elderly people in their residential homes—over 10% of the total number of institutional places vailable in the GDR. There are long waiting lists for vacancies. It is clear that the extra quality of care provided by the Churches is very much appreciated. The chronically ill who are not in hospitals or institutions are given special care by members of the Protestant and Catholic Churches. There are also special ministries for the blind and the deaf. In recent years much attention has been given to the counselling of alcoholics and their families. Special groups have been set up for marriage guidance and the handling of family problems. As well as the Roman Catholic Church and the main Protestant provincial Churches, other Christian denominations—such as the Methodists and the Seventh-day Adventists—have their own facilities.

The training of the Churches' medical personnel has created problems, and was the subject of a detailed agreement separately concluded in 1975 between Protestant and Catholic representatives on the one hand and the state on the other. Certain subjects—namely Marxism-Leninism, psychology, sociology and German—must be taught, and taught only by the state teaching body; for the rest the Churches are responsible. The dual teaching is so arranged that successful candidates receive a state recognised diploma. There are also other types of training for church employees for which the church alone is responsible; in this case there is no state recognition of the qualifications given.

The costs of feeding and caring for patients in hospitals and other church institutions are borne by the state. The payment is made in accordance with a scale fixed annually. Naturally no element to cover the cost of pastoral or spiritual care is included. Nor is the cost of capital investment (medical equipment, maintenance or the erection of new buildings) covered in any way. Were it not for the ready assistance of the West, the costs of capital investment would prove crippling indeed for the Churches of the GDR. One significant source of extra income is the annual street collection undertaken with state permission by the Churches, for the express purpose of aiding social work. To take one example: in 1980 the Protestant provincial Church of Saxony collected over a million marks in this way. The salaries of rather more than a third of the 50,000 or so people employed by the Protestant Churches in all aspects of social work are paid by the Churches in West Germany, as are those of a similar proportion of Catholic employees. The problem of finding a just basis for the level of state subsidy is not an easy one, and supposed state niggardliness has often led to dissatisfaction in church circles.

The church's social work is a fruitful theme for GDR Protestant theologians, particularly those who follow in the footsteps of Bonhoeffer. They are only too well aware of the fact that the Churches in the GDR have no temporal power, and no means of influencing political policies. Social work is a means of obeying Christ's command to uphold the cause of the helpless and the underprivileged. Some Protestant Church leaders see the present situation as a chance for the church to atone for its alleged failure to be concerned with the 'working masses' in the past. There are others, however, who are worried that the Churches might become part of the structure of society, or social agents obediently carrying out the policies of the state. Meanwhile, the social responsibilities of the Churches show no signs of diminishing.

Ecumenical activity

An interesting analysis of the state of ecumenical relations in
the GDR has been made by a Leipzig theologian who, though
a Catholic, has for the last fifteen years been involved with Protestant affairs. The ecumenical spirit has made the most progress at the lowest (the 'grass-roots') level, where true fellowship and solidarity exists. Visible signs of this spirit are the programmes of religious education accepted by both communions,
the care of old people and the jointly undertaken preparation
for preaching. There is a real feeling of unity here. At the level
of Church leaderships, however, it would be more accurate to
describe the relationship as 'cool and distant', in spite of the
well-ordered contacts that exist and the jointly held church
events that are carried on. The basic reason for this lack of cor-
diality is the difference in outlook concerning church-state relations. The Catholic bishops accuse the Protestants of naïve willingness to become incorporated in Marxist society. The
Catholic leaders have always been unwilling to have close contacts with the state; they have always refused 'dialogue' unless
absolutely necessary. Protestant leaders accuse the Catholics of
withdrawing 'behind the drawbridge' into a 'religious' world,
leaving the Protestants alone to challenge the state on many
thorny problems. It is thus very hard for the two denominations to co-operate closely at the highest level. There are fail-
ures, too, at the middle level—in the work of the theological
academies and seminaries. A common approach is urgently
needed towards the sensitive themes of peace-work and
defence of the environment in order to ensure a unified Christian voice. Nevertheless, the Leipzig theologian believes that
the Christian witness borne by many young men during the last
few years on these explosive matters has been astonishingly
vigorous and bold. He describes the ecumenical climate as
immeasurably more free of tensions and problems, and far ful-
ler of goodwill than it is in the West.

The part played by the GDR Protestant Churches in the

worldwide ecumenical movement has been—and still is—
extremely significant. The Protestant provincial Churches, the
Moravian Church and the Old Catholic Church are members of
the World Council of Churches. As early as 1948, Bishop Otto
Dibelius, of the Evangelical Church of Berlin-Brandenburg,
including (at that time) West Berlin, was elected to the Central
Committee of the WCC, and between 1954 and 1960 he served
as one of the WCC's vice-presidents. In 1975 Bishop Johannes
Hempel, of the Evangelical-Lutheran Church of Saxony, was
elected to the Central Committee; later he became a vice-
president. Several high-level conferences of the WCC have
been held on the soil of the GDR, and GDR theologians play
a vital part in the Council's work. The Lutheran Churches are
members of the Lutheran World Federation. The other Protestant Churches play an active part in different worldwide ecumenical groupings. GDR churchmen are usually in evidence at
gatherings held outside the countries of the Soviet bloc, and
observers have frequently been struck by the distinctive and
independent nature of their contributions.

CHAPTER 6

Albania

ALBANIA: OVERVIEW

The country; the people; brief history

The People's Socialist Republic of Albania, which is roughly the size of Belgium, lies in the south-west of the Balkan peninsula on the Adriatic Sea. It shares borders with Yugoslavia and Greece, and has a mountainous interior with a coastal plain. The Albanians are believed to be descended from the ancient Illyrians, thought to be the oldest inhabitants of Europe. Their language, although Indo-European, is unlike any other modern European tongue.

Albania is experiencing an officially encouraged population explosion. Abortions are illegal and contraception discouraged. The population of 2.9 million is expected to reach 4 million by 2000. Only 7% of the population is over 60, and 37% under 15. The average age of the population is only twenty-six.

Albania was part of the Roman province of Illyricum, and several Roman Emperors were Illyrians. In spite of subsequent invasions by Visigoths, Huns and Slavs in the third to seventh centuries, the Albanians retained their language and customs. Turkish invasions began in the fourteenth century, but the Turks met determined resistance led by George Castriota (Skanderbeg), who had been forcibly converted to Islam but later reconverted to Christianity.

From 1467 to 1912 Albania was part of the Ottoman Empire. After independence Albania continued to be under threat of foreign domination, variously from Greece, Italy and Serbia. These experiences confirmed Albanians in their traditional suspicion of all foreign powers. Italy eventually invaded in Spring 1939 and the country remained under Italian, then German, occupation until the Axis withdrew in 1944, whereupon the communist element in the national resistance movement brought about the establishment of a Communist-dominated government under the leadership of Enver Hoxha.

For the next forty years Hoxha ruled Albania until his death, on what he took to be pure Stalinist lines. He criticised the Soviet Union for revisionism after Khrushchev's 'destalinisation' campaign had begun, and broke off relations with the USSR in 1961. Albania then grew closer to China, and withdrew from the Warsaw Pact in 1968. But when China, too, fell prey to revisionism, relations grew sour and in 1978 Albania broke with China as well. Since then, Albania has pursued a completely independent and isolationist course. The régime is one of ruthless internal control based on orthodox Stalinism and nationalism; the ratio of secret police to population is the highest in the communist world. Enver Hoxha died in 1985. His successor Ramiz Alia is said to be more moderate, and some minor relaxations have been noted by foreign visitors.

The economy; social conditions; political life

Albania's isolationism has been made possible by its rich natural resources, including oil. There is no doubt that the economic situation and living standards in Albania have improved during the forty years of Communist power. Infant mortality has been cut, life expectancy has been doubled, illiteracy has been reduced, disease controlled and the basic standard of living raised. However, when compared with the rest of Europe, Albania still lags far behind. Agriculture is completely collectivised and may eventually be unable to cater for the rapidly growing population. A very high proportion of the budget is spent on the army. There are chronic shortages of meat, and rationing is the norm. The highest incomes in Albania are only twice the lowest; and all are low. Luxuries like television and even necessities like shoes have to be saved up for even if they are available. No citizen may own a private car. Public transport is minimal: most workers use bicycles. There is no unemployment in Albania, but obvious overmanning is the result. Manual labour is regularly used where machines would save long hours of exhausting or monotonous work.

THE STATUS OF CHRISTIANITY

The religious complexion of the country

Christianity came early to Albania, probably through Greek traders. When the Roman Empire was divided in 395, Albania was administered from Constantinople, but was under the ecclesiastical jurisdiction of Rome. During the Dark Ages the Albanians came completely under Byzantine rule and Eastern Orthodox Christianity, but after the schism of 1054 the northern part of the country came once again under the ecclesiastical jurisdiction of Rome, and many old bishoprics were re-established. Dominicans, Benedictines and Franciscans became active there. By the time of the Turkish invasions northern Albania was predominantly Catholic, the rest of the country Orthodox. All Albania's leading writers and scholars of the sixteenth and seventeenth centuries were Catholic priests and bishops, and they helped to prevent the Christian faith and Albanian culture from being overwhelmed by Islam.

The Turks placed crippling taxes on Christians, and often adopted cruel measures to persuade the Albanians to adopt Islam. The centuries of Ottoman rule, therefore, saw a steady stream of converts to Islam. Nobles were the first to convert, and later the ordinary people, particularly in the coastal plain and the towns. By 1912 Albania had become the only European country with a Muslim majority. The 1938 census showed that 70% of the population were Muslims, about 20% Orthodox and about 10% Roman Catholics.

The state's attitude to religion

Persecution of religion began immediately after the Communists came to power in 1944. The authorities made the usual Marxist criticism of religious institutions, namely that they had historically been among the exploiters of the poor—although the Albanian Churches had never been big landowners. The Communists also criticised the religions for having been a divisive element from the point of view of the Albanian nation, each major religion having been promoted by various invaders at different times. The negative role of religion was contrasted with the positive role of Albanian nationalism. 'The religion of the Albanians is Albanianism'.

Religious education of young people was forbidden. Sermons and pastoral letters were subjected to censorship. By the land reform of 1945 the Churches were deprived of considerable property, including monasteries, libraries and seminaries. Those clergy who resisted were arrested and sentenced. Terror, murder and torture were also used against individual clergy and believers. The practice of religion had been guaranteed without restriction in the Constitution of 1946, but legislation passed between 1949 and 1951 set the first legal limits to religious freedom. Religious practice should not contravene 'the laws of the state, law and order and good customs'. The latter were not defined, but the only religious freedom specifically allowed was that of holding religious services in a place of worship. Anti-religious activity continued. Religious institutions went through a very difficult phase of restricted and marginalised existence.

A bad situation became qualitatively worse in 1967 when Enver Hoxha launched a campaign to close down all places of worship. By May all 2,169 religious establishments had been boarded up or demolished. In November 1967 all decrees on religion were abolished, religion was forced into complete illegality, and Albania proclaimed itself the 'first atheist state in the world'. The present Constitution was promulgated in 1976: Article 37 declares that 'the state recognises no religion', and Article 55 forbids citizens to set up organisations, produce propaganda or engage in activities 'of a fascist, anti-democratic, religious or anti-socialist nature'. The Penal Code of 1977 states that religious activity of any kind is punishable by 3 to 10 years imprisonment.

THE VARIOUS CHURCHES

The Albanian Orthodox Church

The Orthodox Church of Albania made a unilateral declaration of autocephaly in 1923 and is still under the anathema of the Patriarch of Constantinople. It was divided into four dioceses and was led by a metropolitan and three bishops.

In the period 1945–50 the state attempted to use Orthodox clergy to enlist the support of the faithful for domestic policies. At the same time it infiltrated communist agents and sympathisers into Orthodox churches and monasteries. Most of the leaders of the Church (like those of the Catholic Church and the Muslim community) were gradually eliminated by murder, execution, imprisonment and torture.

The state also tried in this period to use the Orthodox Church to further its foreign policy aims. The legal position of the Church was defined by the Decree on Religious Communities of January 1949 and the Statute of the Autocephalous Orthodox Church of Albania of May 1950. According to the latter, the Orthodox Church (like the Catholic Church and the Islamic community) was 'nationalised', but unlike the Catholic Church, the Orthodox Church was encouraged to co-operate with those of its sister Churches which were working to promote 'peace and true brotherhood'—that is, with the Orthodox Churches in the other countries of the Eastern bloc. One of the first victims of this policy had been the head of the Church, Archbishop Kristofer Kisi, who resisted what he saw as enforced subjection to the Moscow Patriarchate. In August 1949 he was accused of having been involved in 'fascist activities' and of trying to bring his Church under the jurisdiction of the Vatican. He was imprisoned and tortured to death.

Since 1967, the state has dispensed with any show of co-operation with religious bodies. The Orthodox Church has ceased to exist as an organisation. In 1975 the entire hierarchy of the Church and most of the clergy were believed to be in prison, Archbishop Damian, the head of the Church, having died there in 1973.

The Roman Catholic Church

The Catholic Church in Albania consisted of six dioceses. In 1939 it had 203 priests and 165 monks and nuns, a proportion of them foreign.

From the start of the communist period the Catholic Church has been persecuted with even more consistent savagery than the other religious groups. The new rulers of Albania were determined to obliterate the idea that Catholicism had at one point been the upholder of Albanian culture. The Church's links with the Vatican were condemned as dependence on an outside institution intrinsically opposed to communism, and the contacts of churchmen with the 'imperialist and aggressive West' were used as the basis for condemning many of them as fascist fifth-columnists and wartime collaborators with the enemy.

One of the first steps the government took was to expel all foreign monks and nuns. Church presses were confiscated and schools and children's homes taken over by the state. Many priests were murdered by atheist activists. Priests were condemned in show trials. Among the first victims were six bishops, including the Archbishop of Shkodër, head of the Albanian Church. In December 1945 members of the Albanian Union, a mainly Catholic legal political party which existed before the first parliamentary election, printed anti-communist leaflets on the press of the Franciscan seminary without the knowledge of the Order's leaders. As a result, the two leaders of the Albanian Union were sentenced and executed, together with the Rector of the Seminary, the Deputy Father Superior, the editor of a Franciscan journal and five other people unconnected with the incident. Immediately after this the Jesuit order was banned in Albania; the Franciscans followed in 1947.

The Statute of the Catholic Church in Albania of July 1951 was passed some time after the statutes relating to the other religious communities, and evidently caused the state the greatest difficulties. As well as being nationalised, the Catholic Church was henceforth forbidden to 'maintain any organisational, economic or political relations with the Pope'. The authorities were thus attempting, as in China (whose policies were at that time admired in Albania), to create a national Catholic Church entirely separate from Rome. Trials and executions of clergy continued, however.

Since 1967, the aim has been to eliminate the Catholic Church and the Catholic faith altogether. In 1967 the Franciscan Gega Lumay was sentenced to 15 years' imprisonment. The following year one priest was shot and two others sentenced to ten and twenty years imprisonment. In 1971 Bishop Troshani was sentenced to 20 years. In February 1972, the 74-year-old Fr Shtjefen Kurti was executed for baptising the child of a fellow-prisoner in a labour camp. In spring 1971 there were probably only 14 Catholic priests still alive in Albania, 12 of whom were in concentration camps or prisons and 2 in hiding. A list compiled in 1976 estimates that 5 bishops, 56 priests, 28 Franciscans, 13 Jesuits, 10 seminarians and 8 nuns had died since 1945 or were still in prisons or labour camps. Bishop Çoba, who had been in a labour camp for many years, was severely beaten there on Easter Day 1979 for having celebrated Mass and died of his injuries. In 1980 Fr Ndoc Luli, former Director of the Xavier College in Shkodër, who had already spent 15 years in a labour camp, was rearrested and sentenced to life imprisonment for having baptised twin nephews.

The Vatican has spoken up many times since 1967, deploring the Albanian situation. At the end of 1983 Vatican Radio condemned 'the very serious and systematic persecution of the Catholic Church in Albania', and reminded listeners that Pope John Paul II had called on Catholics throughout the world to pray for religious freedom in Albania during November that year.

CHRISTIAN ACTIVITIES

The government of Albania has been entirely successful in destroying institutional religion, but there is continuing evidence that it is finding it much more difficult to kill personal religious belief and private practice. In 1975 the Party newspaper *Zeri i Popullit* reported that religious rites and services were being held in some parts of the country and in 1976 the newspaper *Bashkimi* put this kind of thing down to a decline in 'revolutionary vigilance'. Again in 1975, an atheist specialist wrote that religious ideas were 'still strong and influential' within the family circle. Even today in more than 96% of marriages the two partners both come from the same one of the four major religious traditions (Catholic, Orthodox, Sunni Muslim and Shiite Muslim), although mixed marriages are officially encouraged.

The current anti-religious campaign uses two major techniques. The first is a mass educational programme designed to demonstrate the futile and harmful nature of religion. The second is to prompt local atheists to take 'popular action' and to set up 'confrontations' with believers. There is evidence that physical violence is often involved. A recent decree (May 1979) has stated that any person who is a danger to the system can now be sent to prison without trial.

CHAPTER 7

Romania

ROMANIA: OVERVIEW

The country; the people; brief history

Situated in the south-east of Europe, between the Danube basin in the west and the Black Sea to the east, Romania has within its borders both spectacular mountain scenery (the Carpathian range runs through the middle of the country) and fertile agricultural land, as well as the Danube delta, which provides good fishing and rich wildlife. The country has its own oil-field too, in the plains north of the capital, Bucharest. All Romania's neighbours are communist countries: the longest common border is that with the Soviet Union; Romania's other neighbours are Hungary, Bulgaria and Yugoslavia.

Romanians are a people who physically resemble other southern Europeans, and the language they speak is very much a Latin tongue. They proudly claim their descent from the Romans, who invaded the territory known as Dacia in the second century AD and intermarried with the natives. Only some 88% of Romania's 22 million inhabitants are ethnic Romanian, however: the largest ethnic minority are the 2 million Hungarians of Transylvania; the Germans are another significant—though declining—group; next come the gypsies, thought to be about 1% of the population; and smaller ethnic groups include Jews, Serbians and Ukrainians.

It was not until the settlement at the end of the First World War all the territories peopled mainly by Romanians were united into a single independent country. Transylvania had been one of the Hungarian crown-lands for most of its history, and the former principalities, Moldavia and Wallachia (which were united in 1859 and recognised as independent in 1878), had been under Turkish rule or suzerainty for centuries. For some 20 years, Romania was a constitutional monarchy until, in 1938, the King dissolved Parliament and introduced a new constitution which gave him increased power; two years later he was replaced by General Antonescu, a pro-German dictator. Towards the end of the war, in August 1944, with the Soviet Red Army already invading, Antonescu was ousted and the country changed sides. The Antonescu régime was replaced by a 'government of national unity' within which, over the next three years, the Communist Party gained the upper hand. A People's Republic was proclaimed on 30th December 1947.

The economy; social conditions; political life

Once one of the more prosperous countries of the Balkans, with a good, agriculturally based economy, Romania has now become the poorest in Eastern Europe (excepting, perhaps, Albania). The heavy and enormously costly industrialisation programme begun in the 1960s included a petro-chemical industry whose capacity vastly exceeds Romania's indigenous oil supply. The result is that expensive plants lie idle, the country has to pay hard currency for oil imports, and there is a serious energy shortage, with stringent petrol rationing and frequent power cuts. At the same time, much of Romania's best food is exported to earn hard currency, with the result that many basic food-stuffs are rationed and in short supply. Despite the recent industrialisation, Romania is still primarily a rural society. Few Romanians are more than a generation removed from village life, and most town-dwellers have relations in the country. The 'extended family', with two or three related families living under one roof, is common. It is quite normal to obtain jobs, services or scarce goods by the use of bribery (open, or of varying degrees of subtlety) or 'connections' or some form of barter. The economic decline of recent years has, if anything, exacerbated this problem.

In the early 1960s Romania began to adopt the 'nationalistic' political stance which under Nicolae Ceauşescu, who gained power in 1965, it has maintained ever since. Displaying a measure of foreign-policy independence, Romania has even acquired a reputation as something of a maverick in the Soviet bloc by, for instance, maintaining full diplomatic relations with Israel and by sending its team to the 1984 Olympics in the face of the Soviet-led boycott. The independence of Romania's foreign policy is strictly limited, and it does not mean that the country is 'liberal' or any less communist. In its internal affairs it remains one of the most oppressive régimes in Eastern Europe. The most distinctive aspect of Romanian political life is the personality cult surrounding President Ceauşescu and his family, many of whom have been placed in powerful Party and government positions. He and his wife, Elena, are often portrayed almost as king and queen, and Elena and their son Nicu have both been tipped as possible successors.

THE STATUS OF CHRISTIANITY

The religious complexion of the country

Christianity first came to Romania with the invading Roman army which conquered Dacia in the second century AD. Evidence of this early Christianisation is to be found in the preponderance of words of Latin (rather than Greek or Slavic) origin in the basic church vocabulary. This Christianisation was not a sudden conversion of an entire people, rather a gradual influence, an influence which was, perhaps, deeper on the right bank of the Danube (the Roman province of Moesia), where the first episcopal sees were established by the fourth century: these include Tomis (now known as Constanţa, but its old name is retained for ecclesiastical purposes) and Silistria (in present-day Bulgaria).

At least 20 million of Romania's 22.7 million population are Christians of some kind. Clearly this figure must include some of the 3.5 million (15% of the population) who are members of the Romanian Communist Party, by no means all of whom would profess themselves to be atheists.

The Romanian Orthodox Church claims at least 17 million adherents, making it by far the largest Christian grouping in the country, accounting for more than 75% of the population (and well over 80% of ethnic Romanians). This figure includes, however, a large number of Transylvanian Byzantine-rite Catholics—or Uniates—whose Church was incorporated against its will into the Orthodox Church in 1948. At the time of the enforced merger this Church had about 1.5 million adherents (all ethnic Romanian). Most Orthodox would see their allegiance to that Church simply as a consequence of their Romanian nationality. Even under Communist rule, the Romanian Orthodox Church has continued to enjoy privileged status and might be regarded—though not, of course, officially—as a state church. For many Romanians, their allegiance to the Orthodox Church is only nominal, however.

The next largest groups are the 1.3 million Roman Catholics (mainly Hungarian and German, but including also a significant number of Romanians in Bucharest and Moldavia); the Reformed Church (Hungarian), about 700,000 strong; and the 2 separately recognised Lutheran denominations, one Hungarian, the other German. All these denominations tend, like the Orthodox, to have an ethnically defined 'natural constituency', and Church allegiance often seems to be an expression of national consciousness and little more.

The small Protestant denominations (known in Romania as the 'neo-Protestants'), the Pentecostals, Baptists, Brethren and Adventists, have about half a million members between them, but appear to be the fastest growing. They are now largely Romanian denominations but have many local churches serving the other main ethnic groups. They tend to demand greater commitment from their members and this is reflected in a level of evangelistic and other activity which is, compared with that of other larger denominations, relatively high.

Followers of non-Christian religions in Romania are the Jews, who now number fewer than 30,000 (since the war, more than 10 times that number have emigrated, mainly to Israel), and about the same number of Muslim Turks and Tartars, who live in the Dobrogea region near the Black Sea.

Undoubtedly, the state's negative attitude towards religion is a factor which hinders its spread—or, rather, the growth of active religious commitment. At the same time, the state's attitude, as well as the hardships caused by economic decline and a decline in public and private ethical standards, may have encouraged many to turn their attention to spiritual matters.

Urbanisation has been a negative factor in the past two or three decades. Village populations have declined and many people now live in blocks of flats in vast, newly-built suburbs on the outskirts of the major cities. These new suburbs are not well provided with churches.

The State's attitude to religion

Article 30 of the Romanian Constitution guarantees the 'freedom to practise a religious confession' and states that the religious denominations 'organise themselves and function freely'. Article 318 of the Penal Code lays down a penalty of up to 6 months' imprisonment for anyone who impedes or disturbs the freedom of religious practice enjoyed by any religious group which is organised and functions according to the law. At the same time, the Romanian Communist Party (declared in Article 3 of the Constitution to be the 'leading political force of the whole of society') is firmly committed, in its political educational programme, to the cultivation of the 'dialectical and historical-materialist' world view. This responsibility is frequently reiterated in the Romanian media, and it is made clear that this entails opposition to religion. In common with most other Eastern European countries, then, Romania guarantees—and claims even to protect—freedom of religious practice, while at the same time working towards its eventual elimination. To complicate matters further, it should also be noted that Churches, their official publications and their leaders are quite often enlisted in the support of the régime's propaganda requirements, particularly in the foreign-policy field.

In practice, Romania has been pursuing a policy of restricting the freedom of operation of religious groups, a policy carried out primarily by a state body, the Department of Cults (or—better translation—Religious Affairs). This restriction is achieved more through bureaucratic control than through legislation, and denominational leaders have sometimes been persuaded to accept restrictive rules and adopt them in their own churches as if they themselves had initiated them—thus absolving the state, or any other external organisation, from any 'blame'. Church building and training of clergy are two examples of areas in which restrictions have been achieved in this way. Discrimination against active religious believers in employment and education is—constitutional guarantees notwithstanding—a fact of Romanian life. This is generally indirect, often being a result of barring non-Party members from certain posts, but it is occasionally openly acknowledged.

THE VARIOUS CHURCHES

The Romanian Orthodox Church

History
The history of the Romanian people between the Roman occupiers' withdrawal and the emergence, by the fourteenth century, of the two Romanian principalities remains obscure. The history of their Christianity during this time is likewise unclear. What is known is that in the ninth century the Slavicised Bulgars to the south gained an independent Bulgarian patriarchate, recognised by Constantinople, and it was this Church which, under Bulgarian rule (and later the Byzantine Empire), had jurisdiction over the Romanians north of the Danube. Through the influence of disciples of Cyril and Methodius, the Bulgarian Church had adopted Slavonic as its liturgical language in place of Greek, and Slavonic remained the Romanians' language of worship until the seventeenth century.

It was natural, then, that the Romanians should have found themselves on the 'eastern' side of the great divide which separated Byzantine and Roman Christianity in 1054, part of the branch known as 'Orthodox'. For some time the Romanian churches continued to be dependent upon Bulgarian bishops (at Vidin and Silistra); but even after the foundation of separate episcopal sees north of the Danube, coming under the direct jurisdiction of the Ecumenical Patriarchate in Constantinople, many of the priests serving the churches in Moldavia and Wallachia were Slavs. It was not until the seventeenth century, with the rise of the political and economic influence of the Phanariot Greeks (who were entrusted by the Turks with the administration in Christian parts of the Ottoman Empire), and the replacement of Slavs by Greeks in key positions in Romania's churches and monasteries, that the time came for Slavonic to be supplanted by the vernacular: the first complete Romanian Bible was published in 1688.

The fortunes of the Orthodox Church continued to be dependent very largely upon political developments outside its control. In Transylvania, the Romanians, though a majority of the population, were predominantly peasants, and thus formed the lowest stratum of society. The Romanians' Church—likewise inferior in status—had to accept papal supremacy in an Act of Union completed in 1700, shortly after the principality came under direct Habsburg rule. Thus the Uniate Church was created.

In the other two principalities as well, political changes presaged religious changes. When Wallachia and Moldavia were united into a single state in 1859, the two metropolitanates merged; and in 1865 the Metropolitan of Bucharest took the title of Primate of Romania. Similarly, the country's independence, achieved in 1877, paved the way for the Romanian Orthodox Church to be granted autocephaly—ecclesiastical independence—by the Ecumenical Patriarch in 1885. In 1925, following the addition of Transylvania to the Romanian State, a Romanian patriarchate was founded.

The recognition of the Orthodox Church in the 1866 Constitution as 'the dominant religion of the Romanian state' was granted at some cost to the Church itself, which had to occupy a position of loyal subservience to the state, a relationship which continued well into the twentieth century. A striking illustration of this loyalty is provided by a pastoral letter issued by Patriarch Nicodim in 1941, in which he calls upon his faithful to pray for Adolf Hitler 'and his glorious army' as well as for 'Conducător' Ion Antonescu.

Romania became a Communist state in 1947. Patriarch Nicodim died in 1948 and was succeeded by Justinian Marina, who had only recently emerged from relative obscurity to become Metropolitan of Moldavia. His predecessor, Metropolitan Irineu Mihălcescu, was one of several senior clerics who had resigned in 1947 when 'investigations' commenced against them. Four other bishops were removed the same year by the lowering, by law, of the official retirement age for priests. Thus the new régime was able to rid itself, in a short space of time, of much of the potential opposition in the Church hierarchy; and at the same time hundreds of priests were purged from the lower ranks of the clergy.

What emerged from this was a Romanian Orthodox Church which by the end of the 1940s was no less loyal to the Communist government than it had been to the right-wing régime just a few years earlier. It was led for almost 30 years by a patriarch who could be relied upon—apart from a brief period out of favour in 1959—to give public support to government policy, both when it was unquestioningly pro-Soviet and when it became, in the 1960s, more 'nationalistic'. In his theological writings, collected and published in a series entitled, significantly, *Apostolat social* ('*Social Apostolate*'), he provided a reasoned justification for his concept of a 'servant church' loyally playing its part in the new social order.

Justinian's style of leadership was continued without significant change by Patriarch Justin Moisescu, who succeeded him upon his death in 1977. Justin died in 1986 and was succeeded by Teoctist Arăpas, Metropolitan of Moldavia.

Church structure and membership

The Romanian Orthodox Church is autocephalous: it has its own patriarch and is governed by its own synod. The Patriarchal Cathedral is situated in Bucharest, next to the Parliament building, and much of the central administration is located at the nearby Antim monastery. There are five metropolitanates and these are divided into, in all, seven archbishoprics and six bishoprics. The next administrative level is the deanery, of which there are about a hundred, each consisting of a group of several parishes, generally a town with its surrounding villages. Each deanery is presided over by a rural dean, or 'archpriest'. There are about 8,000 parishes (the total number of places of worship exceeds this slightly).

Although in theory there is devolution of administrative responsibility to diocesan level (each diocese has its own assembly and council) and even to the parishes, the organisation of the Romanian Orthodox Church is in practice highly centralised: considerable power is vested in the synod, the National Church Assembly and its executive organ, the nine-member National Church Council; the patriarch's personal power, too, is substantial.

Romania has a rich monastic tradition, though this has changed drastically, both qualitatively and quantitatively, in the Communist era. There are now 122 monasteries and sketes (a type of monastic community), compared with more than 200 before the wave of repression which began in 1958. The monastic foundations are integrated into the same administrative structure as the rest of the Church.

Other associated institutions include the six seminaries and two theological institutes, as well as the Bible and Orthodox Missionary Institute, which belongs to the patriarchate and which is responsible for, among other things, the printing of Church publications.

The Romanian Orthodox Church is almost entirely ethnic Romanian; there are small communities of Serbian and Bulgarian Orthodox, who come under the jurisdiction of their respective patriarchates, and Ukrainians, who are also independent of the Romanian Church. Regular church attendance is more widespread in the villages than towns, and among the less educated rather than the professionals. This disparity has probably been accentuated by many professionals' understandable reluctance to participate too frequently in the more visible forms of religious observance, for fear that their careers might be adversely affected.

There are about 9,000 priests in service in the Romanian Orthodox Church—a little more than one per parish, or roughly one for every 20,000 out of the church's claimed membership. The number of religious is about 2,000 of which three-quarters are nuns (there were more than 7,000 before the 1958 wave of closures and restrictions of monasteries).

Current growth trends
The lack of reliable figures makes assessment of 'growth' in the Romanian Orthodox Church very difficult. In any case, since a large majority of ethnic Romanians are already counted as 'Orthodox', there is little scope for numerical growth. It would be more meaningful to speak of growth in commitment (measured, perhaps, by church attendance) but here, too, the evidence is—inevitably—fragmentary. There have been reports of a substantial growth in the 1980s in the attendance by young people at some Bucharest churches; but it may be necessary to balance this against the depletion of village churches, caused by population transfer to suburbs having few churches within easy reach.

The Old Believers

The Old Believers, though few in number, constitute one of the fourteen officially recognised 'cults' separate from the Orthodox Church. They are all members of an ethnic Russian fishing community living in the Danube delta. Church leaders are mentioned occasionally in official reports of such events as peace conferences.

The Lord's Army

The Lord's Army is a 'renewal' movement within the Orthodox Church. It enjoys neither the recognition of the state nor the approval of the Church hierarchy. Its size is difficult to determine, but some estimates suggest a membership exceeding half a million.

The movement began in the early 1920s, initially as a campaigning force concerned about the morally degenerate state of Romanian society (and alcoholism in particular), but it soon acquired theological distinctiveness as well. At first it enjoyed the support of the Church hierarchy, but that support turned to opposition by the mid-1930s. In 1948 state opposition was added to that of the Church, and several of the leaders of the Lord's Army spent many years in prison in the 1950s and 1960s. Despite its illegality, it still has many adherents. It continues to regard itself as an Orthodox movement within the Orthodox Church, although it has 'evangelical' characteristics and many of its members enjoy good relations with non-Orthodox evangelicals.

Although it has always enjoyed the active or passive support of some priests, the Lord's Army is primarily a lay movement. Members attend the liturgies of the Orthodox Church, but take part also in unofficial Bible study and prayer meetings in homes. The movement is confined to ethnic Romanians. It has always been relatively strong among the poorer, less educated agricultural workers—but not to the exclusion of people from other backgrounds. It is stronger in the north of the country (especially Moldavia) than the south. Young people are well represented in the movement.

The Roman Catholic Church

History
Latin-rite Catholicism in Romania originated west of the Carpathians where it can be traced back to ninth and tenth century missionary activity and, in particular, to the conversion of the first Hungarian king, István (Stephen), who obtained his crown (still preserved in Hungary today) from the Pope, and in 1083, less than 50 years after his death, was canonised by the Roman Church. Thus a majority of the Hungarians, who settled in Transylvania as well as what is now Hungary proper, became Roman Catholics.

For centuries the Hungarians and Germans in Transylvania,

though fewer in number than the Romanians, enjoyed a privileged position in society. Along with three 'recognised nations'—Magyar, Székel (also Hungarian-speakers) and Saxon—there were four 'received religions' (Catholic, Reformed, Lutheran and Unitarian) recognised by a law passed in 1571. In 1691 Transylvania fell to the Habsburg crown, and Habsburg rule ensured that Catholicism gained predominance, a position that was strengthened by the Union in 1700 of most of Transylvania's Romanian Orthodox with Rome.

The incorporation of Transylvania into Romania after the First World War necessitated a concordat between Romania and the Vatican, reached in 1927, under which such matters as new episcopal boundaries (some of the old bishoprics straddled the new national frontier) were resolved. This concordat was revoked by the new Communist government in 1948; at about the same time, the number of dioceses was cut from five to two; the Catholic religious orders were disbanded, and many institutions such as hospitals and schools closed down or nationalised; all the Church's publications were stopped. For many years the Latin-rite Catholic Church in Romania occupied an anomalous position, without full official recognition, because no agreement could be reached on an organisational charter; the Bucharest archbishopric was headed, from 1954 to 1983, by an 'ordinary' appointed by the state, but never accorded episcopal rank by the Vatican. During the 1980s there has been a slight but significant amelioration of the situation of the Catholic Church: new bishops have been appointed and there is greater freedom for more churchmen to visit Rome.

Church structure and membership

The Roman Catholic Church in Romania now has its five dioceses functioning again. They are the archdiocese of Bucharest, and the dioceses of Iaşi (Moldavia), Alba Iulia and Oradea-Satu Mare (Transylvania) and Timişoara (Banat). The archdiocese is headed only by a bishop (Ioan Robu, appointed in 1984), but he is recognised as the 'leader' of his Church in Romania. The combined diocese of Oradea-Satu Mare consists of the parts of two larger dioceses which came into Romania when the post-First World War boundary with Hungary was drawn; Timişoara diocese is, similarly, part of a once larger unit. A large majority of Romania's Catholics are concentrated in the three western dioceses.

There are now two Roman Catholic seminaries in Romania: at Alba Iulia, where the teaching is in Hungarian; and at Iaşi, where it is conducted in Romanian.

Next to the Hungarians, who make up by far the largest part of the Church, it is another ethnic minority, the Germans, who are most significant. It is they who dominate the Catholic Church in the Banat, where it is attended also by people from the smaller ethnic minorities (such as Serbians) found in that area. In the Bucharest and Iaşi dioceses, Romanians are relatively strong numerically in what is, in those areas, a much smaller Catholic community. A large proportion of Moldavian Catholics are Changos, a group thought to be of Hungarian origin (though this is disputed) but who speak Romanian.

The number of priests available to care for the 1.3 million Catholics in Romania is uncertain. In 1978, 800 was given as the total, but the figure is now believed to be as low as 600. Well over half the existing priests are over sixty and admissions to the seminaries are so restricted that the number of newly-trained priests still fails to compensate for losses due to sickness, retirement and death.

Current growth trends
The strongest growth experienced by the Catholic Church over the past decades has been in Moldavia. This has been due largely to the higher birth-rate in Moldavia, but there have also been reports of greater levels of commitment and activity from Catholics in that part of the country.

Another cause of growth has been the transfer of Uniates who have chosen to worship with Latin-rite Catholics instead of joining the Orthodox Church.

The Eastern-rite Catholic Church

History
The Eastern-rite (or Uniate) Church, which acknowledged

papal supremacy and accepted the 'filioque' clause of the Roman Catholic creed while retaining its married clergy and Orthodox liturgy, was created for political reasons. Although a return to Orthodoxy began 50 years later, around 1750, at least half the Transylvanian Romanians stayed with the new Church, which acquired an identity of its own and even became an important custodian of Romanian culture and national consciousness in the foreign-ruled province. It officially ceased to exist in 1948 when—for reasons no less political than those which created it—it was forced to merge with the Orthodox Church.

Church structure and membership; current growth trends
The Eastern-rite Catholic Church has continued in being, outside the law, and without formal structure. The six bishops in office in 1948 were all imprisoned and died in detention; of the six who were secretly ordained to replace them only two survive. It is thought that at least 600 priests are now practising unofficially (they have secular full-time employment), compared with more than 1,700 in 1948. Some Uniate believers have chosen to worship in Roman Catholic churches, although they are all Romanian and the churches are Hungarian. For this reason the state has restricted the use of Romanian in Roman Catholic churches except in Bucharest and Moldavia.

The Baptist Church

History
The Baptist denomination in Romania began in the nineteenth century with evangelistic work within the minority communities. Conversion of Romanians—who made up two-thirds of the denomination by the time a Baptist Union was founded, in 1919—attracted the opposition of both the Orthodox Church and the state, which restricted the activities of this 'sect' and even banned it altogether in 1942. The new coalition government lifted the ban in 1944, but the respite proved to be short-lived: government pressure in the 1950s and 1960s resulted in

more serious restrictions, many of which are still effective.

Church structure and membership; current growth trends
Contrary to the traditional Baptist principle of local church autonomy, the Romanian Baptist Union wields considerable power over its local churches, which are grouped also into area associations. The Baptist seminary in Bucharest (established in 1921) is, similarly, very much under central Union control.

Although the Baptist denomination was formerly considered 'foreign', its membership is now very largely Romanian, and socially mixed. At present there are about 170 Baptist pastors in Romania (compared with more than 500 in the 1950s) to look after 1,000 local churches and a total community of around 200,000.

The Romanian Baptist denomination's membership is, as a proportion of the population, by far the largest in Eastern Europe and it is acknowledged to be one of the fastest-growing religious groups. The most spectacular growth has, though, been achieved by a relatively small number of individual churches, mainly in the west of the country, and these may give an exaggerated picture of the general growth trend. Most churches, however, report a yearly increase in their membership.

The Reformed Church

History
The Reformation had a strong impact in Hungary in the sixteenth century and, for various reasons, Transylvania proved to be particularly fertile ground; Cluj (Kolozsvár) became an important centre for the Calvinist faith, which came to be closely identified with Hungarian nationality. This close identity has continued to the present day.

Church structure and membership; current growth trends
The Reformed Church in Transylvania is still exclusively Hungarian. It has an episcopal organisational structure (there are

two bishops) and its 700,000 members are led by about 700 pastors—slightly fewer than the number of parishes. No notable numerical growth has been reported in recent years.

The Pentecostal Church

History

Unlike the Baptist denomination, the Pentecostals won their first converts among Romanians rather than other national groups; although there was some foreign influence, the inception and spread of Pentecostalism in Romania was due primarily to native Romanians.

The first Pentecostal church was founded in the early 1920s, in a village in the west of Romania. Before long Pentecostalism attracted the unfavourable attention of the Orthodox Church and the state, and the movement was—like that of the Baptists—banned for a time. Official recognition came in 1950, but this was followed by many restrictive measures imposed by the Ministry (later Department) of Cults.

Church structure and membership; current growth trends

As with the Baptist Union, the Pentecostal denomination has a high degree of centralised control by an Executive Committee. National denominational conferences, held theoretically every four years, have not in fact always taken place, though a conference was held in June 1986. Meetings of area associations (there are three) are held, however. A seminary was opened in 1976.

The Pentecostal denomination is largely Romanian, but other ethnic groups (including gypsies) are represented as well. The social balance is towards those with unskilled occupations. There are about 140 pastors, but this includes several who are in fact retired and no longer functioning; they care for a community about 200,000 strong.

The Pentecostals are a relatively rapidly growing group, though this growth is unevenly spread; as with the Baptists, there is a small number of particularly successful local churches. One reason for the Pentecostals' growth is their relatively high birth-rate (they have a reputation for having large families); besides attracting new converts, they have gained also by transfer from other evangelical denominations.

Other Protestant Denominations

Four other Protestant groups are worthy of mention, two of them old, two having appeared more recently.

The Lutheran Church is a Transylvanian Church with Hungarian and German membership. It is not growing significantly; the German Lutherans have been losing many members—and, more damagingly, pastors in particular—by emigration to West Germany.

The *Creştini după Evanghelie* ('Christians According to the Gospel') denomination was formed by the amalgamation of three existing religious groups shortly after the war. Of these, two were Brethren groups, similar in doctrine and style of worship to Western Brethren; the other was an indigenous group called (after their founder) the 'Tudorişti', which was originally an evangelical movement within the Orthodox Church. The latter group still preserves a separate identity within the combined denomination. The Brethren are relatively few in number (about 50,000) but growing; a large majority are Romanian, but there are several assemblies serving the other main national groups.

The Seventh-day Adventists are also about 50,000 in number, from all three main ethnic groups. Adventism came to Romania early this century. Their 500 churches are organised into four regional associations.

Quasi-Christian Groups

Very little is known about quasi-Christian groups in Romania except that they do exist, that they are small, and that the state's attitude to them is one of strong hostility. Propaganda articles against such groups appear in the Romanian press from time to time, though in general the articles describe sects outside Romania (often in the USA). The only group which is frequently mentioned by name in connection with people and events within Romania is the Jehovah's Witnesses; there is a clear admission, then, that the Jehovah's Witnesses do exist in Romania, and it is stated that they are 'outside the law'. One source suggests a total membership of about 2,500. The Unitarian church has ethnic Germans and Hungarians in its membership, but is not growing significantly.

CHRISTIAN ACTIVITIES

Evangelism and mission

As might be expected, it is the evangelical Churches that are most involved in evangelism, though the official possibilities for evangelism are extremely limited. Some local churches do from time to time designate a meeting—or even a series of meetings—as 'evangelistic' and members would make a special effort to invite outsiders to such meetings. Apart from this, most evangelistic activity takes place on the personal level.

The only religious group able to send 'missionaries' abroad is the Orthodox Church. There have been as many as a hundred priests, monks and nuns abroad at one time. This number would include those living in the Mount Athos monastic communities and priests serving Romanian émigré communities in various parts of the world (for example, the 'Romanian Orthodox Missionary Archdiocese of America and Canada'). This is not, then, missionary work in the normal sense: many priests sent abroad by the patriarchate are known to work for the Romanian secret police.

Broadcasting

No religious broadcasting is possible in Romania. Several foreign radio stations broadcast religious programmes into Romania, however; these include religious programmes on secular radio stations (such as the BBC and Radio Free Europe) as well as programmes on radio stations whose primary purpose is religious (such as Vatican Radio and Trans World Radio).

Literature

The Romanian Orthodox Church has a substantial publishing programme with—for an Eastern European Church—a remarkable range of both periodicals and books. There are in all nine periodical publications in Romanian, three of which are published by the patriarchate (through the Bible and Orthodox Missionary Institute), the others by the various metropolitanates. These include theological journals which—despite their obligation to print propaganda extolling the virtues of the President and supporting current government policy—do publish articles of scholarly merit. In addition, there is *Romanian Orthodox Church News,* published in English and intended primarily for foreign readership.

Most of the other recognised religious bodies also have a regular magazine or journal. These are, of course, heavily censored —though in practice this is now normally self-censorship. A large part of them consists of the exposition of biblical passages or themes. Church news usually amounts to little more than such items as obituaries and reports of baptisms; a small amount of secular news is often included—generally reports of 'successes' in agriculture and industry culled direct from the secular press. Reports of 'peace conferences' and the like and loyal telegrams of support addressed to the President are commonly featured.

With the publication of books, likewise, the Orthodox Church has been much more successful than other denominations. Books published include liturgical material and theological writings; one particularly important work is a Romanian translation, in several volumes, of the *Philokalia*.

There is little religious *samizdat* produced and circulated in Romania. There is, however, a considerable hunger for devotional and ethical literature and aids to Bible study, particularly among the so-called neo-Protestants. Unofficial imports of literature produced outside the country go some way towards fulfilling these needs, though at some risk to those who receive and handle it. The main recipients of unofficially imported literature are the Baptists, Pentecostals and Brethren.

Bible translation and distribution

The last complete translation of the Bible undertaken in Romania dates from 1944; revised editions of that translation have appeared in 1968, 1975 and 1982. These have been the work of the Orthodox Church.

Printing equipment, as well as considerable quantities of paper and other necessary materials, have been supplied to the press of the Orthodox patriarchate by the United Bible Societies for Bible production. In recent years several print-runs of 50,000 or 100,000 have been claimed; in addition, there have been printings of New Testaments and 'Shorter Bibles' (selected passages of Scripture). Distribution of the Bibles printed in this way is via parish priests, for sale to their parishioners. Disincentives to potential customers at this point include the high price of the Bibles and the fact that the priest has to inform his superiors of the identity of every individual purchasing one. There is, moreover, cause to doubt whether the full quantities of Bibles really have been printed and distributed.

Similar doubts have been expressed over the fate of some of the officially sanctioned imports of Bibles sent to the other denominations by foreign organisations. A consignment of

20,000 Hungarian Bibles supplied in 1980 to the Reformed Church by the World Reformed Alliance is a case in point. In any event, even if it were certain that all official imports and official printings of Bibles reached their intended destinations, the quantities supplied would still be insufficient to meet the needs. A substantial part of the need continues to be met by unofficial imports of Bibles.

Education

The only education that Romanian religious bodies are officially involved in is the training of their own clergy. Once again, it is the Orthodox Church which enjoys by far the most favourable situation: it has six seminaries and two university-level theological institutes. The seminaries have 'middle-school' status: entry to them generally follows the normal eight years of primary education. Graduates of the seminaries can become cantors (after two years) or exceptionally, and after a five-year course, priests in rural parishes; or they may proceed to one of the theological institutes. Completion of a four-year degree course is the normal requirement for admission to the Orthodox priesthood; the institutes also offer facilities for post-graduate study. The Orthodox institutions of theological education do not appear to have been as seriously affected by restrictions on the number of new students as have other denominations' seminaries.

The number of students at the Baptist seminary in Bucharest currently (Spring 1988) stands at 19, of whom 10 are due to complete the 4-year course in 1989 and the other 9 in 1990. At the end of 1985, 10 new students were admitted to the combined Protestant Seminary in Cluj, which trains clergy for the Reformed, Lutheran and Unitarian Churches. Catholic theological students have two seminaries available to them, though both have been obliged to restrict their intakes severely. The 1985 intake at Iaşi was down to 20 (120 had applied). Physical conditions for study there and, more especially, at Alba Iulia have been reported to be seriously inadequate.

Social concerns

The only sort of social activity that Romanian Churches are officially involved in is the care of retired and sick members of their own clergy: some of the Orthodox monasteries have this as one of their major functions. Any other work in the 'social' sphere is carried out on an informal basis by individual believers or local fellowships, not by any denominational organisations acting officially.

CHAPTER 8

Bulgaria

BULGARIA: OVERVIEW

The country; the people; brief history

The People's Republic of Bulgaria occupies an area a little smaller than that of England in the eastern Balkans, sharing frontiers with Romania, Yugoslavia, Greece and Turkey and bounded to the east by the Black Sea. It is a country of great geographical diversity and beauty. The Balkan mountain range divides Bulgaria into two parts: to the north, the hilly Danube plain, known as the country's granary, and, to the south, the Valley of Roses, the Sredna Gora mountains, the fertile Thracian plain and the massif of the Rhodopes. Northern Bulgaria has a temperate-continental climate, while that of the south is more Mediterranean in type. An industrial-agrarian country, Bulgaria has a variety of natural resources, including deposits of minerals, ores and coal. It is also famous for its production of rose-oil—'attar of roses'. For many centuries—and still today—the country has stood at the crossroads of nations and as an important staging-post on the road to and from the Orient.

The ancient forebears of the Bulgarian people consisted of Thracians, Illyrians, Proto-Bulgarians and Slavs; more recent times have seen a variety of other peoples contributing, to a greater or lesser extent, to Bulgaria's ethnic composition. Of the country's present population of about 9 million, some 2 million live in the urban areas of Sofia (1.1 million), Plovdiv, Varna, Ruse, Burgas, Stara Zagora and Pleven. Bulgaria is officially described as a 'uninational state' and a vigorous campaign aiming at the complete assimilation of national minorities has been conducted by the present régime. A census carried out in 1965 indicated that minorities accounted for 12.1% of the population (and 19.6% of children under 8). No figures on nationality were published following the 1975 census. However, by far the largest minority group is of Turkish origin; there is also a sizeable gypsy community. The Macedonians, who are no longer recognised by the Bulgarians as a separate ethnic group, numbered over 250,000 in the 1945 census. Other minority groups include Armenians (about 22,000 in 1956), Jews (currently under 6,000), and small Tatar and Greek communities.

The first Bulgarian state was founded in the year 681 and lasted until 1018, when the country came under the domination of Byzantium. Re-established at the end of the twelfth century, the state flourished for a period. However, divisions developed within the country and the Ottomans, taking advantage of this process of fragmentation, eventually succeeded in subjugating Bulgaria completely by 1396.

After some five centuries of Turkish domination, the country was liberated by Russian arms in 1878. Little lasting peace and stability were to follow, however, for many decades. Eventually, at the end of the Second World War, when Soviet forces entered the country, communist revolutionaries were ready to seize power and pave the way for the post-war Communist government. Today, under long-serving Party and state leader Todor Zhivkov, Bulgaria stands as a faithful 'hard-line' member of the Soviet bloc.

The economy; social conditions; political life

Economically, Bulgaria has long been considered one of the more successful of the Eastern European states. Industrial production has risen steadily in the post-war period, progress in science and technology has been made and the mechanisation and automation of production processes introduced. Full employment is claimed, with the manpower released from agriculture being absorbed by the widespread development of industry. Recently, however, a variety of factors, including management inefficiency, indiscipline among workers, the poor quality of goods manufactured for export and the insufficiency of fuel and energy supplies, have combined to raise serious questions about the country's continuing economic health.

Bulgaria claims that her long-term economic progress has been reflected in the field of social devleopment. Since 1944, the material well-being of the people as a whole has undoubtedly improved, with strong state financial support in the spheres of education, social security and medical care in particular. Working conditions, housing and living standards generally, although well below the norms to be found in Western Europe, have shown progress in recent decades. However, the country has experienced problems over the last few years, in particular a shortage of energy, bringing in its wake drastic increases in the prices of household electricity, gas, oil, petrol and even drinking water. Difficulties such as these have resulted in a significant setback to the achievement of the country's social aims. In March 1985, extensive measures designed to rectify the situation were proposed by the Council of Ministers and in 1987 the Politburo and Council of Ministers, following the Soviet line of *perestroika,* anticipated major legislation to implement policies of economic renovation and reconstruction. Efforts are now being made to put this into practice, but many obstacles remain to be overcome and observers are forecasting a period of very slow economic progress.

The virtually uninterrupted period of political stability in Bulgaria since the war has been due, in no small measure, to the country's traditionally very close ties with the Soviet Union. Bulgaria is sometimes even referred to as 'the USSR's sixteenth republic'. However, even this 'special relationship' has appeared recently to come under some degree of threat. Gorbachev has taken a more demanding line and Soviet criticisms of Bulgaria have been directed at her lack of investment policy and planning, as well as at the quality of the goods that she sends to the USSR. Another important problem facing the Bulgarian government at present is the active opposition from the Turkish minority (as well as from Turkey herself) to the state policy of forced assimilation. Elsewhere, in recent years, allegations of participation in the plot to assassinate Pope John Paul II and of the country's involvement in drug-trafficking and international terrorism have contributed to injure Bulgaria's reputation abroad.

Of all the peoples of the Soviet-bloc countries, the Bulgarians are probably the least known and understood in the West. Since the government tourist department decided, some years ago, to develop the Black Sea resorts and the winter sports centres, a number of Westerners have acquired some superficial knowledge of the country—but few have had more than fleeting contact with the people and their way of life. In many ways, this remains a mysterious and enigmatic land, and anyone setting out to discover, in any detail, the situation of Christians in contemporary Bulgaria is faced with a difficult task. For a variety of reasons the Churches (and particularly the Orthodox Church) tend to be inward-looking and uncommunicative.

THE STATUS OF CHRISTIANITY

The religious complexion of the country

The Christian church in Bulgaria traces its origins back to the first centuries AD, when flourishing communities and churches were established in the Balkan peninsula. These were damaged by, but survived, the Slav and Proto-Bulgarian incursions of the sixth and seventh centuries, and the faith eventually began to spread among these peoples. By the ninth century, Christianity had become the official religion of the Bulgarian state. An ecclesiastical council was held in Constantinople in 870, attended by envoys from Rome and representatives of the Eastern patriarchates, and following prolonged debates, revealing deep divisions between Rome and Constantinople, it was decided that Bulgaria should belong to the Christian East. Thus, the foundations of what is now the Bulgarian Orthodox Church were laid.

In the absence of any recent information from official Bulgarian sources—which itself would be open to question—we are faced with a fair range of estimates of Christian denominational membership in the country, particularly as regards the vastly predominant Orthodox faith. Professor Todor Sabev, a Bulgarian theologian and Deputy General Secretary of the World Council of Churches, has spoken of 'six million' baptised members of the Orthodox Church—although he allowed that not all of these were believers. A study made by the Bulgarian Academy of Sciences some years ago concluded that just over one third of the population (about three million) held 'some religious belief'. Taking other estimates into account, regular Christian worshippers in Bulgaria seem unlikely to exceed two million in all and may indeed number little more than 10% of the population.

The state readily acknowledges that for many centuries, particularly during the period of the 'Ottoman yoke', the Orthodox Church stood as a symbol of Bulgarian national identity and guardian of Bulgarian culture. Since the advent of communism, dialectical materialism has become the official philosophy and atheist education is compulsory for all. Despite this, the Orthodox Church is still defined, for those who choose to be Christian, as 'the traditional religion of the Bulgarian people'. The relatively very small non-Orthodox Christian Churches in the country tend to be seen by the state as distinctly 'foreign' bodies, if not extensions of 'Western imperialism'.

The 500-year occupation of Bulgaria by the Ottomans, which ended little more than a century ago, explains the fact that, today, something like 10% of the population are Muslims. There are probably between 750,000 and 1,000,000 ethnic Turkish Muslims, together with a considerable number (estimated to be more than 200,000) of Pomaks (Muslims of Bulgarian extraction). The gypsies, a minority of whom are Christian, tend largely towards Islam and may number between 200,000 and 400,000. (They, like the ethnic Turks, are no longer officially recognised as a distinct national minority and reliable statistics regarding religious affiliations and ethnic origins are virtually impossible to obtain.) Only about 5,500 Jews remain in the country; of these, some 3,200 live in Sofia, where only about 50 attend public worship.

The state's attitude to religion

The Bulgarian Constitution closely reflects that of the USSR.

Article 53.1 states that 'citizens shall be guaranteed freedom of conscience and religion. They may perform religious rites and conduct anti-religious propaganda'. The guiding force in Bulgarian society is, of course, the Communist Party, and members are expected to 'fight determinedly against the influences of...religious prejudices'.

The 'Committee for the Affairs of the Bulgarian Orthodox Church and the Religious Cults' must give its consent to the appointment of denominational leaders and ministers. It has the power to suspend clergy and other religious officials who 'violate laws, the public order or good morals, or whose acts are in conflict with the democratic institutions of the state'. It exercises control over all church activities, including meetings, processions, publications, budgets and theological training. All contacts with, and support from, churches abroad are regulated by this committee. (There is an official ban on donations of money and the sending of other gifts by persons outside the country to Bulgarian citizens who are not members of the donor's family.) Christian theological training is officially permitted only for the Bulgarian Orthodox Church at its one seminary and at its one theological academy. On rare occasions, non-Orthodox candidates are allowed entry to these institutions. Clergy are forbidden to give religious instruction to under-16s. (This ban was reiterated in 1982 and is currently being strictly enforced.)

In a Party document on 'communist education and the working people', we read that 'an inseparable part of the education of the new human being is the fight against bourgeois ideology, with its reactionary opinions, religious prejudices and antiquated moral ideas and customs....' Religious faith is represented by the authorities as irrelevant and outdated; the sentiment that educated people will shun religion is nurtured and, indeed, known church-goers can face discrimination at their work. However, conscious of the sensitivity of many Bulgarians to the question of their traditional Church, the Party and its organs tend to avoid out-and-out frontal attacks on religion generally and Orthodoxy in particular. Among the more indirect methods used by the state to propagate atheism is that of the substitution of secular rituals and festivals for the traditional Christian ones—but only limited success has been achieved in this sphere. Christian baptisms, marriages and funerals are still sought by many.

THE VARIOUS CHURCHES

The Bulgarian Orthodox Church

History

The Bulgarian Orthodox Church began its life in the ninth century as an autonomous archbishopric under the Constantinople patriarchate. Its establishment came eighth in succession, after the four Eastern patriarchates of Constantinople, Alexandria, Antioch and Jerusalem and the three ancient archbishoprics of Cyprus, Sinai and Georgia. By the end of that century, under the influence of the great Slav educators Ss Cyril and Methodius, Bulgarian had become the recognised language of both church and state, an Orthodox hierarchy had evolved, and churches and monasteries were being built.

The tenth century saw the first Bulgarian state at the height of its development. Under Prince Simeon, in accordance with the Byzantine concept *'Imperium sine Patriarcha non staret'* ('There can be no Empire without a Patriarch'), the Bulgarian Church was proclaimed autocephalous and raised to the status of patriarchate. In 1018, Bulgaria fell under Byzantine domination. Emperor Basil II accepted the autocephaly of the archbishopric of Ohrid (which had become the Bulgarian patriarchal see), but removed the patriarchal title. During the twelfth and thirteenth centuries, under the second Bulgarian state, an independent archbishopric was established at the then capital, Turnovo, and here the Bulgarian Orthodox Church eventually resumed its patriarchal status.

However, the long occupation of the country by the Ottoman Turks was to begin in 1393. The eminent Patriarch Eftimi was sent into exile and the Bulgarian Church was subordinated to the patriarchate of Constantinople. Although the religious centre at

Ohrid (then in Bulgaria) survived well into the eighteenth century, the Orthodox faith of the country generally was severely tested under the brutal Turkish régime. There were many Christian martyrs, many emigrated and a great number were converted, willingly or unwillingly, to Islam. The Patriarchal Cathedral at Turnovo was among the number of churches destroyed or turned into mosques. At a time when the country was in danger of losing completely its Bulgarian identity and even its language, the surviving Orthodox Church—and, in particular, the monasteries—became the outstanding symbol of enduring Bulgarian faith, culture and patriotism.

Eventually, in 1870, shortly before the country's liberation, a strong resurgence of national religious consciousness resulted in the acceptance by the Ottoman government of a restored Church hierarchy or 'Bulgarian exarchate'. In the following year, at a 'Council of Church and People', the 'Statute of the Bulgarian Exarchate' was adopted and, thus reconstituted, the Orthodox Church was able, gradually, to consolidate and reorganise itself and lay the foundations for the restoration of the patriarchate.

In 1945, the year following the Communist take-over, the patriarchate of Constantinople again recognised the autocephaly of the Bulgarian Church. Between 1946 and 1953, Christians generally underwent severe persecution from the new régime, particularly following the enactment of the 1949 Religious Denominations law. The Orthodox Church made important concessions of principle to the state, but managed to keep its outward structure intact. By 1950, the Church was already designated a patriarchate and eventually, in May 1953, Kiril of Plovdiv, having sufficiently demonstrated his acceptability to the government, was formally elected Patriarch of Bulgaria and Metropolitan of Sofia. This election of a very competent administrator and outstanding scholar brought unity and stability to the Church's hierarchy.

When Kiril died in 1971, Maksim, the present Orthodox leader, was elected Patriarch. Relations between the state and the Orthodox hierarchy have, for some decades, appeared to be smooth and even cordial. Both parties seem to have accepted a very one-sided compromise: the continued existence of an institution to which many Bulgarians are still at least sentimentally and patriotically attached is permitted—in return for the surrender of much basic religious freedom and independence, and the acceptance of firm and comprehensive state supervision and control.

Church structure and membership

The Church in Bulgaria is, of course, constitutionally separate from the state. According to a statute endorsed by the Third Council of the Church and People in 1953, the Bulgarian Orthodox Church is 'an inseparable member of the one, holy synodal and apostolic church', but also 'a self-governing body under the name of Patriarchate'.

There are eleven Orthodox dioceses within Bulgaria, each with its bishop or 'metropolitan', two overseas dioceses (New York and Akron, Ohio), a diocese for Western Europe, with headquarters in Budapest, several individual parishes abroad, and a small group of monks on Mount Athos. The general administration of the Church is in the hands of the Holy Synod, which includes the Patriarch and all the diocesan prelates. (There are about ten other bishops, each bearing the title of an ancient diocese.)

The Theological Academy of St Clement of Ohrid, governed directly by the Holy Synod, is in Sofia and the Orthodox Seminary is at the Cherepish Monastery, in the Iskar Gorge, north of the capital. Together, these cater for some 380 students, according to figures published in 1984 by the Church (although another source suggests that the numbers are smaller). There is a synodal publishing house, but its output is minimal and largely devoted to uncontroversial ecclesiastical topics. The Church is allowed to produce a newspaper, *Tsurkoven vestnik* ('Church Gazette'), appearing every ten days, and a monthly journal, *Duhovna kultura* ('Spiritual Culture'). There are Orthodox holiday and rest homes, church farms (totalling about 9,000 acres) and workshops for the manufacture of candles and other religious objects. (Of the Church's revenue, estimated in 1983, 13% came from state subsidy, but well over half was derived from the sale of candles and calendars.) Other institutions associated with the Orthodox Church include planning and building departments and a church history and archival institute (containing a historical and archaeological museum).

Most indigenous Bulgarians are at least sympathetic towards the Orthodox Church and, if challenged, many, from a wide variety of social groups, would claim it to be 'their Church'. No relevant statistics are available to permit a serious sociological analysis of the Church's present composition. As is the case in many Christian churches (in both East and West), the older generation appears to predominate, although not to the complete exclusion of the young.

According to figures appearing fairly recently in the Orthodox press (which bear a remarkable resemblance to those published about 10 years previously), the Bulgarian Orthodox Church has 3,720 churches and chapels, administered by about 1,500 parish priests. The number of Orthodox monasteries in the country is given as 120, but it is not clear how many of these remain as functioning religious houses. (At the two most famous monasteries of Rila and Bachkovo, the numbers of monks in 1984 were 8 and 15 respectively.) The total number of monks and nuns—about 200 of each—has apparently remained constant since 1975.

At the beginning of this decade, the Orthodox *bratstva* or parish brotherhoods were becoming increasingly active. They were composed of lay members of the congregation who helped the local priests in such activities as cleaning the church and tending the churchyard. However, these developed into fellowship groups to which the priests would address a short homily when they gathered to carry out their work, and they were formally banned by the government in 1982.

Current growth trends

It is not possible to make a really objective analysis of the degree and nature of the commitment of those who would claim to be ordinary Orthodox believers today. The state continues to promote an ideology of which atheism is an intrinsic element. It has succeeded in imposing such controls on the Church as to render it politically impotent and socially inoffensive. Today, the compliant hierarchy of the Bulgarian Church gives enthusiastic support to the régime and its leaders—who can afford to be polite in return. Far from encouraging the faithful to scrutinise the ideology of the régime with which they have to co-exist, the Orthodox leaders speak, through their official journal, of 'the normal and loyal relationship between Church and state in our country' and pledge that the Church 'will continue to cultivate in its youth a love for our socialist motherland' and 'encourage creative work towards its further blossoming.' Orthodoxy represents no apparent threat to the evolution of the country along communist lines and consequently it seems unlikely at present that the authorities will go out of their way to disturb the status quo.

It is not possible to assess how many of the Orthodox clergy or laity dissent from this line of least resistance. There is virtually no *samizdat,* and very little evidence of dissident activity within the Orthodox Church. There have been rumours of the existence of an underground Orthodox Church, but these have not so far been confirmed. There are suggestions that some young people, disillusioned with the shallowness of the communist ideology, are beginning to turn to their national Church; but in general it would be hazardous to make any predictions about the future of Orthodoxy in Bulgaria.

The Roman Catholic and Eastern-rite Catholic Churches

History

As we have seen, Catholicism was rejected in favour of Orthodoxy in Bulgaria in the ninth century and Catholic influence was insignificant in the country until the counter-reformation. In the sixteenth century Apostolic Visitors with responsibility for Bulgaria were appointed by Rome, and the following century saw the beginning of a real Roman Catholic mission in the country, with the establishment of two archbishoprics. Following the abortive Chiprovtsi uprising against the Turkish occupiers in 1688, the Catholics suffered persecution and survived only in scattered groups.

The year 1861 saw the establishment of the Eastern-rite Catholic Church in Bulgaria, following moves by some Orthodox clergy and laity, who resented the way in which they were being subjected to the power of the patriarchate of Constantinople. Numerically, this has always been a small denomination in Bulgaria and that probably explains why its survival has been allowed, even under the present régime.

Following the liberation from Turkish occupation in 1878, Catholic schools, hospitals and orphanages were founded and, by the beginning of the Second World War, Catholicism had regained a certain prestige and influence.

Since the Communist take-over in 1944, the scene has changed radically. During the late 1940s and early 1950s, Bulgarian Catholics were severely persecuted and repressed. Religious education was banned and all Catholic educational and social institutions closed. Many Catholics were arrested and some were put to death. More recently, repression has continued, but the state has used much less violent means to achieve its ends. The ban on religious instruction for minors by the clergy, strongly emphasised in 1982, has been keenly felt by the Catholic community. Clergy and religious suffer great privations and, for the most part, live in very poor conditions.

Church structure and membership; current growth trends
Bishop Dobranov of Sofia-Plovdiv, who died in 1983, was replaced only in 1988, thus increasing the number of Latin-rite bishops to two; the Eastern-rite faithful have an apostolic exarch. There are believed to be some 60,000 Latin-rite Catholics in Bulgaria, served by about 25 priests; for the Eastern-rite, the numbers are about 10,000 and 15 respectively. The two rites have, for many years, worked harmoniously together and their relations with the Orthodox have been good. There are a few tiny communities of religious. No Catholic seminaries or theological institutions are permitted by the authorities; most of the priests are very elderly and it is extremely difficult to replace those who die. In 1987, however, it was reliably reported that the Bulgarian authorities had given permission for the ordination of 3 new priests annually. Under the present régime, the Catholics have remained uncompromising and consistently true to their faith. They have endured much in consequence and, in human terms, the state

of Catholicism in the country can only be described as precarious.

Protestant Denominations

History

The Protestant Churches in Bulgaria are of comparatively recent origin and include only a tiny proportion of the practising Christians in the country. The American Congregational Church and the American Methodist Church had missionaries in the country from about the middle of the last century; they divided their activities geographically, with the Congregationalists influential in the south and the Methodists in the north. (This division survives today.) The Baptist movement in Bulgaria, initiated by German members who came into the country from Russia, began a little later. They were followed by the Adventists, whose adherents first settled in Bulgaria in 1891. The Pentecostal Church became established in 1921 and is now by far the largest Protestant denomination.

During the Stalinist period, the Protestants, like other Christians in the country, were subjected to violent repression. Some pastors were shot and a number of Church leaders were given long terms of imprisonment. Comprehensive restrictions were imposed on the Churches' activities. Since the early 1950s, the violence has eased considerably, but the constraints remain. The authorities are particularly sensitive to East-West church contacts, other than those organised with the government's express approval. In 1979, five leading Pentecostals were imprisoned, having been found guilty of receiving currency and/or literature from the West. As recently as 1984, a Pentecostal imprisoned for refusing to bear arms was severely beaten by the guards when he insisted on celebrating Christmas in gaol. Pastors who refuse to comply with state directives can still find themselves suspended, imprisoned or sent into internal exile.

Church membership; current growth trends
The mainstream Pentecostals in Bulgaria are thought to

number about 7,000 at present, the Congregationalists about 4,000, the Methodists 1,500, the Baptists 800 and the Adventists possibly 3,000. There are also a number of other small Protestant groups including Free and Tinchevist Pentecostals, Christian Brethren and Reformed Adventists.

Numerically, Protestantism in Bulgaria seems to have at least held its own over recent decades. Despite the absence of any facilities for theological training (other than Orthodox) within the country and restrictions on travel abroad for this purpose, some younger Protestant pastors seem to have been forthcoming—about a third of the fifty-five or so mainstream Pentecostal pastors are said to be under forty. On the other hand, the authorities seem to have had considerable success recently in their clear policy of infiltrating the denominational leaderships with pastors who are prepared to implement the wishes of the government. From the state's point of view, this has had the desired effect in that debilitating divisions have arisen among members of the same Church—and these obviously threaten the future well-being and effectiveness of Bulgarian Protestantism.

CHRISTIAN ACTIVITIES

Evangelism and mission

What the Bulgarian Constitution terms 'freedom of religion' represents, in terms of Christian activities, little more than the ability of approved denominations to conduct religious services of an agreed character under the direction of acceptable religious leaders. Atheist propaganda is encouraged, but Christian missionary campaigns are forbidden. Evangelism outside the church can take place only unofficially, generally on a person-to-person basis.

Broadcasting

There is no question of permitting the Christian view any representation on Bulgarian radio or television. Christian broadcasts from Vatican radio and Trans World Radio are beamed to Bulgaria.

Literature

There are very few outlets for the books emanating from the Orthodox Synodal Publishing House (the only organisation producing any significant Christian literature). The few works that are printed seem, for the most part, to be on learned theological or historical topics, of concern to the clergy and scholars rather than to the laity. Much the same interests are served by the Orthodox periodicals mentioned above. Practical, everyday problems and issues are largely ignored and matters of a controversial nature studiously avoided.

There seems to be very little, if any, religious *samizdat* circulating in Bulgaria; certainly none finds its way abroad.

Bible translation and distribution

In 1983 a slightly revised edition of the Bulgarian Bible was printed by the Bulgarian Orthodox Church, on paper supplied by the United Bible Societies. The UBS reported (in October 1983) that until then there had been no production of Bibles in the country at least since the Second World War. It is known that many Protestants either possess or have access to a Bible, but a shortage still exists. A traveller was told at the Synodal bookshop in Sofia in successive years (1984 and 1985) that no Bibles were available.

Bibles are taken unofficially into Bulgaria by Western organisations and concerned individuals, and these go some way towards meeting the general shortage.

Education

The Bulgarian Orthodox Church has special government authorisation to administer its Seminary and Theological Academy, but these are the only exceptions in the country to the Religious Denominations law of 1949, which forbade religious denominations to maintain any kind of school. This law states that the education of the young shall be carried out 'under the care of the government and shall not be within the province of the religious denominations and their ministers of religion'. At the Cherepish Seminary, there were, until 1987, 5-year and 3-year courses; now there is only a 3-year course. All the seminarians are full boarders and receive scholarships. Most of the students at the Theological Academy come directly from the Seminary. There are some extramural students, seeking to improve their theological qualifications. Although some of its graduates enter other professions than the ministry, the Academy is referred to as the 'intellectual power-house' of the Orthodox Church. (One of its members is Professor Todor Sabev, Deputy General Secretary of the World Council of Churches.)

Social concerns

All Church-sponsored hospitals, orphanages and similar institutions were taken over by the state in 1949 and the Churches generally are excluded from performing any significant social funtion in the country. Under the Religious Denominations law, all such activity has become the exclusive responsibility of the state. The Bulgarian Orthodox Church is, however, allowed some latitude in caring for its 'clergy and other church personnel working in its enterprises and offices'. Some houses have been constructed for them by the church building organisation 'Synstro' and special Orthodox summer holiday and rest homes exist for their benefit.

CHAPTER 9

Yugoslavia

YUGOSLAVIA: OVERVIEW

The country; the people; brief history

Yugoslavia came into being only after the First World War, partly as a consequence of the break-up of the Austro-Hungarian Empire. Former south Slav territories of the Empire united with the independent kingdoms of Serbia and Montenegro to produce a country of 98,766 square miles. Today it comprises six republics (Serbia, Croatia, Bosnia-Hercegovina, Slovenia, Macedonia and Montenegro) and two autonomous regions (Kosovo and Vojvodina). Four principal languages are spoken and each republic and region retains its own strong national identity. Yugoslavia shares borders with Italy, Austria, Hungary, Romania, Bulgaria, Greece and Albania. In the north and east the fertile valleys of the Danube and the Sava link the country with Central Europe; the narrow coastal strip links it to the Mediterranean world, and in between two-thirds of the country is occupied by complex rugged mountain ranges over which migrating peoples and invaders have passed in all directions for centuries.

The population of Yugoslavia is about twenty-two million. Apart from the national groups belonging to the different republics, there are several national minorities. The most important national groups are the Croats (traditionally Catholic) and the Serbs (traditionally Orthodox). Catholics also predominate in Slovenia while the Macedonians and Montenegrins are Orthodox. There is a minority group of Albanian Moslems (in Kosovo), as well as a group of Albanian Catholics, and in Bosnia there are Moslems of Slavic origin. In 1968 Tito created an official Moslem nationality in order to end disputes as to whether the Slavic Moslems were of Serbian or Croatian stock.

As suggested above, the history of the countries and

nationalities which now comprise Yugoslavia is extremely complex. The Slavs entered the western Balkans in the sixth and seventh centuries. From the twelfth century to about the middle of the fourteenth century the kingdom of Serbia was the centre of independent south Slav power. The Turks eventually conquered Serbia and Bosnia, and held on to them until the nineteenth century; meanwhile the northern areas of the peninsula came under the control of the Austrian Empire. Only mountainous Montenegro kept its independence. Serbia regained its independence during the nineteenth century, but the Balkans continued to be the theatre for rivalry among the great powers, chiefly Austria and Russia. It was the murder of an Austrian archduke by a Bosnian revolutionary which finally sparked off the First World War.

The kingdom of Yugoslavia, founded in 1919, suffered from the beginning from Serb-Croat rivalry, and tension between the two lay behind virtually all the country's political problems between 1919 and 1941. King Alexander, a Serb, followed a policy of centralisation (resented by Croats, who wanted a federal state with considerable local autonomy). The king's policies led to his institution of a dictatorship in 1929. From the 1920s Croat émigrés established groups called *ustaše* (singular: *ustaša*) organised on fascist lines and aiming to set up an independent Catholic Croatia.

In 1941 Hitler invaded Yugoslavia and the country was dismembered. The only nominally independent part was Croatia, under the puppet government of the *ustaša* leader Dr Ante Pavelić. Systematic anti-Serb and anti-Orthodox atrocities sowed the seeds of the hatred which persists to this day.

Meanwhile, the Partisans, the indigenous resistance movement led by the communist Josip Broz (Tito), were working to free Yugoslavia from German occupation. A long guerrilla campaign led in 1944 to formal Allied support for Tito. The Croatian government disintegrated and its members fled at the end of the war; and with the help of the Soviet Red Army, Tito finally succeeded in liberating the whole of Yugoslavia.

The Federal People's Republic of Yugoslavia was proclaimed in November 1945. Initially, Tito followed a strict Leninist line and dealt harshly with any opposition, including

that based on religious belief. Soon, however, he found himself
in disagreement with the Soviet leaders and Yugoslavia was
expelled from the Soviet bloc in 1948. Since then, the country
has followed its own road and has evolved a relatively humane
political system.

The economy; social conditions; political life

The first 5-Year Plan, introduced in 1947, envisaged highly
centralised economic planning on the Stalinist line; and an
attempt was made to collectivise agriculture. During the 1950s,
however, a new system of 'socialist self-management' was
introduced, characterised by liberalisation and devolution.
Peasants can now own a certain amount of land and factories
have a real say in setting their own targets for output. The
Party, of course, exercises ultimate control; this is effective at
local level, but less so at federal and national level. During the
later years of Tito's presidency economic mismanagement led
to inflation and unemployment, and to a drop of about 30% in
living standards. The government introduced a quasi-market
economy, private enterprise being encouraged in both agriculture and industry. There is a well-developed tourist industry,
bringing in much-needed Western currency; and despite
Yugoslavia's non-aligned status, she is heavily dependent on
COMECON for trade.

There is a marked division between the living standards in
northern and southern Yugoslavia. In the northern parts it is
much higher, as is the level of cultural sophistication; in
Slovenia and parts of Croatia there is almost total literacy and
the 'feel' is that of northern Italy or Austria. Parts of the south
are by contrast still very poor and many peasants are illiterate.
Of the one million unemployed in Yugoslavia, about two-
thirds are young people.

Yugoslavia is a one-party state and the political system is not
democratic in the Western sense. There is a relatively high
degree of personal freedom, however, and relatively free political and religious debate (though this varies from region to

region, Slovenia and Croatia being the most advanced); but the authorities are likely to be sensitive about activities of a political and religious nature which seem to disguise nationalist motives, and to punish those involved.

Tito died in 1980, and since then the country has been run by a rotating collective presidency.

THE STATUS OF CHRISTIANITY

The religious complexion of the country

The Slavs who settled in the western Balkan lands in the sixth and seventh centuries comprised three main groups. To the north were the Slovenes, in the centre the Croats and to the south the Serbs. The last two share two very similar languages; but it was the first two which came under Western and Roman Catholic influence, while the Serbs came into the orbit of Constantinople and the Orthodox Church. The Slovenes were converted chiefly as a result of the missionary efforts of the Frankish kings (especially Charlemagne); the Croats were converted from the bishoprics of the Adriatic cities and north-western Italy. Meanwhile, the missionary work of St Sava and others led to the confirmation of the Serbs in Orthodoxy.

Protestantism has always had a negligible presence in the Yugoslav lands. However, in the twelfth century the Bogomil heresy took hold in Bosnia and became the faith of the majority of the common people, landowners and nobility. The Bogomils were a dualistic religious sect combining neo-Manichaean doctrines with reformist aspirations inspired by an evangelical Christianity. A Bogomil 'Bosnian Church' was founded. The Ottoman conquest of Serbia and Bosnia in the mid-fifteenth century led to the conversion to Islam of the Albanians of the Kosovo region; but Islam was also welcomed by the Bogomils of Bosnia, who proceeded to convert to the new faith. Islam had a number of points of resemblance to their own heresy and it gave the practical advantage that converts could keep their lands. Thus Bosnia produced the unique phenomenon of an Islamic Slav state.

Accurate statistics about the religious allegiance of the Yugoslav population today are hard to establish, but the broad picture is clear. The Serbian Orthodox Church has the nominal allegiance of some 40% of the population, and the Roman Catholic Church that of 32%. Only 0.8% of the population are Protestants.

About 10% of the population are Muslims (Slav or Albanian). They have over 1,500 imams and between 2,000 and 3,000 mosques. Yugoslavia is the only Eastern European country with Muslim theological educational institutions. Imams are trained at two medressehs (in Sarajevo and Pristina), and a Muslim theological faculty was opened in Sarajevo in 1977. There are three Muslim periodicals. *Glasnik* ('The Herald'), *Preporod* ('Renewal') and *Islamska Misao* ('Islamic Thought'). The Koran has been printed since the war. The Islamic community is very well organised. The chief religious official, the *Reis-ul-Ulema,* resides in Sarajevo, and there are four area assemblies or seniorates (Sarajevo, Pristina, Skopje and Titograd). Since Tito officially recognised a Muslim nationality in Yugoslavia, Muslims have enjoyed an increasing sense of identity and have developed fruitful links with Muslims in other countries. In 1983, 3,000 went on a pilgrimage to Mecca. The authorities have become sensitive to any hint of interest in the setting up of a specifically Islamic republic in Yugoslavia and in 1983, 13 Muslims were sentenced to terms ranging from 6 months to 15 years for allegedly advocating this.

Before the Second World War there were about 75,000 Jews in Yugoslavia. 80% of them died in the war; and then in 1948 all Jews who wished to do so were allowed to go to Israel. Today there may be as many as 6,000 Jews in Yugoslavia, although only 1,384 citizens declared themselves as Jews in the 1981 census. There is only one rabbi in Yugoslavia, and the National Federation of the thirty-five Jewish communities in the country is primarily a secular body. Many Jews have changed their names to Slavonic ones, and it seems likely that assimilation will continue to completion.

The Yugoslav authorities are not concerned systematically to attack religion, and regulations on religious activity are at worst inconvenient and restrictive rather than crippling to religious witness. The major factor posing a threat to religion is growing materialism and the secularisation which normally affects industrialised societies. Attendance at Catholic Masses in the cities is much lower than in the countryside; the same is true for the Orthodox.

The state's attitude to religion

There has not been a consistent offensive against religion as such in Yugoslavia since the 1950s. The late 1950s and early 1960s were marked by a gradual relaxation of tight Party control and efforts by the government to involve all citizens, including religious believers, in the socialist self-management system. The process of liberalisation in all spheres accelerated its pace after the fall of the head of the secret police and the country's leading conservative, Aleksandar Ranković, in 1966.

One of the reasons why the government has been anxious to accommodate religious believers is that any offensive on religion would be likely to provoke not only religious but also nationalist and political opposition. On the other hand, the government is always sensitive about religious activity when it appears to mask nationalist motives or to involve interference by believers in political affairs. Hence there is a built-in dilemma in the attitude of the Party to religion which has never been fully resolved.

The period of liberalisation from the late 1960s until early 1972 did indeed see a rise in nationalist feeling throughout Yugoslavia; and the consequence was that in 1972 Tito put a definite brake on relaxations of Party control. Liberals both at the centre and in the republics were replaced by more conservative men. The churches felt the effect of this tightening of control: the authorities became less tolerant of the manifold social and cultural activities organised by the churches (for example, choirs, free medical services provided by religious organisations, study grants by churches), fearing that these might condition citizens to look to their various religious communities as protectors not only of their religious interests but also of their social and hence perhaps even political interests as well.

In general, lack of a clear and consistent Party programme on religion—laws differ from republic to republic—and problems consequent on the policy of decentralisation have encouraged the importance of religious communities at local level. The authorities have recently expressed concern over the growing involvement of young people in religious activities. In the 1985 session of the commission of the Central Committee for Ideological Work one of the speakers made it clear that the various religious bodies are gaining increasing influence among the young because the Party is inert and inactive in this sphere. There has been a certain amount of discussion at high levels over whether religious belief should be incompatible with membership of the Communist Party. However, it is a fact that certain types of employment are in practice closed to believers: higher ranks in the armed forces; senior posts in the government and economy; the diplomatic service. There are frequent public debates about whether believers may be teachers, and considerable variation in local practice. In this area, as in other areas of activity by believers, practice in general has become more restrictive since the early 1970s.

THE VARIOUS CHURCHES

The Serbian Orthodox Church

History
The patriarchate of the Serbian Orthodox Church was established in 1919 when Yugoslavia came into being. The Church saw this move as a revival of the mediaeval Serbian Church which achieved autocephaly under St Sava in 1219; but in fact

the new Church combined six separate Orthodox jurisdictions which had existed for centuries in different parts of Yugoslavia with their own traditions, and these now had to be accommodated. Another difficulty for the new Church was that instead of enjoying the rights of a state Church, it was now just one among many theoretically equal religious communities.

During the 1930s the Serbian Orthodox Church, and in particular its Patriarch Gavrilo Dožić, was prominent in resisting the growing friendship between Yugoslavia on the one hand, and Fascist Italy and Nazi Germany on the other. Serbs feared a betrayal of their national and religious traditions. When the Nazis invaded in 1941 the Patriarch was arrested and spent the war in prison and in Dachau concentration camp. It fell to Metropolitan Josif to administer and defend the Church. The nine Serbian Orthodox dioceses in the new fascist-led state of Croatia were the principal casualties: during the course of a few months the structure of the Church there was almost totally destroyed by the *ustaše*. Under Nazi control in Serbia itself, the Church agreed to observe the laws of the occupiers and to preserve peace.

After the Axis defeat the first task for the Church was to regather its congregations and restore parish life. Priests had been killed, or were missing, or had been forced to join the Croatian Orthodox Church. Property, libraries and treasures had been stolen and scattered. One-sixth of the pre-war total of 4,200 churches were destroyed or seriously damaged.

At the same time, the Church had to come to terms with restrictions on religious life being introduced by the new government. Land reforms deprived the churches of the major source of their income. Religious education in schools was officially stopped in 1952, and although permitted in churches, was beset by administrative obstacles. Restrictions were placed on the seminaries which the Church was trying to reopen. The new Yugoslav leaders in general wanted an accommodation rather than a confrontation with religious communities in this difficult period, but this did not alter their determination to punish any priests for alleged collaboration during the war; and throughout Yugoslavia there was widespread harassment of clergy and believers: the first show trial of an Orthodox bishop took place in 1946. The government sponsored the formation of priests' associations to encourage clergy who would be favourable to the new régime. By 1952, 80% of Orthodox priests were reported to be members of associations; the bishops viewed these associations with concern as they tried to reassert their own contol over the Church. At the same time, the government was able to use the Orthodox Church to keep up links with Orthodox Churches in other Eastern European countries as an adjunct to Yugoslav foreign policy.

The law on the Legal Status of Religious Communities of 1953 finally defined the Churches' rights, although it was a number of years before these began to be respected. The second major trial of an Orthodox bishop, Arsenije, took place in 1954.

From the mid-1950s, however, relations between the Orthodox Church and the state began to improve. Patriarch Vikentije became more prominent in relations with other religious communities throughout the world. His death in 1958 was front-page news in the national press; the newspaper *Politika* published a sympathetic obituary. Under his successor, Patriarch German, relations between the Serbian Orthodox Church and the government improved still further. They have continued cordial to this day, as part of the liberalisation of all aspects of Yugoslavian society, although from 1972 there was a certain hardening of the state's attitude, which referred not only to political but also to religious life. The government once again attacked the Churches for excessive nationalism and for exceeding their constitutional rights to concern themselves with purely 'religious' affairs, and it sought to define more closely the permitted areas in which priests may concern themselves. Clauses banning Churches from involvement in social activities which do not directly serve religious interests were introduced into new laws on religion promulgated in 1974-5. The ever-present spectre of nationalism was the main factor here, however, and no all-out attack on religious belief has been forthcoming. In any case, these new clauses have had more effect on the Catholic than on the Orthodox Church.

In general relations since the 1970s between the state and the Orthodox Church have been smoother than those between the state and the Catholic Church, and improvement has been steady. In 1984 the Orthodox Church opened a new 4-storey theological faculty in Belgrade. In 1986 the Yugoslav news agency Tanjug stated that the Party in Belgrade had noted with approval 'positive changes and a less clericalist approach in religious publications' on the part of the Orthodox Church.

Church structure and membership; current growth trends
The Serbian Orthodox Church, led by the patriarch who resides in Belgrade, has twenty-one dioceses in Yugoslavia and four more abroad. They include about 2,400 parishes served by about 1,400 priests. The shortage of priests is partly a consequence of the massacres during the Second World War. The Church had about 8 million members in 1964. There are 83 monasteries but only some 200 monks; since the Second World War, there has been a revival of women's monasticism and there are now about 700 nuns in 72 convents. The Church, like all religious communities in Yugoslavia, is allowed to publish, and has ten regular newspapers and journals. There are almost 600 theological students in 5 seminaries and an average of about 100 students in the higher Orthodox theological faculty in Belgrade. The foundation-stone of a new building for the faculty in Belgrade to accommodate about 200 students was laid in 1984 in the presence of Patriarch German.

Orthodox churches are well attended on major festivals, but more sparsely at other times. By no means every parish organises religious education for young people, partly because of a shortage of priests, but often as a result of administrative pressure. There are no signs that the Serbian Orthodox Church is growing in numbers. Recently, however, there have been some signs of an intellectual and spiritual revival: some younger monks and one bishop are known to be involved.

The Macedonian Orthodox Church

Macedonia has always been disputed between Serbia, Bulgaria and Greece as part of the integral territory of each. An independent archbishopric in Ohrid had been abolished by the Ottoman Turks in 1767, but after the formation of Yugoslavia the Orthodox in Macedonia were taken into the Serbian Orthodox Church (1920). Macedonia was under Bulgarian occupation during the Second World War, but the Comintern decided that it should eventually revert to Yugoslav control, and after the war the new Yugoslav government was committed to the establishment of a separate Macedonian republic within the new federation, partly as a deterrent to possible further Bulgarian claims to the area. This was welcomed by Macedonian Orthodox clergy who called in turn for ecclesiastical independence from the Serbian Orthodox Church. The leadership of the latter, however, resisted this idea vigorously, and the Macedonian clergy set themselves as their interim aim to obtain their own bishops. Eventually losing patience with the Serbian hierarchy, however, the Macedonian priests in 1958 declared their Church 'autonomous', while still under the ultimate headship of the Serbian patriarch. Under pressure from the government Patriarch German was reduced to silence. Further problems, however, led the Macedonians to claim complete autocephaly in 1967, but although the Yugoslav government approves, the Serbian Orthodox Church has never recognised Macedonian autocephaly, nor has any other Orthodox Church.

The Church has between 600,000 and one million members in four dioceses. It has 250 priests and one seminary.

The Roman Catholic Church

History
The creation of the kingdom of Yugoslavia in 1919 brought the Catholic Croats and Slovenes, in territories formerly belonging to the Austro-Hungarian Empire, into an uneasy political union under the Serbian Orthodox crown. Inter-war discrimination against Croats by the dominant Serbs contributed to the political and religious enmity between the two groups which came to a head in the Second World War. The fascist-led

independent state of Croatia was determined to purify itself of
Serbs, and by deporting, murdering or converting the Serbian
population of Croatia the *ustaše* succeeded in destroying
Orthodoxy as well.

The Catholic clergy in Croatia were in an unhappy and
divided state. Most of them welcomed an independent Croatia,
but while some supported the *ustaše*, others including
Archbishop Stepinac of Zagreb were appalled at the atrocities
and denounced them, at first privately but later in sermons in
public.

Immediately after the war the new Yugoslav government
was determined to punish clergy who had collaborated with the
fascists, and its attention turned naturally to the Catholic
Church. Additional political charges which could be laid
against Catholic clergy arose from the suspicious attitude of the
new government towards the Vatican, which in supporting
Italy during the war could be said to have endorsed Italian
claims to Yugoslav territory. Show trials of clergy took place
from the mid-1940s. The most famous of these was the trial of
Archbishop Stepinac in 1946. He was sentenced to sixteen
years in prison. In fact he served only five, and then lived in
exile in his native village until his death in 1960. He was then
partially rehabilitated and given a massively attended funeral
and burial in Zagreb Cathedral.

Other pressures on the Catholic Church in the late 1940s
were similar to those felt by the Orthodox Church, and arose
from legislation being introduced by the government depriving
Churches of the greater part of their lands and possessions,
restricting religious education and so on. As in the Orthodox
Church, the government promoted the founding of priests'
associations as a means of dividing the clergy and undermining
the authority of the bishops.

In 1953 the Churches were given a legal definition of their
rights, and from the mid-1950s their situation began to
improve. In 1966 the Yugoslav government signed a protocol
with the Vatican and in 1970 became the first socialist government to restore full diplomatic relations. During the late 1960s
the Catholic Church in Croatia experienced an intellectual and
spiritual renaissance upon which the government looked

benevolently. In 1972, however, Tito launched an attack on Croat 'nationalist euphoria' and purged the Croatian League of Communists. For several years the Catholic Church was subjected to criticism for allegedly disseminating nationalist propaganda in its paper *Glas Koncila,* and the Catholic Archbishop Kuharić of Zagreb was attacked in the press for allegedly supporting the dismissed Croatian leaders. In the mid-1970s new legislation deprived Churches of the right to become involved in social and economic activities. As originally drafted the law would have put a stop to the extensive charitable activities of the Catholic Church in Croatia, but the Church protested and subsequent long discussions meant that the law in Croatia was not published until 1978. It now bans all activities by the Church not directly related to religious ends; but even in its present form it is not strictly applied in Croatia.

Since the 1970s relations between the state and the Catholic Church have been much less smooth than between the state and the Orthodox Church, partly as a consequence of the boldness of the bishops and clergy in standing up to state pressure, partly as a consequence of the religious revival in the Church. By the early 1980s Catholic bishops were being subjected to frequent attacks in the Yugoslav media, couched in a language reminiscent of the early 1950s, and courts were sentencing priests to relatively lengthy terms of imprisonment for apparently minor misdemeanours construed as 'religio-nationalistic activity'.

Church structure and membership; current growth trends
The Roman Catholic Church, under the leadership of the Cardinal Archbishop of Zagreb, has 14 dioceses divided into 2,782 parishes. These figures are comparable with those for the Serbian Orthodox Church. The Catholic Church, however, has about 3,000 priests, 1,750 monks in 180 monasteries, 6,500 nuns in over 400 convents, and 30 seminaries and 2 theological faculties with a total of some 1,700 students. The publishing activity of the Church has been very vigorous over the last twenty years and there are nearly seventy regular Catholic publications. All these figures are substantially higher than those for the Orthodox Church, and indicate in general the greater

spiritual vitality of the Catholic Church.

The Church has traditionally organised a wide variety of social, cultural and welfare activities, and in the late 1960s began evangelistic activity on a large scale among young people, starting up youth clubs and sponsoring musical and sporting events to bring young people together. It was against these kinds of activities that the new religious legislation of the mid-1970s was principally directed. The development of this work among young people and the religious revival in Croatia coincided with a period of growing Croatian national feeling—the 'Croatian Spring'. A massive festival organised by the Church in 1971 near Zagreb in order to foster devotion to the Virgin Mary attracted some 200,000 people, and in the same year an international Mariological conference was held in Zagreb.

In the less tolerant climate towards religious activity since 1972 the Catholic Church remains the boldest of the religious organisations. In 1980, for example, some 40 leading Croatian intellectuals and priests signed a petition demanding an amnesty for all Yugoslavia's political prisoners. The election of a Polish Pope in 1978 has given a further boost to the Church's vitality, and from time to time government spokesmen find it necessary to remind the Church that Yugoslavia is not Poland.

A remarkable recent event affecting the Catholic community in Yugoslavia has been the series of appearances of the Virgin Mary to six children in the parish of Medjugorje in Hercegovina. These began in the summer of 1981 and within days large crowds were gathering from all parts of Yugoslavia—more than 10,000 on weekdays and several times that number at weekends. It is estimated that within four months at least half a million people had visited the parish. The authorities reacted in a hostile manner to the manifestations. A senior Party figure said that 'clerico-nationalists' were using the alleged appearances for purposes hostile to the Yugoslav state. The Bishop of Mostar, however, refused to dissociate the Church from the events. The priest of the parish was arrested and sentenced to three and a half years in prison for remarks made in sermons, and soon afterwards two of his close associates were accused of hostile activity and sentenced to eight and five and a half years respectively (though these sentences were later reduced). Meanwhile, eleven local

Party members were expelled and forty-eight punished for having visited Medjugorje. By 1988 the Vatican had still not reached a definite verdict on whether the alleged appearances were genuine, but reports continued to indicate that the result has been a new sense of mission and purpose among priests and nuns in the parish, and a general religious revival amongst the local people.

Other Denominations

Protestants comprise less than 1% of the population. There are four Churches, which serve a separate national minority: the Slovak Lutheran (Evangelical-Christian) Church, the Evangelical Church in Serbia, the Evangelical Christian Church of the Augsburg Confession in Slovenia, and the Reformed Church. None has more than some 55,000 members. There are about 3,500 Baptists, about 300 Adventist churches, about 3,700 Methodists, 72 congregations of Pentecostals, and 24 congregations of the Church of United Brethren. All these groups are well supplied with pastors, all have at least one regular publication and all have facilities for training clergy. A Protestant theological faculty open to students from all Protestant Churches was opened in 1976 in Zagreb. The Protestant denominations have made most progress in small rural communities, particularly, some feel, where the local Orthodox church lacks a priest. There is a certain amount of youth work in the cities and Protestant denominations have organised summer camps, conferences and crusades by visiting evangelists. In 1985 it was reported that in general the Protestant denominations had experienced significant growth in recent years.

Other denominations include Old Catholics (eleven parishes) and a small number of Eastern-rite Catholics under the administration of an Eastern-rite Bishop of Križevci.

Quasi-Christian groups

There are 104 congregations of Jehovah's Witnesses. They operate legally in Yugoslavia.

CHRISTIAN ACTIVITIES

Evangelism and mission

There is very little active evangelism by the Orthodox Church except by the clergy in church.

The Catholic clergy are more active, but tend to concentrate on their own lapsed members and on those national groups which have traditionally been Catholic (the Croats and Slovenes). It should be noted that since the signing of the protocol between the Yugoslav government and the Vatican in 1966, Catholic priests have been allowed to travel to Western countries to carry out pastoral work among expatriate Croats and Slovenes. As noted earlier, the Catholic Church since the late 1960s has been noted for its spiritual and intellectual vitality, and the Medjugorje appearances have recently stimulated further revival, in this case attracting pilgrims of other denominations too.

Protestant groups, as noted above, probably have more success in small rural communities than in the larger cities where they tend to have inadequate resources, both material and numerical, to combat the pressures of secularisation. Summer groups and conferences often attract large numbers: about 800 young people attended a Baptist conference in Novi Sad in 1978. A crusade conducted by Billy Graham in Zagreb in 1967 was, however, judged only a partial success.

Broadcasting

Requests by religious leaders, notably Catholic bishops, that the Churches should have access to radio and television have consistently been turned down by the authorities. There is then, no religious broadcasting in Yugoslavia organised by the Churches, although from time to time programmes do deal

with religious questions: in 1977 for example, several high-ranking clergy participated in a television programme which was
described at the time as the 'first religious programme on Yugoslav television'. In 1985 a series of 4 programmes was broadcast
on Yugoslav television about the Protestant Churches. Church
authorities had had some say in the making of the programmes
and were in general satisfied with the result.

In recent years Vatican Radio has been broadcasting regular
programmes in Serbo-Croat which are heard in Yugoslavia and
these contain information on the religious situation there.

Literature

All religious communities in Yugoslavia are allowed to publish
literature. As in other areas of religious activity, the laws differ
in detail from republic to republic. The laws in Croatia, in Bosnia
and Hercegovina and in Macedonia give comprehensive permission, but those in Slovenia and Serbia are more precise and
specify that the religious press shall confine itself exclusively to
religious and spiritual matters. The Serbian law also prohibits
the distribution of religious literature outside church premises,
except in special shops or by subscription. In fact in all the republics religious publications are vulnerable to action by the
authorities if they contain material which the authorities feel
promotes nationalist sentiments or intrudes into the political
realm. In 1980 a Croatian priest was sentenced to five years in
prison for writing to the Catholic newspaper *Glas Koncila* complaining of forced entry to churches and physical attacks on a
priest, which the authorities claimed had not taken place. The
Croatian Committee for Social Questions of Religion reported
in 1982 that 134 newspapers are published by the religious communities in Croatia, in an annual total of over 9 million copies;
but the Committee went on to criticise those who abused the
right to publish in order to give circulation to ideas alien to the
goals of Yugoslav society, and called on the Party to discuss
appropriate measures to be taken in cases when the religious
press exceeds its brief.

There are over 200 regular religious publications in Yugoslavia, and almost all religious communities have at least one. The Roman Catholic press continues to be the most active: it now has sixty-seven regular publications. The most important is the fortnightly Croatian newspaper *Glas Koncila*, which first appeared in 1962 and has a circulation of 120,000. It was intended by Archbishop Šeper of Zagreb as an information bulletin reporting on the Second Vatican Council, but has moved over the years to an authoritative position on the front line between church and state. The authorities have occasionally had to ban issues they have considered offensive. In 1966 Cardinal Šeper authorised the founding in Zagreb of *Kršćanska Sadašnjost* ('Contemporary Christianity'), a Catholic centre for the study of the Second Vatican Council. It supports itself by publishing liturgical books, and also produced a range of journals: *Svesci* is the main Catholic theological journal, which aims to communicate Western theological developments to its readers in Yugoslavia; *Kana* (circulation 53,000) is an illustrated family monthly magazine in colour; and *AKSA* is a weekly news service, which reports every mention of religion in the Yugoslav press as well as surveying the situation of religion in the countries throughout the world. In Slovenia, *Družina* (125,000) is the Catholic newspaper and *Ognjišće* (83,000) the magazine.

The Serbian Orthodox Church has ten publications. The most important is the fortnightly *Pravoslavlje* (24,000) published by the patriarchate in Belgrade. *Vesnik* (3,500) is also a fortnightly, intended mainly for the clergy. *Pravoslavni misionar* (50,000) appears six times a year, and *Svetosavsko zvonce* (30,000) is a monthly magazine.

The small Protestant denominations each have at least one regular publication. *Reformatus elet* (4,000) is the organ in Hungarian of the Reformed Church. The Baptists produce the fortnightly *Glas Evandjelja* (3,000) and the monthly *Glasnik* (3,000). *Glas Jevandjelja* (note the different spelling) is a Methodist publication. The Pentecostals publish the monthly *Izvori* in Croatian and the bimonthly *Hriscanski Pregled* in Serbian.

In addition to religious newspapers and journals, the churches produce books, calendars, pamphlets, epistles, postcards, records of church music and even religious films.

In 1983 books published by a number of religious communities, including the Orthodox, Catholic, Baptist and Evangelical Churches and the Muslims, were on show at the International Book Fair in Belgrade.

Bible translation and distribution

In the 10 years before 1970, the annual import of 25,000 Bibles by the United Bible Society was permitted and the Bible was printed in Yugoslavia in both Cyrillic and Roman script. Since the late 1960s, the Bible has been translated into all the major languages of Yugoslavia.

There is now no shortage of Bibles in Yugoslavia and they are freely available. There is a shop run by the United Bible Societies in Belgrade and copies of the Croat translation of the Bible are sold in many other bookshops. In 1971 the United Bible Societies decided to transfer to Yugoslavia the production of all Scriptures in the languages spoken in that country. The translation work is nearly always carried out on an inter-confessional basis, although the Croatian Catholics produced their own new translation in 1971. In 1981, 20,000 Bibles were published in each of the 3 languages Serbian, Croatian and Slovene, as well as 10,000 New Testaments in Albanian. In 1982, after 10 years' translation, editing and printing work, the first edition of the Living New Testament became available in Croatian and was in such demand that an immediate reprint was necessary. Called *The Book about Christ,* it is designed primarily for the secular market, for those who have had little or no previous exposure to the Bible. A New Testament in Serbo-Croat, published in 1984, was exhibited at the Belgrade International Book Fair. A translation of the Old Testament into Macedonian was handed to the typesetter in 1985 and when it is published, it will constitute, together with the Macedonian New Testament which appeared in 1967, the first complete Bible in Macedonian.

A New Testament commentary in 20 volumes, produced by

the Protestants, was published in Serbo-Croat in 1983–6 and went on sale in bookshops. It was funded by a £4,000 grant from Eurolit, an ecumenical body which facilitates the official publishing of religious literature in Eastern Europe. An Old Testament commentary is also planned.

Religious Education

The religious instruction of children is provided for in all the republics. It must be held on religious premises which are places of public access (ie a church or church building), it must not clash with school hours or school-linked activities, and must have the consent of both parents and the child. Slovenia, Serbia and Bosnia and Hercegovina do not specify the child's age of consent, but Croatia and the Vojvodina specify that the child must be over fourteen and Macedonia alone specifies ten. The Macedonian draft law was to have contained a clause forbidding religious instruction of children under the age of seventeen, but this was leaked in advance and picked up by *Glas Koncila,* the Zagreb religious fortnightly. There was such an outcry that the proposal was dropped. Clearly the phrase 'school-linked activities' lends itself to abuse. One of the most common complaints is that teachers frequently arrange out-of-school activities which clash with religious instruction or other religious activities, and this is done sometimes with the object of making it impossible for a child to take part in religious activities. There are great variations in practice: as well as many incidents which have led to complaints, there have also been reports of places where the priest and the school reach an informal understanding. There are also many complaints about teachers who, quite illegally, bring pressure on children not to go to religious instruction, or single them out for public ridicule. A determined priest or bishop can very often obtain redress by complaining immediately to the local authorities: for example, in Slovenia Archbishop Pogačnik of Ljubljana referred to this abuse in a sermon and asked the authorities to take steps to curb it.

All republics allow religious communities to found schools for the education and training of priests, pastors and imams. There is no significant variation in the conditions laid down. Schools and halls of residence must be registered—they come under the general supervision of the competent ministry—but the curriculum and the appointment of teachers are under the control of the religious community. There have been no reports of instances of improper interference. Nobody who is not a Yugoslav citizen may teach in a religious school except with the permission of the authorities. Nobody may attend until he or she has completed compulsory education between the ages of seven and fifteen. Slovenia specifically allows persons who assist the priest, but are not going to be ordained, to attend religious schools, and in practice this is common in all republics: for example, nuns attend the theological faculties and teach in some of the seminaries, and young men who attend both Orthodox and Catholic seminaries and faculties may go on to work in the offices of religious communities, or became catechists, without proceeding to ordination. Bosnia and Hercegovina is more specific than other republics and stipulates that the authorities must be notified of the curriculum and that nothing in the curriculum shall be in opposition to the Constitution. In some republics students at religious schools have gained some of the rights (social and health insurance, travel concessions) enjoyed by students at state schools and universities, except the right to shorter and deferred military service until the completion of education.

Social concerns

As soon as the Partisans came to power the Churches were deprived of their property and establishments, including hospitals, orphanages and homes for the elderly. These expropriations affected the Catholic Church much more seriously than the Orthodox Church: the former had a rich tradition of social activity. The Catholic hierarchy protested and, as a result, the government gave permission in 1946 for the work of *'Caritas'* to continue: under this name the church continued to give financial assistance and food to the needy.

The gradual liberalisation of Yugoslav political life especially between 1966 and 1971 produced a climate in which the Catholic Church could seek to extend its social involvement. It opened numerous youth centres and recreation clubs and began sponsoring musical and sports events.

After 1972, as we have seen, the government once again sought to cut back on the social activities of the Churches. New laws were drafted for the various republics. That for Croatia would have banned all the social and charitable activities of the Catholic Church, but the bishops protested so strongly that the draft was modified. Now only social activities not related to religious requirements are banned, and thus the work of *Caritas* can continue. The Croatian Catholic Church is now the only Church in Yugoslavia which owns its own welfare institutions. It has no hospitals, but runs homes for old people, abandoned children and unmarried mothers, and these are available to the general public, not only to Catholics.

Legislation in all the republics allows people in hospitals, sanatoria and old people's homes to practise their religion and to receive visits from priests, as long as house rules are obeyed and other inmates are not disturbed. Visits by priests to prison inmates have never been allowed, however, nor the practice of religion in the armed forces. As in other areas of religious activity, local practice varies widely. In 1986 the Catholic newspaper *Glas Koncila* reported that a notice had been hung in all corridors of a hospital in one town (Lipik) stating that 'all religious rites are forbidden in the hospital, except for those expressly authorised by the hospital authorities, and in these cases only on the express demand of the patient or his closest relatives'. It was reported that some patients were afraid that applications for a visit by a priest would bring mockery from hospital staff, and that processing of applications can take so long that dying patients do not receive the last rites in time.

Ecumenical relations

Enmity and suspicion have traditionally characterised relations between Catholics and Orthodox in Yugoslavia; but there have been some efforts by both denominations to overcome these barriers and work towards real ecumenical co-operation. There are two-yearly conferences between the two Catholic and the one Orthodox theological faculties, and a certain amount of friendly contact between believers at local level. Bible translation projects have been effective in bringing about co-operation among the denominations. Since the election of Pope John Paul II, the Catholic Church has experienced a growth in self-confidence under the influence of the Pope's strategy to give Christians of East and West of all denominations a sense of unity. In 1980 government and Roman Catholic representatives attended the installation of an Orthodox bishop. The Catholic newspaper *Glas Koncila* reports on developments in the Orthodox, Protestant and Islamic communities.

The Protestants also seem to be co-operating among themselves to an ever greater degree. In April 1980 the first working interdenominational conference on evangelism was held in Novi Sad, and members of a wide range of Protestant denominations attended.

Christian-Marxist dialogue

After the invasion of Czechoslovakia and the crushing of the 'Prague Spring' in 1968 it was for many years only in Yugoslavia that there was any serious attempt to maintain some form of constructive dialogue between Christians and Marxists. (Recently new attempts have also been made in Hungary.) On the Christian side the dialogue in Yugoslavia is confined almost entirely to the Catholic Church, and it involves occasional meetings of Catholic intellectuals with their communist counterparts to discuss how more fruitful co-operation can be achieved.

NOTES

1. See *Religious Prisoners in the USSR* (Marc/Keston College, London, 1987)
2. Metropolitan: the title of a bishop exercising provincial and not merely diocesan powers.
3. The Council of Chalcedon in 451 affirmed that Christ has two natures, human and divine, which while inseparable are unconfused. This doctrine has been accepted by the majority of churches, but not by those churches now known as Monophysite, of which the most important are the Copts, the Syrian Jacobites and the Armenians.
4. 'Kenotic' theories explain the way in which Christ restrained, limited or 'emptied' himself in order to become incarnate.
5. Autocephalous: independent and self-governing. It describes the status of the modern national Orthodox Churches which, while in communion with Constantinople, are governed by their own national synods.
6. Exarch: local plenipotentiary representing a Church leader—in this case, the Patriarch of the Russian Orthodox Church.
7. Catholicos-Patriarch: title of the head of the Georgian Orthodox Church.
8. The Molokan sect originated in the late eighteenth century. The Molokans taught a spiritual Christianity freed from church rituals and canons.
9. Monophysite—see Note 3 above.
10. Catholicos: title of the head of the Armenian Apostolic Church.

A FEW WORDS ABOUT KESTON COLLEGE

The founder and director of Keston College, the Rev Michael Bourdeaux, was told by a group of Christians in the Soviet Union in 1964: 'The most important single way you can help us is by telling our story. Give the facts exactly as they are. The world must know.' Keston College was established as a direct response to this particular call which was later repeated by many other Christians—a call to give the facts, to let the world know what is happening in the realms of spiritual life and growth and in problems encountered by believers from atheist propaganda and discrimination because of their religious activity.

Keston College has remained faithful to that call. The research and archive staff speak the languages of the countries which they study; most have travelled and lived within a country of Eastern Europe for some time. The reputation of the College for accuracy, expertise and equal treatment of all believers seeking to tell us about themselves has grown over the years. As the College has been faithful to speak for them, other organisations and individuals have also been faithful to act on the basis of that information. Keston College is unique for its comprehensiveness and ecumenical approach to the cause of religious liberty in the Soviet Union and other communist countries. You can help religious believers in the Soviet Union by supporting the work of Keston College.

Please write to the appropriate address if you would like to be put on the mailing list to receive (free of charge) *The Right to Believe* each time it appears. Please also ask for details of subscriptions to *Keston News Service*, *Frontier* and *Religion in*

Communist Lands, recommended reading lists, and other information. The work depends upon donations entirely, and your gifts to help will always be welcome.

Keston College,
Heathfield Road,
Keston,
Kent BR2 6BA,
England.

North America:
Keston USA,
PO Box 1310,
Framingham,
MA 10710,
U.S.A.

Australia:
Keston College Australia,
19 Sloane Street,
Stawell,
VIC 3380,
Australia.

New Zealand:
Keston College New Zealand,
PO Box 28131,
Kelburn,
Wellington 5,
New Zealand.

C000048803

TAILS
OF THE
UNEXPECTED

**A JOURNAL OF MEMORIES &
MISADVENTURES FOR MY DOG**

Hardie Grant

QUADRILLE

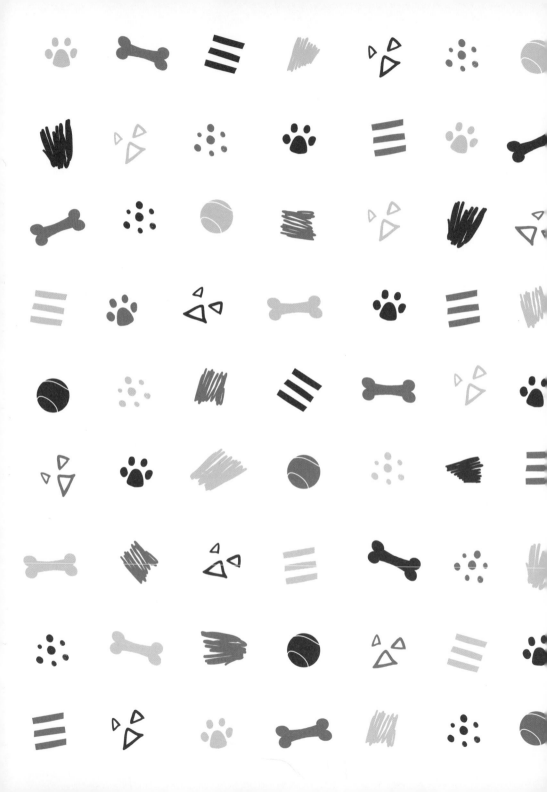

THIS JOURNAL BELONGS TO

_____

FIRST
YEAR

How did you choose your furry friend?

What is their gender and breed?

What did you first notice about them?

What makes them top dog in your eyes?

Did you choose to adopt or buy your furry friend?

Was your dog raised with its mother?

By the end of your first visit was your dog friendly? Nervous? Fearful?

How long did you have to wait between the first and second visit?

What were you most excited for with your new four-legged friend? Cuddles? Playtime?

_____

_____

_____

_____

_____

_____

_____

_____

_____

_____

_____

_____

How did you first meet? Was it love at first sight?

_____

_____

_____

_____

_____

_____

_____

_____

_____

_____

_____

_____

As a new owner of a dog, did you have any worries or fears?

How was the journey home with your precious pooch?

How did you spend your first day together?

Bringing a new family member home for the first time can be a special and un-fur-gettable experience. What are some of your favourite memories from this day?

How did you prepare your home for the new arrival?

Was there any confusion when you first brought your dog home?

Were there any family pets that they needed to be introduced to?

What was the first food you fed them?

Make a list of all the things you needed to make them feel at home (bed/lead/bowl/toys).

-
-
-
-
-

Make a list of anything you still need.

-
-
-
-
-

STICK PHOTOGRAPHS HERE FROM THEIR FIRST YEAR

How and why did you choose your dog's name?

Describe the first time you used their name and they recognised it.

How did you introduce your new family member to your home and family?

What happened the first time you both went for a walk together?

How did you celebrate their first birthday?

What was the first gift you got for them?

Describe a special day out together.

_____

_____

_____

_____

_____

_____

_____

_____

_____

_____

_____

_____

STICK PHOTOGRAPHS HERE FROM ONE YEAR LATER

What happened the first time you went away, with or without your pup? Describe the experience.

How does your dog get along with other humans?

How does your dog get on with other animals?

Who is your pooch's BFF (best furry friend) and what do they get up to together?

DIP YOUR DOG'S PAW IN (NON-TOXIC) PAINT OR INK, THEN GENTLY PRESS IT ONTO THE PAGE FOR A COUPLE OF SECONDS. LIFT THE PAW STRAIGHT UP AND WASH IT.

ROUTINE

DESCRIBE YOUR DOG'S TYPICAL DAY

MEALS

Breakfast:

Lunch:

Dinner:

Snacks:

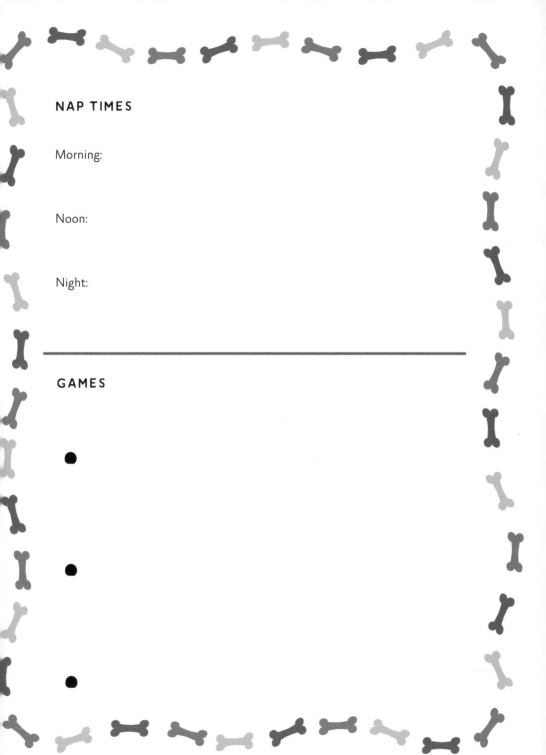

NAP TIMES

Morning:

Noon:

Night:

GAMES

-
-
-

Describe your training routine.

_____

_____

_____

_____

_____

_____

_____

_____

_____

_____

_____

_____

_____

What's your pup's favourite reward?

What is their favourite exercise?

And their least favourite exercise?

What are they really good at, and what needs work?

How well behaved is your dog on a lead? Any doggy disasters or surprising experiences?

Describe your first attempts at toilet training.

Pack-loving pooches like making friends; who runs in your dog's tribe?

DRAW OR STICK IN PHOTOGRAPHS OF YOUR PUP'S PALS

Where does your pooch like to exercise?

_____

Is your dog a city slicker or an off-the-beaten-track adventurer?

From surfing to doggy dancing, what surprising things does your pup enjoy doing?

Describe your first trip to the vet together.

Describe your canine's personality.

Where's your dog's safe place?

What do you love most about training with your furry friend?

FAVOURITES

Whether relishing doggy delicacies or chewing a rubber bone, food is the stuff of woof! What are your pooch's top three favourite dinners?

-

-

-

Do you have any funny food-related stories about your dog?

How about human food?

List any special dietary requirements.

-
-
-

Where is your dog's preferred snoozing spot?

_____

Where is your preferred spot to snooze together?

What about sleeping positions? Describe or draw their cutest pose.

PAP YOUR PUP IN THEIR FAVOURITE SNOOZING SPOTS

Whether it's your bed, their bed or the couch, every dog has a slumber schedule. What's your dog's bedtime ritual?

What is your favourite game to play with them?

What is their favourite game to play with you?

Top dogs have top toys; what's your pooch's favourite plaything?

What sends your pooch into tail-wagging overdrive?

How does your pooch like to be pampered?

A scratch behind the ear is a pleasurable experience for giver and receiver; what's your dog's itching spot of choice?

What is your favourite part of the day with your dog and why?

_____

_____

_____

_____

_____

_____

_____

_____

_____

_____

_____

What makes them bark out loud?

.

What's their favourite foodie treat?

Describe an adventure you've shared together.

Describe a misadventure you've shared together.

What is it about your furry chum that makes you laugh out loud?

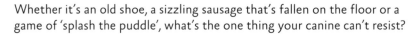

Whether it's an old shoe, a sizzling sausage that's fallen on the floor or a game of 'splash the puddle', what's the one thing your canine can't resist?

When have you felt proud of your pooch? Explain why.

How does your furry friend make you feel special?

_____

_____

_____

_____

_____

_____

_____

_____

_____

_____

_____

_____

Describe a treasured memory of your dog, whether it's an experience you've shared or just a moment in time.

_____

_____

_____

_____

_____

_____

_____

_____

_____

_____

_____

_____

Name the lap of choice for your pup.

Who is your dog's favourite human and how can you tell?

Who is their master and how can you tell?

STICK PHOTOGRAPHS HERE OF YOUR DOG WITH THEIR
FAVOURITE HUMAN

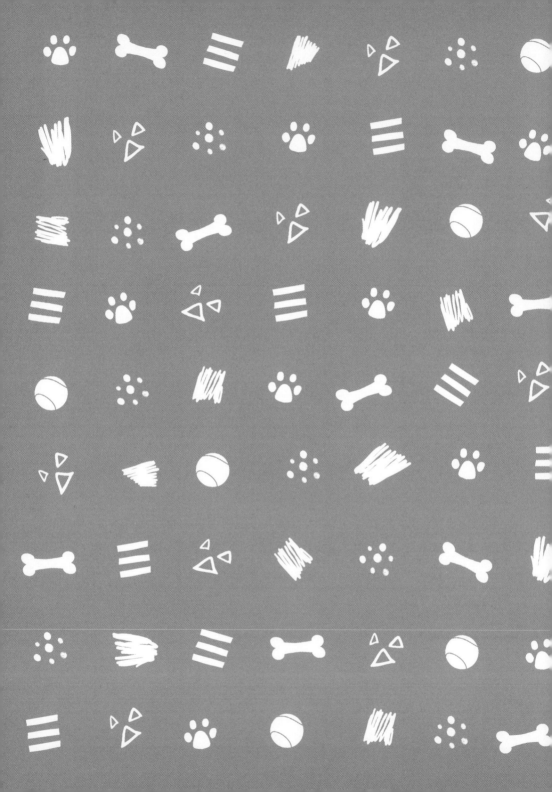

ECCENTRICITIES

Does your dog have a nickname, or respond to different calls?

-
-
-
-
-

What freaks out your fur buddy?

What is the strangest noise your dog makes and what do you think it means?

What's the funniest thing they've done since joining the family?

What's the weirdest thing they've done since joining the family?

Is there anything in particular that gives your dog the 'zoomies'?

What is your dog's strangest habit?

Has your pooch taken a dislike to anyone or anything? Why do you think this is?

Do you watch TV together, and if so, which shows top your canine's list?

From digging up the garden to riding pillion on the motorbike, what unusual activities do you enjoy doing together?

Is your pooch a music lover, and what makes them strut their furry stuff?

Where does your dog like to hide, and what is their oddest bolt hole?

Is your dog a fashion hound, and if so, what's their outfit of choice?

Is your dog a water baby or a mucky pup?

From the ability to sniff out trouble or just that hidden jar of cookies at the back of the cupboard, dogs are gifted sleuths. What other hidden talents does your canine possess?

And what can't they master, no matter how hard they try?

What superpowers do you think they have?

What superpowers do they think they have?

What's your dog's most annoying habit?

What's your pooch's most lovable trait?

Describe a standout moment in your life together.

How well behaved is your dog at the vet?

Are they a freaked-out canine or a take-it-easy top dog?

What are their views on dog cages: a cosy safe haven or a doggy dungeon?

What calms them down when the going gets tough?

From vacuum cleaners to toilet lids, what household objects strike fear into your otherwise fearless canine?

Have they ever been in a fight with another dog?

From pen lids to paper clips, has your dog ever eaten something they shouldn't have?

Do you regularly have to discourage your pup from being naughty?

Describe the naughtiest thing your dog has ever done.

PRACTICAL INFO

What's your dog's name?

What's their official date of birth?

What date did they join the family?

Do they have any known illnesses?

What's your dog's microchip number?

How much do they weigh?

What's your vet's name, address and contact details?

_____

_____

_____

_____

_____

_____

_____

_____

_____

_____

_____

_____

List any numbers and contact details in case of emergencies.

What vaccinations does your dog need? List details and dates.

-

-

-

-

How often do they need them?

When did your dog have its first flea and worm treatment?

_____

How often do they need flea and worm treatments?

Does your dog have any allergies?

-

-

-

Give details of illnesses since joining the family.

-

-

-

List any regular medications, including times and dosages.

-
-
-
-
-

What is the condition of your dog's teeth?

How do you keep them clean?

List their grooming details (tools, dates and times).

-
-
-
-
-

Is anyone in your family allergic to dogs?

What precautions will you take when family are visiting?

Will you spay or neuter your dog? Make a note of your arrangements for this.

_____

_____

_____

_____

_____

_____

_____

_____

_____

_____

_____

How often do they need to be walked?

Do you have a code word for 'walks'?

Make a list of some of your favourite routes.

_____

_____

_____

_____

_____

_____

_____

_____

_____

_____

_____

List your insurance details, reference numbers and any exclusions to the policy.

-
-
-
-
-

Do you have a dog sitter or a kennels you use? List the details.

_____

_____

_____

_____

_____

_____

_____

_____

_____

_____

_____

_____

USE THIS PAGE TO WRITE INSTRUCTIONS FOR YOUR DOG SITTER

Breakfast:

Lunch:

Dinner:

Snacks:

How often do you take them out for a walk?

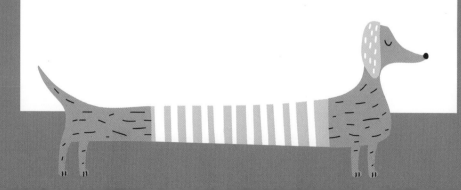

How long are their daily walks?

How regularly do they need to be let out?

Make a note of any other useful information.

-
-
-

Make a list of useful stores and websites for your dog's needs
and belongings.

-
-
-
-
-

NOTES

PUBLISHING DIRECTOR Sarah Lavelle

BUSINESS DEVELOPMENT DIRECTOR Melanie Gray

EDITOR Stacey Cleworth

WORDS Alison Davies

JUNIOR DESIGNER Alicia House

HEAD OF PRODUCTION Stephen Lang

PRODUCTION CONTROLLER Katie Jarvis

Published in 2021 by Quadrille,
an imprint of Hardie Grant Publishing

Quadrille
52–54 Southwark Street
London SE1 1UN
quadrille.com

All rights reserved. No part of this publication may be
reproduced, stored in a retrieval system or transmitted
in any form by any means, electronic, mechanical,
photocopying, recording or otherwise, without the
prior written permission of the publishers and
copyright holders.

The moral rights of the author have been asserted.

Text © Quadrille 2021
Design and layout © Quadrille 2021

ISBN 978 1 78713 543 7

Printed in China